T0352462

PIANO GIRL
PLAYBOOK

PIANO GIRL
PLAYBOOK

notes on a musical life

ROBIN MELOY GOLDSBY

Backbeat
Books

Guilford, Connecticut

Backbeat Books
An imprint of The Rowman & Littlefield Publishing Group, Inc.
4501 Forbes Blvd., Ste. 200
Lanham, MD 20706
www.rowman.com

Distributed by NATIONAL BOOK NETWORK

British Library Cataloguing in Publication Information available

Library of Congress Cataloging-in-Publication Data available

ISBN 978-1-4930-5619-4 (hardcover)
ISBN 978-1-4930-5620-0 (e-book)

♾™ The paper used in this publication meets the minimum requirements of
American National Standard for Information Sciences—Permanence of Paper for
Printed Library Materials, ANSI/NISO Z39.48-1992

To musicians young and old,
from all corners of the world.
I hear you.

Contents

Foreword

by Mike Edison

As a race, musicians are not the smartest people. Have you ever tried to talk to a guitar player? A rock guitar player? Or, god forbid, a bass player? At least drummers know how to count.

Piano players, of course, are a breed apart. They control a palette the equivalent of a scaled-down orchestra that (if you are the Piano Girl in question) can run the range from elves leaping about an enchanted forest, to the Sturm und Drang of apocalyptic doom, to romantic themes more suitable for drunken hookups and lurid affairs. Robin has mastered them all, from enchanting pianissimo doodles to the fortississimo clusters necessary for crowd control in Europe's grandest castles, to the lush, post-Bacharach chords that are hotel-bar accelerants for drink sales and never-to-be-spoken-of-again sex. She is also a wizard at composing new-age lullabies for naked people, a talent of which neither Brubeck nor Basie could boast.

Robin has no Cinderella dreams—hers is a self-realized stardom that skirts the unreality of a profession notorious for lauding hard-rock lunks as gods while marginalizing jazz innovators as outliers, has vacillated on Beethoven (once called unlistenable, now the cornerstone of a flagging classical music industry), and rewards the flavor-of-the-day pop star with giant sacks of gold but has made little room to celebrate the real talent in the room, the warrior poets such as Robin whose heroics keep the music flowing.

As a genius of the lounge piano, her musicality, humor, and mettle are unquestionable and resonate not only in her arsenal of discretely dispatched glissandos (which come filigreed with gig-appropriate degrees of irony and Liberace-in-heels rococo flair), but in her gleefully honest writing and storytelling. She sees not just herself—solipsism being a high risk in the music biz—but everything around her. She is the Mata Hari of the piano. From the panopticon behind the Steinway, she has seen things that people wouldn't believe: the hotel-lounge equivalents of attack ships on fire off the shoulder of Orion and C-beams glittering in the dark near the Tannhäuser Gate.

She is part lifeguard and part mystic; and like all great gurus, her heightened sense of the absurd and saint-like patience transcend most mortals. Playing the piano in the sleazy lounge in one of Donald Trump's New York City hotels, it's amazing she didn't throw it at someone. I've been to that bar, and it was everything that was wrong about New York City in the 1980s but had to have been a step up from the airport lounge in Newark, New Jersey . . . or was it?

Robin's career is unexpected, yet vital—seriously, who dreams of growing up and becoming the piano player in a hotel bar? Or paying the rent by scoring a million sweaty listeners in high-end European spas? Or thinks that solo piano background music is somehow the path to playing for the future king of England at Buckingham Palace? And is a reminder that music is literally everywhere. She is a witness to its curing powers and a testimony to the cats and kittens who make beautiful, timeless music, almost anonymously but without whose gifts it would be a sad world indeed. It breaks my heart into pieces just to think that she may be the last of a dying breed, holding a gig that is fading into a cloud of digital streaming and a new world of boozy philistines and bourgeois barflies who lack the proper breeding to worship the Piano Girl.

You will not learn how to play the piano from reading this book, but it may help you become a better human. It is a potent reminder to laugh and to love, and that good-spirited contempt and mockery have plenty of place even in the hearts and minds of the enlightened.

Introduction

The Piano Zone

I play the piano.

I'm over sixty and lead a pretty respectable life, which is saying something, considering my spotty past as a Chopin-playing stripper. For decades, I've shaped my career by experiencing success and failure in real time in front of a live audience.

Chances are you've never heard of me, although you might stream my music in your home without even knowing my name. Perhaps you're old school and still purchase and play CDs in your undigitized car, but most of my fans these days are streamers, grabbing music from the internet and consuming playlists like salted bar pretzels in a bottomless bowl.

These days I play hundreds of solo piano jobs a year—probably an average of four times a week, all year long. Compare that to my hyper-gig years in New York (on the bench for fifteen or more sessions per week), and you might say I'm on easy street now. I've played more gigs than the Rolling Stones have ever played, more than Madonna has worked, even during her busiest "Material Girl" years. For more than four decades, I've been playing for lounge lizards, mobsters, and moguls; lovely ladies who love to lunch, jet-lagged bedraggled global travelers, the up-and-coming and down-and-out, princes and paupers, smooth talkers and potty mouths. My music, when I'm in the zone, sands the edges of tumultuous, noisy lives with the salve of a Mozart-ish adagio for the forlorn, a pretty pop tune for the Gen X Aperol Spritz sippers, or something new age-y in E minor for the wistful nondrinkers dressed in boring hues of blue. Ah, look at all the lonely people. I'm constantly connecting to my listeners, face-to-face and heart to heart.

I represent career musicians who continue to perform live in the world's best hotels, seediest airport lounges, and piano rooms of every stripe. We are a rare but noble breed—the endangered species of the music industry, dedicated souls producing gentle music in a noisy world. Now, more than ever, we are needed. Live music offers something more than recorded music: it demands a human connection, nudges us forward, encourages our shared humanity, and forges new collective memories. Because live music relies on the synergy of audience and musician, it creates compassion on both sides.

Regardless of the venue, my connection to the audience is everything. I've played ambient music in roadside dives from Pittsburgh, Pennsylvania, to Waterbury, Connecticut, and enter-tained aristocrats and monarchy in glitzy five-star Manhattan hotels and third-world countries. I've been a hit on the Miche-lin three-star European castle circuit—tasting deviled quail eggs, lobster-infused ice cream, and pigeon mousse while sipping glasses of luscious, viscous burgundy that cost as much as my mortgage payment. I've played concerts for naked people in sau-nas, misbehaving children in elf hats, drunken tourists in coastal resorts, and for the future king of England at Buckingham Palace—where seventy white-gloved servers floated through the ballroom carrying silver-domed plates of royal free-range chicken.

The gig gods do not always look favorably in my direction. Sometimes the braying, braless pig lady shows up, the happy-go-lucky shit-faced Dutch bowling team crashes and trashes the room, or the perfectly-coiffed parents of screaming twin babies park the parade-float stroller next to the Steinway and go off to a far corner to sip martinis and eat salted cashews, leaving me in loco parentis. I loathe those people, but I can hardly blame them. The melodies I spin across the room are occasionally drowned out by drunken, doltish behavior, or the maddening din of the blender, the yapper, the dropped tray of champagne glasses.

It's all good. My dad was in the jazz trio on the *Mister Rogers' Neighborhood* program for more than thirty years. At one of my first gigs on Nantucket Island, Fred Rogers himself, the nicest man of all time, pointed out to me, "There's always someone listening."

In my first book, *Piano Girl*, I tell tales of how to handle unruly piano lounge guests, of which there is never a shortage: the choking priest; the gentleman who mistook the inside of the grand piano for a coat check; a marauding gang of bagpipers (on their way to a private party at the back of the hotel) droning their way through the middle of my sensitive Michel Legrand medley; a matched set of interpretive dancers in silver catsuits who gyrated to my music for three hours; a periodontist, complete with a set of chattering teeth, determined to bellow "Love Me Tender" through my entire performance.

You might laugh. I do. I used to be offended, but by now I've learned to be amused.

Today I'm in Cologne, Germany, where I've found my home, doing my steady teatime job playing the piano at Excelsior Hotel Ernst. I lean into my first set of background music just as our guests are settling in. I play the opening cadence to a quiet piece called "The Village" and eye the lobby lounge like a CIA spook. I let the harmonies hang in the air, slowly drifting through the room like the subtle scent of expensive perfume.

I connect with my upscale, sophisticated guests, who hail from all corners of the planet. They sip tea and champagne and, sometimes, they listen. They are unique and private individuals, yet when they are thrown together as a group for this unplanned public gathering, a beautiful social accident unfolds—framed and orchestrated by the music wafting through the room. I wonder who is the oldest, the youngest, who will die first, or live the longest. I wonder who among them might be hiding secrets, or illness, or shame. I wonder who had to fight the hardest to make it into this room. That very well might be me.

The music bonds us in some small, impeccably human way. I stay in the moment, reach into my quiver of songs, and let the next piece flow through my fingers. Time is on my side; balance always returns to the space that music occupies. That's the best,

most miraculous part of playing live: witnessing the effect music has on my audience and what they give back to me. The connection.

When I'm in the piano zone, each melody carries a fleeting message of calm into the world—like a vote for kindness, or a raised hand for peace. Playing a song can be a simple act of grace offered to an aggressive, broken world. Call it love, or revenge, or passion. It's the least—and the most—I can do.

One

Blonde Ambition

I am scheduled to perform today for afternoon tea. The Excelsior Hotel Ernst lobby—an oasis of old-money elegance—offers a plush, peaceful shelter for upscale Cologne residents and well-groomed voyagers from distant lands. Today's guest of distinction, however, has created a hubbub. Madonna is staying with us this week. It's not unusual for us to host a classical music celebrity or a government official from a distant land, but pop stars are a novelty at our grand European hotel.

The last time I was here, I played for a multinational group of lobby people. To my left was a table of six German women "of a certain age": blown-out hair, manicured hands, cashmere frocks in soft shades of navy, burgundy, beige. Painfully tasteful jewelry.

On my right were six Emirati gentlemen from London: painfully perfect Oxford English accents, equally precise fade haircuts and trimmed beards, bespoke suits with embroidered vests. Velvet slippers. Brit chic, Dubai dash.

In the middle sat a recently engaged, middle-aged gay couple, suave, painfully happy, and obviously in love. Not glamorous, but perfect. Fluffy sweater vests.

In the back I spotted a clump of four American businessmen: casual Friday jeans and blazers. They hovered around one laptop, their unblinking eyes glued to the screen. Dow Jones? NFL updates? Free porn?

Far-left corner—two PhD candidates from Ghana: gleaming ebony skin, pale yellow and pink button-down shirts. Biochemists.

Far-right corner—one Korean woman: translucent complexion, skinny black pants, hoop earrings. She tap-tap-tapped her dating app. Sipped a latte, ignored the Pierre Hermé pastel macarons.

As for me, I was, as usual, in the piano zone—the vortex of music and love—where all seems right with the world. Even if it's not.

Incredibly, the German women, the Africans, and the Emiratis were all celebrating birthdays. I played "Happy Birthday," anticipating a train wreck when we got to the name part of the song.

Happy Birthday, dear Gisela,
Happy Birthday, dear Xavier,
Happy Birthday, dear Mohammed . . .

The result sounded a little like Happy Birthday, dear Exgiselamohamahdala.

They applauded, laughed, leaned back, closed their eyes, and tuned in. The lone Korean woman smiled and put down her phone. "Happy Birthday" has always been like money in the bank. Even the Americans closed their laptops.

Score one for the humans.

That was yesterday, a classic gig right out of the *Piano Girl Playbook*. Today's challenges are likely to be different. Management has kept Madonna's presence a secret from the press (and from me), but now the blonde's out of the bag, and about a thousand people hover by the hotel's front door, waiting for a glimpse of their favorite pop icon.

Exciting, I suppose, but the huddled masses make it impossible for me to get anywhere near the hotel's entrance. Middle-aged women (some of them wearing leopard-print pants) and gay men (tastefully dressed) stand alongside pierced and tattooed teens—necks craned, toes tipped, autograph pens at the ready.

The human wall seems impenetrable. But I'm good in situations like this—all those years of weaving through Puerto Rican Day crowds on Fifth Avenue in Manhattan trained me well. I put on my sunglasses, square my shoulders, assume an attitude of arrogance, and use my "emergency pianist voice": *"Coming through, coming through! Musician! Musician!"*

I figure this particular group might respond to pushy, New York-accented English—they'll be less likely to argue with me. It works. The seas part, I make it to the velvet rope. One of the doormen greets me and lets me through. I should mention that no one asks for my autograph, in spite of the sunglasses.

I sit at the Steinway, a 1939 Model A. The lobby area at this time of day usually hums along at a pleasant, lazy afternoon tempo, but it's unusually quiet right now. Because of our celebrity visitor, the hotel is closed to walk-in pedestrian traffic, and management has politely requested that hotel guests refrain from loitering in the lobby. The result? I am playing to an empty room.

I love this.

Some performers slip into a low-grade funk when no one shows up to hear them, but not me. Yesterday I had a crowd; today the place is empty. No reason to take it personally.

A gorgeous piano, a room that's an acoustic dream, and solitude—what's not to like? I play "Flight of the Cranes," one of my compositions. The music spills into the lobby. I catch the eye of the hotel director. He smiles. I feel like one of the cranes in my song, coasting along, gliding through the autumn afternoon. I remind myself how lucky I am to be a musician.

"Nice," says a leather-clad man with spiky hair and a face full of stubble. Where did he come from? Sometimes I close my eyes when I play, and when I open them again—*surprise!* People pop up like creepy mannequins in an amusement park house of horrors. The pop-up people really freak me out sometimes.

"Thank you," I say. He grunts. This guy looks like he's auditioning for the *Spinal Tap* sequel.

Pulling the number one choice out of the *Idiotic Things to Say to a Musician Handbook*, he (let's call him Spinal Tap) leans on the piano and asks, "So, can you actually make a living doing this?" I have been in this business forty years, and I still haven't come up with an appropriate response. I consider telling him I'm actually a brain surgeon down on my luck, but, instead, settle on a condescending tone without sarcasm. It's a fine line.

"Yes," I say, with one of those fake smiles I reserve for drooling fools and drunks. "And what do you do for a living?"

"I'm a music journalist," Spinal Tap says.

"And can *you* make a living doing that?"

"I make documentary films about musicians. But not musicians like you."

"Excuse me?" Hackles now officially raised.

"What you do is kind of old fashioned."

"I prefer to think of it as timeless."

He laughs, or something like it. "You know what I mean."

"No, actually, I don't. There is nothing old fashioned about what I do."

"These days there aren't many hotels with piano players."

"And?" I ask. "Does that make me old fashioned? Or does that make me valuable? Or does that mean most hotels are too cheap to provide this little luxury for their guests?"

I keep smiling, but I can feel steam coming out of my ears. I'm a little angry, but I'm also amused. The older I get, the more often I find myself entertained by the stupidity of middle-aged men with overinflated egos. Better to laugh than to fall victim to cocktail lounge road rage. What am I going to do, anyway? Throw a napkin and a handful of toasted almonds at him?

"Classy hotel, here," Spinal Tap says.

"Yes. And maybe one of the reasons it's classy is because they have a pianist."

"Whatever." He rolls his eyes. "I'm not going to discuss music trends with you. I'm here to interview your colleague."

"My colleague?"

"Yes. Madonna. The star. That's the kind of musician I write about."

Visions of Madonna swirl through my fifty-year-old brain—cone bra, fingerless gloves, leg warmers, and a bad perm. Eighties Madonna, but there you have it. My Madonna. "Old fashioned" is a relative term, I guess. If you worshipped a particular phase of pop culture, its glossy icons stay hip and up to date until you drop dead.

I remember hearing Madonna's "Borderline" in a disco in Haiti in 1984. I was crossing a few borderlines myself that year, working as a lounge pianist in a third-world country and attempting to play songs such as "Skylark" for a Merengue-crazed audience. Madonna's music, spunky and fresh, didn't appeal to my own sense of musicality, but I loved it despite itself. There was something edgy about her breakout feminist message.

Be who you want to be, she seemed to be shouting from the center of the dance floor. *Be sexy, be strong, be wrong. Don't be afraid.* My music may have veered in a completely different direction from her disco and dance-driven style, but I learned a lot from her business savvy. *Don't be afraid.* In 1984 I needed to hear that as often as possible. I still do.

I continue to play while Spinal Tap yaps at me. I want to douse him with my glass of Ruinart champagne, but that would be a ghastly waste of good grape. I've lost my Zen piano vibe, but I'm sure I'll get it back sometime later this afternoon. It never wanders too far.

I wonder what Madonna is doing right now, as she prepares to greet her fans—the crowd outside has doubled in the past hour. Is she checking her lipstick? Calling her kids? Eating a vegetarian club sandwich and worrying about bloat? Trying to remember her set list for tonight's concert? Dealing with an annoying case of tennis elbow?

"You know," I say to Spinal Tap, "Madonna and I have a lot in common."

"*Really?*" he says, looking sideways at my little black dress and pearls.

"*Really*. We're the same age, we're both mothers, and we're both still working at the thing we love. All the time. Not bad for a couple of women in their fifties."

He never gets a chance to consider this. Madonna enters the lobby, and normal conversation ceases. Spinal Tap rushes out to watch her, more like a goofy fan than a professional journalist. It is kind of pathetic. From the corner of my eye, I see a swirl of black, a tumbleweed clump of security, and a gazillion flashes. Wouldn't it be nice if she stopped by the piano to say hello?

"*Have a fun gig,*" she might say.

"*Thanks,*" I would say. "*You, too. And good luck with that tennis elbow.*"

She doesn't notice me at the piano. She is Material Girl. I'm Invisible Girl.

Happy but invisible. The irony doesn't escape me. Here I sit, playing beautiful music on a beautiful instrument to a completely empty lobby. Twenty-five feet away, thousands of people wait to see another blonde musician—the famous one—sashay through a sliding glass door and climb into a van. Her fans have waited for hours to watch a journey that takes thirty seconds.

Madonna, of course, might argue that her thirty-second journey to the black van actually took thirty years.

Madonna and I have that in common. My own musical road trip has taken equally as long. But on most days only a select few—Gisela, Mohammed, Xavier—get to witness my progress. I coast along, sort of like the cranes in my composition, following the seasons, squawking at the pop-up people, content to be doing what I love. Blonde or not, in this ego-bloated business it takes a lot of ambition to get off the ground. And even more to keep flying.

Two

The Notes That Got Away

"See that Burger King? I played there once, before it was a Burger King."

I'm in the car with my musician father, and he's pointing out places where he used to perform. "The Burger King used to be a Moose Club. Before it was a Moose Club it was a Masonic Lodge. I played there, too. And down the highway, over by the Southland Shopping Mall? That used to be the Ankara. Big night club. Six nights a week, live music, different acts all the time. I was in the house band in the sixties. Mr. Cenemie was the manager. Called him Mr. Centipede. He hated me. I'm telling you, beautiful dancers from the Philippines in that place. Made no sense since it was called the Ankara, but whatever. And up on the hill? That nursing home? I played there for about two years, when it was still a hotel. They had great shrimp cocktail."

"Was that the place with the singer of small stature and the Desi Arnaz look-alike?" I ask.

"What? The singing dwarf? No, that place was across from the nursing home. And the dwarf worked with the stripper, not with Desi. The Desi impersonator usually worked with the ice-skater, but sometimes with a ventriloquist."

"Wait, the nightclub had an ice-skating rink?"

"Back in the day they spared no expense."

"Jesus."

"Hey, that's no joke—I worked for Him, too. That Catholic Church over by Wendy's? Al Dilernia was extremely popular at that church. I used to play with his band for church events. The priest liked jazz. Al used to listen to Pirate games on his transistor radio during prayers. He once yelled, 'God damn it, you assholes,' during the blessing when the Cleveland Indians hit a home run. He usually had spaghetti stains on his shirt."

"I remember Al," I say. "And the spaghetti sauce. He tried to kiss me on the lips once when I was, like, sixteen."

"Which Dilernia was that? Albert or Alfred? There were two brothers, both named Al. Both great players. Both liked spaghetti. Either one would have tried to kiss you."

"The guitar player."

"That would be Al. I always said they should start a band with Edmond and Edward Manganelli. Al and Al and Ed and Ed."

Driving anywhere in the greater Pittsburgh area with my dad, octogenarian drummer Bob Rawsthorne, means listening to dozens of stories pulled from more than six decades of gigs in vanished venues. We can hardly cross a strip-malled intersection without him pointing at a corner and blurting out a tale that involves skullduggery, musical madness, or management idiocy.

"Ah, there's the VFW Post 5111," Dad says as we drive on Pittsburgh's Mt. Washington. "I hated playing there. Rotten piano. Rotten manager—that guy actually snapped off the TV during the moon landing. We wanted to take a break to watch it. The damn moon landing! 'I ain't payin' you guys to watch television,' he said. I'll never forget the bartender's reaction. He went outside and looked up at the stars, hoping to see Neil Armstrong. Sad. So sad."

In just one trip to the Giant Eagle grocery store I hear about a drunken host with a mynah bird that spewed racial insults, a greedy nightclub owner with a drawer full of stolen watches, and a drunken girl singer with balloon boobs who would always blank out when trying to remember the words to "Accentuate the Positive."

My father was, and is, an accomplished musician, a big fish in Pittsburgh's smallish pond of high-quality players. He stayed in Pittsburgh because the city's many nightlife outlets once rewarded good musicians with plenty of work. For most of his career he stayed busy. Crazy busy.

We've often talked about the roller-coaster lives of working musicians—the way a five-star gig on Tuesday turns into a dumpster-dive engagement on Wednesday.

Here's an actual conversation from 1986:

"Hey, Robin, guess where I'm playing this week? The White House."

"Great, Dad. Is that the new restaurant in Bloomfield?"

"No, man." (Jazz musicians often call their wives and daughters "man," which manages to be slightly insulting and endearing all at once.) "No, no, man. The White House. Like, where President Reagan lives. I'm going with the Johnny Costa Trio from the *Mister Rogers'* show to play for Nancy Reagan. Dig that."

He went. The trio played "Nancy with the Laughing Face," but the First Lady didn't recognize it, or maybe she just couldn't dig it. The next night Dad was back in town, playing for a drunken sing-along at the Swissvale Moose Club.

The day after that, he returned to the television studio. Dad held on to that *Mister Rogers'* gig for more than thirty years. He also had a thirteen-year steady engagement in a popular pizza and beer joint called Bimbo's, a warehouse-sized restaurant that catered to gaggles of fun-loving folks celebrating life with oily pepperoni slices and mugs of watery swill. "Don't eat there on an empty stomach," he used to tell us.

Dad also subbed occasionally in the percussion sections of the Pittsburgh Symphony, Opera, and Ballet orchestras, often racing from the beer hall to the concert stage and back in one evening. "You know how many times I have to hit those drums to pay for a semester of college?" he used to ask me. Now that I have my own college-age kids, I can guess it was quite a few.

"I'm so old Stephen Foster was my first duo partner."

This is one of Dad's lines—a joke he pulls out of his trap case whenever the topic of old age comes up. He used to tell this joke about other musicians. Now, approaching his eighty-fifth birthday, he tells it about himself. The genius, of course, is that you have to be pretty old just to get the joke, never mind make it.

"I'm so old my wife says I make the same sounds as the coffeemaker."

Dad is still playing gigs. He's the proud owner of two drum sets (a faded greenish-blue Premier and a silver sparkle Ludwig kit), two new hips (also silver sparkle), a collection of ancient Zildjian cymbals, and a vast repertoire of funny stories. Today he has received a call from a perky young woman (let's call her Becky) who wants to book him—a year in advance—for a gig in February 2020. The gig is at a fancy-pants senior residence, the kind of venue where Bob's band, a sophisticated mix of great music and comedy, tends to be a big hit.

"I told Becky the date will be fine," Dad tells me. "And then she wants to know if I have video. Video? What the hell does she want video for?"

"Well," I say, "that's how people book bands these days. People have videos. On the internet."

"The internet? I told Becky, 'Look, I'm almost eighty-five; I'm really good at what I do, even though I'm not exactly sure what it is I do. I have no videos on the internet.' I asked her where she got my name, and she said that the Saint Barnabas senior center told her we were absolutely the best band in the world for the gig. And I said, 'You still need the internet after that recommendation?'"

"And?"

"Get this: she wanted to know if it was 'safe' to book me that far in advance."

"Because you're almost eighty-five."

"Because I'm almost eighty-five."

"Dad, please don't tell me you hit her with the Stephen Foster joke."

"Of course, I did. But she didn't laugh—never heard of Stephen Foster—so I kept going. 'Becky,' I said, 'I'm so old I don't even buy green bananas. I'm so old my Social Security number is thirteen. I'm so old John Philip Sousa was my roommate at music school. I need ten strokes to play a five-stroke roll. It takes me a half hour to play the *Minute Waltz*. I'm so old I was in the house band at Ford's Theater. One of my students was the drummer boy in Pickett's Charge. I'm so old I've seen Halley's comet three times.'"

"Stop!"

"Funny stuff, right?"

"Uh, sure, Dad."

"But Becky didn't laugh. Not once. Can you imagine? Event planners these days have no sense of humor. But I kept going. I said, 'At my age everything is either dried up or it leaks.'"

"So, what happened?"

"I think I wore her down. She gave me the gig. Now all I have to do is stay alive."

"Remember the time the chimpanzee in the burlesque show slapped Red French [the pit drummer] on the forehead and left a palm-shaped welt that took days to fade?" Dad has an endless number of stories in locations that range from seedy to suave. I listen and try to catalog and edit his words for my selfish, writerly purposes. But the dime-store philosopher in me—the halfway serious woman who occasionally questions the meaning of a life in the arts—starts to wonder about the music itself.

Where do all the notes go?

Perhaps that's the attraction of real, live music—that it flies and falls exactly where it's welcomed or needed—in a dancer's happy feet, in the heavy heart of a jilted woman, in the romantic soul of an aging poet, in the noisy mind of a student hoping to restore order to a chaotic life.

Or maybe the notes land on the beer hall floor, and that's that.

Talking around the music feels easier than talking about the music itself. To do that a player must talk about musical technique. Or beauty. Or love. And that gets personal. So instead, musicians such as my father reminisce about nasty nightclub owners or foolish food and beverage managers or knackered brides who insisted on singing "Summertime" in a key that was way too high. Or a drummer with a chimp paw print on his forehead. Or the White House, man.

Today we're in Cranberry Township, near Pittsburgh. As my father's drummer-friendly SUV reaches the top of a rise and descends into the valley, we pass an Olive Garden, a Starbucks, a Walmart, and a KFC. At the bottom of the hill is a scrappy field, the last vacant lot on a congested strip of potholed concrete. Grass grows. Wildflowers stretch their faded heads toward the blazing sky.

"There!" my father says, pointing to the empty lot. "I played there once. On that very corner."

"Nothing there now," I say.

"No. But there used to be," he says. "I'm telling you, man, there used to be."

Three

The Bear

*I*n 1966 I played the Bach Minuet in G at my first piano recital, at the Joseph Horne Company in downtown Pittsburgh. I practiced efficiently, memorized the music, and prepared for the recital by performing in front of other students.

I was nine years old.

The Minuet in G has two "A" sections and two "B" sections—the form is AABB. I plowed through the first half of the piece perfectly, gaining more confidence with every note I tossed behind me. Puffed up and full of pride, I finished the first half and launched into the second section. The first note of the second section is a B natural.

Clam! With great conviction I played an A sharp, the quintessential wrong note, because it's a half step away from the right note. In jazz that wouldn't matter so much—people might even think I was a nine-year-old genius, stealing riffs from Thelonious Monk—but with Bach it sounded like nails on a chalkboard. And I didn't skim the key lightly, I hammered it. Bang! The hundred delicate, perfect notes I had played until this point fizzled and died. All that counted now was the wrong note.

Trembling knees, sweating palms, burning face. The piano recital fight-or-flight response kicked in—I felt like a hungry bear was chasing me through deep, crusty snow. I sensed the

13

audience cringing. I saw my father in the front row raise one eyebrow. My teacher clapped his hand to his forehead.

In survival mode, I relied on muscle memory to propel me through the rest of the piece. In my mind I fled the scene, climbed a tree, and dangled upside-down from a low-hanging limb. I hung on for dear life. The bear licked his chops, growled, and snapped at my hands.

Overly dramatic? I think not. Any music student who has experienced a cortisol-induced hysterical brain freeze while attempting to play a complicated passage will tell you the bear analogy is spot-on.

Back to my nine-year-old self: I had to finish the piece, and that involved repeating the B section. With a kid's logic I thought that if I played the B section correctly the second time, the audience would know I had played it incorrectly the first time. So, I intentionally played the wrong note again, figuring that my listeners would never know I had screwed up the first time.

I repeated the B section and hit that same really wrong note on purpose. *Ha*, I thought, *I've fooled everyone.*

The bear, obviously bored with my refusal to slip from the tree into his slobbering maw, ambled away, checking occasionally to make sure that I hadn't dropped to the ground. I didn't know this yet, but he would be back. Next time I wouldn't be so lucky.

At a certain point in a teenage musician's life, the bear wins more often than not. No one tells you this in music school, but learning to ignore mistakes and move on to the next moment can mean the difference between having a career or not.

Failure—just as much as success—determines who we become as artists. We start out as idealistic musical messengers carrying copious notes of sadness and wonder and love. At some point—to get where we want to go—we must blow a lot of clams. We must learn, as C. S. Lewis wrote, to "fail forward."

At age fifteen, I became paralyzed by the fear of making a mistake while playing a piano concert. Paralyzed! Once the bear showed up, the party was over. Playing a musical instrument well in a solo concert performance has to be one of the most difficult tasks in the world. Staying focused through a Molotov cocktail of eye-hand coordination, memory, insane detail, nuance—it's almost too much for a kid to think about. As a teenager, when we believe we're being judged for every skin blemish, fashion choice, or wrong note, it's damn near impossible.

Benyamin Nuss, a brilliant young classical pianist living in Germany—and currently touring the world with his *Final Fantasy* program of computer-game music arranged for solo piano—has been gracing concert stages for twenty of his thirty years, playing an extremely difficult classical repertoire with the emotional poise and technical wizardry of a seasoned musician twice his age. Benny is the kind of performer who never seems to have a bad day, never makes a mistake, never lets the bear chase him. I ask Benny if he can remember ever screwing up while performing. He laughs.

"There have been so many times," he says. "But the one that comes to mind happened when I was sixteen. I had my first girlfriend, and we had only been together for a couple of weeks. For the first time, there was something in my life other than music. I was playing Beethoven's Piano Sonata no. 7 in D Major. The fourth movement is a rondo with a figure that always repeats three notes. I was coming to the end, after the last repeat of this motive. I got stuck and stopped. Jumped some bars back because nothing better came to mind. Played the motive again. The same thing happened. Then I jumped back again. And again. And failed again. And again. Finally, I just stopped. Didn't know what else to do."

The bear was nipping at Benny's heels. Or the heels of his hands.

"Beethoven ditched you at the finish line?" I ask.

"Yeah, or I ditched myself."

"What did you do?"

"I gave up. I stood, took a pathetic bow, and said, 'Sorry.'"

"Oh, no."

"Here's the thing: I could have improvised my way out of that rondo, but it never occurred to me that I could mess with Beethoven just to save myself. Really—I could have made something up and no one, other than my teacher, my parents, and maybe a couple of classical music experts would have known."

"I bet if that happened to you now, you'd own it. Beethoven meets Nuss. Improvise through a memory lapse? Is that what you learned from that mistake?"

"Yeah. That. And to never think about my girlfriend when I should be focusing on the music."

The night of the rondo breakdown, shortly after suffering what he considered a monumental defeat, Benny took some deep breaths in the wings, returned to the stage, took another bow, sat down, and whipped through his encore—Prokofiev's *Toccata*—twice as fast and furious as the piece he had just flubbed.

Boy versus bear. Boy wins. Sometimes you eat the bear, and sometimes the bear eats you.

Back to me and a chance meeting with the bear, in 1978.

I had been working as a cocktail pianist to make money while attending college. I liked the work—I sat in the corner, played the piano, and no one paid much attention to me. During the day I attended classes, took piano lessons, and practiced for classical music recitals.

I was scheduled to play Maurice Ravel's *Piano Sonatine* for the spring music department recital at the Chatham College chapel. I knew the material. I loved the material. I had practiced it until the piece was playing me. I was confident and secure with my interpretation of the composer's intention and looking forward to the night's performance.

I was nineteen years old and wearing a frilly black frock and strappy heels. I walked onstage, sat at the Steinway concert grand, and adjusted the bench height. About seventy-five people were in attendance, a small crowd for such a big space.

Something felt wrong. My body seemed, I don't know, hollow. My hands tingled. I took a deep breath and began playing the first movement of the *Sonatine*.

That's when it hit me. About sixteen bars into Mr. Ravel's elegantly written composition, my heart started pounding. Boom. Boom. Boom. It was the fucking bear.

My hands began to sweat and tremble, and I moved in slow motion, except for my right knee, which developed a high-speed twitch.

You can do this, you can do this, I said to myself five or six times.

Another voice, a new, strange one coming from inside my head, poked at my self-confidence. A talking bear? Seriously?

You're a fake, and it's about time you realized it. Fake, fake, fake! You're gonna massacre this piece big-time, and all these people will hear you do it. You're nothing but a big faking faker. Fake, fake, fake, fake, fake.

He yelled at me from inside my brain, somewhere between my ears and the top of my skull, and he kept getting louder and louder.

I tried to argue back but couldn't get a word in edgewise. I couldn't locate the notes. Or if I found them, I played them so slowly that I had no idea where I was in the piece. Everything I had memorized was gone—out the window, like bubbles blown through a ring on a windy day.

I stole a glance at the audience. Grandma Curtis and Grandma Rawsthorne sat in the second row with Aunt Jean and Uncle Bill. They were all smiles and didn't seem to notice anything wrong. Good. My parents sat in the row behind them, but I looked away before I caught their reaction to my train wreck. Oh, no. Bill Chrystal, my teacher, with a pained expression on his normally placid face, hovered on the side of the chapel, looking like he might dash out the fire exit if things got any worse.

I could hardly breathe. I was having a full-blown anxiety attack.

Several painful moments passed before I realized the problem. I had gotten so used to the chatter and the laughter of the cocktail lounge that the forced stillness of people actually listening had caused a meltdown. I wanted clinking glasses, whirring blenders, and waiters barking orders at bartenders; instead, I got seventy-five pairs of eyes watching me duke it out with the bear in a silent, one-sided fight against my own demons.

No, no, no, no, no! Don't just sit there and listen! Talk! Smoke a cigarette! Have an argument with your neighbor. Dispute the check with your overworked waitress, because you did, after all, only have two gin and tonics, and you're being charged for three. Order another round of strawberry margaritas or some of those tasty chicken fingers. Do something, anything, but please, please, please, don't listen to me. It is enough for me to listen to myself. Really, it's enough.

I played a C sharp minor chord in a misguided attempt to resolve the cadence—I couldn't even remember what key I was in—and sneaked offstage. Difficult in stiletto heels.

Well, there you have it. Another concert career comes to a screeching halt.

The next day I decided to audition to be a showgirl with Ringling Bros. and Barnum & Bailey. Maybe I would be good enough for the circus. Much easier than playing the piano.

Girl versus bear. Bear eats girl.

I never did join the circus, but I abandoned my concert pianist plans and returned to my cocktail lounge gig, which, in a way, shared certain elements with the Big Top. Clowns, for instance. Scantily clad women. Salty snacks.

In my late twenties, long after I should have settled into my own sense of self, I still felt the brutally judgmental eyes of the world upon me. At home, practicing, I connected with my artistic side, but in public I worried about being loved, or at the very least, liked. My neediness fueled the bear's desire to eat me alive. His hunger grew in direct proportion to my thirst for acceptance in a competitive world. So . . . anxiety . . . dread . . . and the worst, the fear of fear.

Well, there you have it. Another concert career comes to a screeching halt. Girl versus bear. Bear eats girl.

I put up with myself for a very long time.

Finally, somewhere around my forty-fifth birthday, the bear skulked away hungry and never came back. I could tell you that I donned my I AM FIERCE T-shirt and scared the bejesus out of the bear, but that's not what happened. It was more like this: Real life—kids, aging parents, death of friends, love, illness, making a living, paying the bills—reminded me that I have nothing to prove, to anyone, least of all some imaginary bear. I am not a competitor with a finish line; I am a pianist. I play the way I play because I love music that reflects life. My mistakes are part of that process. Making them in public is part of the gig. Why be afraid?

Most musicians don't like to talk about their failures—who does? But I think it's a good idea to let young musicians know that learning to outrun the bear is an essential part of their development. Perhaps not as important as good technique and discipline, but if you can't outrun the bear, you could play like the bastard child of Liberace and Liszt, and it wouldn't make a difference. You'd still be bear food.

A readiness to fail often—and fail well—is a good indicator of future accomplishment. If at first you don't succeed, fail, fail again. If I had given up the piano after that first ill-fated Bach Minuet in G, I might have avoided future scraps with the bear, but I surely would have missed out on the joy of sharing my musical stories with you, with anyone willing to listen.

In a video clip I adore, composer Maria Schneider talks about working with David Bowie. She expresses her many legitimate concerns about screwing up an expensive, risky assignment. This is what Bowie says: "The great thing about music is if the plane goes down, everyone walks away."

Everyone walks away—how I wish I could have heard this as a young adult. It's not life or death; it's music. It means everything in the moment but nothing in the long run. All jokes aside, no one has ever gotten hurt by a wrong note. Why not take a chance on turning a couple of those wrong notes into something beautiful?

These days, I play a few formal concerts a year, but most of the time I stick to background music engagements in fancy rooms. In my current gig, at an old, gold-dusted hotel in Cologne, Germany, I play a 1939 Steinway Model A. The keys of the instrument, contoured by the accumulated blunders of decades of players before me, feel smooth to my fingers when I sit down to play. My musical flaws add another layer of humanity to a piano that has witnessed eighty years of gaffes, all of them, thankfully, forgotten and forgiven by the fleet and reckless tempo of life. Toccata, double time.

Big-band arranger Jörg Achim Keller, one of Germany's most respected leaders of jazz ensembles, says this about the art and craft of playing in a hotel lounge or bar: "There's a lot of value to playing a background music job. For one thing, *the bottom comes up.* When you're playing so often in front of people, your worst moments get less noticeable. The bottom comes up, so to speak. In my opinion, that's the best way to assess someone's playing—not by their flashes of genius, but by their worst moments. Even a complete amateur can have sparks of brilliance. But how low is their bottom? Pretty low, usually. But decades of playing for an audience in a no-pressure situation, the bottom keeps getting higher and higher."

I like that. Bottoms up. One of the benefits of aging.

I consider my career a fortuitous success built on a shaky foundation of multiple screwups and some sort of warped, magical thinking that has propelled me—clinging to the security blanket of my mistakes—into the brawny arms of opportunity. Opportunity, it turns out, sometimes wears a bear costume. I've outsmarted the bear by hugging him, feeding him marshmallows, and teaching him how to dance. Off we go—we're a clumsy twosome, but I've trained him to follow my lead.

Four

Music for Naked People

*I*t's ten minutes to noon at Mediterana, a pastel-colored award-winning sauna and wellness spa located in Bergisch Glad-bach, Germany, about twenty minutes from my front door.

Mediterana, with its spacious gardens and multiple thermal pools, saunas, and steam baths, hosts up to twelve hundred guests a day. For me—a middle-aged, health-obsessed woman—having this place so close to home is like having Disneyland in my backyard. Spending a day here offers the bargain-basement equivalent of a mini-vacation in the south of France, on a Spanish island or a Moroccan beach. For thirty-eight euros (about fifty dollars), I can show up at nine in the morning, sweat, soak, soap, sleep the day away, and emerge in the evening feeling like I've peeled off a couple of years. Amazing what a little exfoliating can do.

Today I'm meeting Andrea, my friend and the resident director of Mediterana. Her expert team of employees has put together a sauna ceremony called Piano del Sol, which features solo piano music from two of my recordings piped through an expensive sound system. Piano del Sol, a twelve-minute sauna odyssey with music, happens five times a day. Five times a day people get naked and sweat to my music. It is almost too much to, well, "bare." We will attend the noon ceremony and, along with thirty other naked people, listen to my piano music and perspire. I'm not sure how I feel about this. I've been known to sweat while playing and, honestly, I feel naked enough when performing. Actually being naked sounds like one naked too many.

I've covered myself with a plain white bathrobe and a pair of flip-flops. I pace on a lavender-lined path and wait for Andrea to show up. Guests of all shapes and sizes—don't ask—carefully hang their terry-cloth (or fairy cloth, as my daughter once called it) designer robes on wrought-iron hooks attached to Moroccan-tiled walls. One by one, naked as the day they were born, they open the door to the Candlelight Sauna and meander into the heat.

Andrea, the busiest gal in the sauna biz, careens around the corner at one minute to noon. She is wearing a pink bathrobe—not her normal workday uniform but an appropriate costume for onsite inspections of the dozens of ceremonies and aromatherapy sessions that Mediterana offers.

"Woo," she says, glancing at the clock on the wall. "Just made it. Busy day!" It's not easy to look professional and stylish in a fluffy pink bathrobe, but she manages to exude an air of complete confidence. I am fascinated by her job. I can't imagine working for a multimillion-dollar business where all of the clients are buck naked.

"You ready?" she says, shedding her robe and revealing a plaid cotton wrap around her midsection, discreetly covering all of her private parts.

"Hey!" I ask, "what's that? You get to wear a towel in there?"

"Yeah. I'm the boss."

"Oh, great," I say. "But what about me? The featured piano player?"

She laughs and offers me nothing. I take off my robe.

I'm at ease in the naked sauna these days but only when I can be anonymous. Because they'll be playing my music, and because a framed poster with my photo is hanging next to the sauna door, I feel a little, uh, exposed.

"Wait a minute," I say. "The sauna guy conducting the ceremony isn't going to introduce me or anything is he? I mean, he'll just turn on the music and conduct the ceremony, and no one will know I'm here, right?"

"Hmmm. I'm not sure."

"OK," I say. "But if I have to stand up and take a bow, I'm going to die. I draw the line at naked bowing. As Elly May Clampett would say, 'It just ain't dignified.'"

"Who's Elly May Clampett?" Andrea asks. I guess *The Beverly Hillbillies* never made it to Germany.

I've performed live in fancy-pants concert halls, strip-mall dumps, castle cocktail lounges, embassies, and third-world countries. My recordings have been used occasionally in television and film productions, but they also have been played in hospitals and schools, funeral homes and birthing rooms, hotel restaurants and furniture store cafeterias. As far as I know, no one is playing my music in elevators, at least not yet.

I like to think—and *hope*—that the songs I compose and perform are relaxing without being mind-numbing, meditative without being boring. I live with two sophisticated teenage pop-music experts and a jazz-bassist husband whom I've nicknamed the "Chord Doctor." The three of them keep me from falling into a New Age tedium pit. I admit to having a fondness for the key of A minor and frilly, trilly grace notes, so I'm lucky that my kids and the Chord Doctor patrol my practice sessions like an in-house harmony task force, making sure I don't write anything that sounds like whale song, a Celtic dirge, or subliminal chimes.

Everyone in my house has suggestions about how to make my music hipper. In a nice way, they let me know when I'm too boring, too lackluster, too monotonous.

John: "Maybe you could add a flat nine to that F sharp seven chord."

Curtis: "That bridge needs some kind of groove. Try *this.* And play it *faster.*"

Julia: "Have you heard the new Ludovico Einaudi soundtrack? You should go in *that* direction."

When I'm smart and feeling open-minded, I listen to their tips. When I'm stubborn, I don't. It's composition by committee. I end up with a kind of meno-mom-meets-Meldau fusion that, in the best-case scenario, has the desired effect of chilling folks out too much when they should be shopping or ordering more drinks.

I write music, record it, and release it into the world. But, ultimately, I have very little control over where it ends up or how it will be used. I like to think that what I record belongs to me—and during the creative process, even with the input of my in-house advisory team, it does. But once it's out there? All bets are off. Some people listen to me at home after they've heard me play live at a concert (I'm big in Oslo and Charleston) or at my steady hotel gig, but most people become familiar with my solo piano musings when a streaming algorithm dumps a few of my tracks into their daily playlist—somehow, I've logged hundreds of millions of streams of my music.

Not long ago, on a storybook-perfect Christmas morning at Schlosshotel Lerbach, a castle hotel not far from the sauna, Frau Eggrich-Bimmelstein—an aging wraith wrapped in satin and sable—charged into the lobby and zigzagged through the crowd to the piano.

"Merry Christmas, Frau Eggrich-Bimmelstein," I said.

"Merry Christmas," she replied. Then, right there in the midst of all of the ridiculously baroque German Christmas cheer—we're talking gingerbread in every conceivable form, mulled wine that filled the room with the scent of nutmeg, thousands of candles, and real chestnuts roasting on a real open fire—she burst into tears. I abruptly stopped playing my joyous version of "Hark! The Herald Angels Sing," stood up, and hugged her.

"Whatever is wrong, Frau Eggrich-Bimmelstein?" I asked.

"My father died last week," she said.

I had known her father. Detlev was a sweet old man with a winning smile and a chronic dripping nose. I would dodge the drips while he stood over me at the piano and showed me American business cards he had collected in the early thirties, before the war. He kept the cards in his wallet, held together with an old rubber band. In halting English, he would read the addresses to me and ask if I knew any of the men. I always suspected there was something more to the story, but our conversations never progressed to the point where I felt comfortable asking.

"I am so sorry, Frau Eggrich-Bimmelstein. You must be very sad."

"He was a day short of his ninety-seventh birthday. When he took his last breath, he was listening to your music."

I paused for a moment. "Really?" I replied, halfway hoping this wasn't true.

"Echt," she said, German for "really."

I sighed. I knew she meant this as the highest compliment. I gave Frau Eggrich-Bimmelstein one more hug, perhaps a tad less sincere than the first. She composed herself, dried her tears, and went off to eat the Christmas goose.

I got a little weepy and nostalgic, thinking about Detlev with his drip, drip, dripping nose and his stack of antique business cards. (I recall one that said Mr. Dick Dahlrimple, III, Purveyor of Hoboken's Finest Leather and Woolen Goods.) The last thing I wanted to do at that moment was play "Jingle Bells." My husband, on a break from his jazz gig in the castle's brasserie, came to meet me in the lobby. He noticed my blotchy face and smeared mascara.

"What's wrong?" he said. "It's Christmas! Joy to the world! Deck the halls!"

"Detlev Eggrich-Bimmelstein died last week while listening to my *Songs from the Castle* CD."

"Really?" he said.

"Echt."

"Huh," said John. "I wonder which track killed him."

Back to the sauna. Here we are, naked and waiting for the music to start. I am not the thinnest, but neither am I the fattest. I have a front-row seat at the penis parade, and I try, really, I do, not to stare.

About thirty very toasty Germans sit or recline on tiered wooden benches. They look pretty relaxed. They look *hot*. I mean that in the literal sense. Maybe my melodies will help the naked folks unwind. Maybe the songs will help cleanse away the effects of too much stress, too much gin, too little sleep. Maybe they will like what I play, maybe they won't. I just hope they won't die while they are trying to decide. I really hope they don't dance. If anything is worse than naked bowing, it's naked dancing. I don't know. Hope this, hope that. But maybe that's what making music is all about. High hopes.

I clutch my towel to my chest. The towel is a critical accessory in the German sauna. Skin is not allowed to touch any part of the wood. To comply with this very strict rule, you need a very long sauna towel, or you need two bath towels capable of stretching the length of your body. Getting your feet, your butt, your head, and your arms all lined up on the towel can seem like a round of naked Twister.

Not that anyone is looking, but I doubt that I'll be recognized in here. In the photo hanging outside I'm cloaked in black silk, spackled with M.A.C. Studio Fix, and face tuned. In here, I'm stripped bare, clean-faced, and well worn. I look around carefully. Nope. No one cares, as is so often the case. I wrestle with my towel and get all of my body parts situated on a lower bench. Better to stay on the bottom—reaching the higher benches involves stepping over other people, which I refuse to do without underpants. Plus, heat rises. It gets really hot up there.

Andrea lounges on one of the top benches—she is a sauna pro and can take it. I eye her wrap. Because everyone else is naked, the wrap gives her an air of authority. I never thought I would covet an orange plaid cloth (with fringe!) that looks like a North African dishtowel—but I would give anything to be covered up right now.

At the stroke of noon, Sauna Guy enters the room and closes the door behind him. Like most of the employees at Mediterana, Sauna Guy is pony-tailed, buff, tan, and looks like he never breaks a sweat, even in a thermonuclear German sauna. He carries a huge wooden bucket of ice. He adds a few drops of aromatherapy essential oil to the ice and places it in a large Moroccan metal bowl—suspended from a pendulum in the center of the wooden ceiling. He sets the pendulum swinging back and forth over the sauna rocks. The ice drips onto the hot stones and sizzles.

We have only been in here for forty-five seconds, and it already feels like it's one million degrees. Celsius.

What better time for a little music?

"Good afternoon, ladies and gentlemen, and welcome to the Piano del Sol sauna ceremony. The ceremony will take approximately twelve minutes and will be divided into two parts, featuring two solo piano recordings composed by American musician Robin Meloy Goldsby."

Sauna Guy seems a little nervous, but I'm sure it's because Andrea, his boss, is in the audience. By the way, Sauna Guy is also wearing one of those plaid dishrags. He has it wrapped around his waist like a loincloth. It's now officially a "look."

"We'll be enjoying lemongrass and eucalyptus essential oils during the ceremony. You'll have the chance to leave the sauna between songs. Otherwise, please remain seated. And please remain silent."

This is new for me—I like the idea of a guard in a loincloth who forces people to sit still, listen, and not talk.

The music starts.

The ice pendulum drips.

The rocks sizzle.

Sauna Guy parades around the room, majestically waving a white linen flag on a wooden pole. This circulates the scented, superheated air, ideally, I suppose, to help expedite the detox effect. I can't decide if this experience is ridiculous or wonderful. Maybe a little of both. Once again—and this happens to me about twice a week here in Germany—I feel as if I've been drop-kicked into the middle of a Mel Brooks film.

My neighbors on the lower bench take deep cleansing breaths. Inhale. Exhale. The first song, "Flying, Falling," comes to an end. Sauna Guy opens the door for a moment, but no one leaves. *Ich schwitze wie ein Schwein,* and would like to flee, but I can't run out on my own recorded performance. Even in a room full of sweaty naked bodies that would be gauche, so I stay put.

My second song, "Magnolia," begins. Because I recorded the damn thing, I know that it will play for exactly four minutes and fifteen seconds. Inhale. Exhale. I float into the music and listen, halfway expecting to hear careless phrasing, places where I should have listened to the Chord Doctor, or slipshod technique. But it all sounds OK to me—not great or glorious, but somehow perfect for this weird moment. At one point, I even forget I'm listening to myself. It's an out-of-body experience in A minor.

No one dies. No one dances. Everyone sweats. No one complains. I do not have to take a naked bow—the applause at the conclusion of the ceremony is not for me but for Sauna Guy, who has expertly guided us through our twelve-minute easy-bake musical ritual. I collect my towel and file out of the sauna with the other naked guests. I'm hungry for cool air. I'm relaxed, naked, and one of the crowd. I'm—dare I say?—hopeful.

Over the course of a few years, my solo piano recordings have become a tradition at Mediterana. Wellness plus soothing solo piano—the concept makes good sense. And just because your audience is naked and asleep doesn't mean they're not listening.

As the naked gods of fate and good fortune would have it, Mediterana asked me to compose and record sixteen new pieces—four for each season—for continued use in the *Piano del Sol* ceremony. They've licensed the music from our record company and purchased the exclusive rights to sell the physical CD to their visitors over the next five years. I keep hearing rumors that music fans have stopped buying CDs. Hopefully this doesn't apply to those who are naked, asleep, or both.

Mediterana released *Piano del Sol* on October 13, 2015. In keeping with the industry tradition of presenting a launch concert, they booked me for a live performance on the *drop date*. Don't you just love those music-biz terms? *Drop, release, launch.* Maybe not such fitting words when your audience is naked.

It's three o'clock. In one hour, I'll be performing in the *Indische Hof*, Mediterana's East Indian indoor garden. The English translation of *Indische Hof* is Indian Square, which makes the event sound like a concert in a teepee. I hope no one asks me to do a white girl rain dance. Circle your wagons while you can.

The *Indische Hof*—a mecca of mosaic tile in soothing shades of green and blue—features a large granite fountain with floating rose petals, palm trees, ferns, and a skylight that filters the dusky German light into something a bit gauzier and more gilded. The garden vibrates with mingled fragrances of eucalyptus and lavender, myrrh and sandalwood. It is a refuge for meditation and reflection; a place to lie naked next to a complete stranger and hallucinate.

The Yamaha grand piano looks like a stout hostess at an embassy cocktail party in Mumbai—a sitar would be more appropriate in this space, but it's *Piano del Sol*, not sitar del sol, so we'll work with what we have.

What we have is me, dressed in my dream pajamas—a black, piano-lounge outfit with a vaguely East Indian-looking cape tossed over my shoulders. With the exception of my blingy flip-flops (you can't wear real shoes here), I'm dressed for a concert in Jaipur or a hotel gig in a posh Punjab hotel lobby.

This is not true of my audience. Generic, white, hotel-issued terry cloth covers most of the guests. Towels, wraps, bathrobes, more towels. At the perimeter of the performance space, naked people stroll from one sauna area to another, but they don't spook me. My nearsightedness blurs them into an impressionistic tableau of brown and beige skin. Mostly beige.

It's plenty hot in here, but I still need to warm up. I want to get the sense of the keys under my fingers. Every piano feels different, and this one, delivered in a rush this morning, schlepped from the cool autumn air into a man-made tropical retreat, might have unique issues. The slightest temperature shift can mess with a piano's tuning—a meteorological event like this could crank the piano way sharp and make it sound like Great Aunt Edna's 1957 spinet. It is pin-drop quiet, people are sleeping, and other audience members are silently taking their places in beds and on brocade sofas. Not a good time for a sound check. I figure I'll take my chances and wait until showtime before playing anything at all. I open the piano to full stick, then sit and check the position and height of the bench.

Uh-oh. Not good. Right in my sight line—at the end of the piano—is a corpulent man in a robe. He's asleep. Not a problem—sleeping seems to be the activity of choice in this space. But he's got a bad case of man spread, the robe gaps open, and there, right at eye level, are things no self-respecting Piano Girl should have to see, at least not while performing, and certainly not while attempting to focus on a new composition that features complex chord clusters that are a bit ambitious for tentative fingers. Concentration is key for this performance. Am I really going to play something called "April Tango" while looking at "Benny and the Jets" at the end of my piano?

I escape to the "dressing room" and try to get hold of myself. The dressing room doubles as a first aid station. I hope there are no medical emergencies between now and showtime. I check out the defibrillators on the wall and measure them for wear and tear. Forty minutes until I go on. I look around for the bear. Thankfully, he seems to have another gig.

I sip a cup of chamomile tea and ponder the potential for cardiac events. The beautiful J, a sauna supervisor, wears a cotton sarong. She's rosy-cheeked and cheerful, excited about the concert but concerned that there won't be enough beds for the audience. Mediterana has twelve hundred visitors today—about one hundred of them will recline and hear my performance. That's a lot of beds.

I think about the guy in the front bed, and then I try not to think about him. Family jewels. Right. Obviously, a term that a man invented.

Voice of Reason, a reliable friend from my Piano Girl past, resonates in my head: *Keep your eyes closed, Mrs. Goldsby, and imagine your listeners dressed in gabardine and silk. Or at the very least, underpants.*

A loudspeaker voice blares through the building: "Please head to the Indische Hof in five minutes for the *Piano del Sol* concert!" The voice sounds like one of those "stand by for evacuation" announcements I used to hear during a fire alarm or bomb threat when I worked the Marriott Marquis in Times Square. Scary. I remind myself that I'm twenty-one years and 3,755 miles away from Times Square. Sure, we had the occasional naked person roaming Forty-Second Street—usually a PETA activist or an escaped convict—but for the most part my daiquiri-swilling Manhattan fans were clothed. They weren't always wide-awake, but at least their private parts weren't flapping in a Broadway breeze.

I sit on the paper-covered exam table in the first-aid/dressing room and go through my set list—I am scheduled to play all sixteen compositions with musical transitions between the pieces. There won't be any applause until the end—an intense sixty minutes of new music for me, but a swell opportunity for music lovers to chill out and take a nap.

It's time. I take another gulp of tea and leave the first aid area. J introduces me. I take a bow and sit at the piano. It's very quiet; management has turned off the fountains, and my naked audience, swaddled like big babies in towels and blankets, has settled in for an hour of meditative music.

Voice of Reason: *Concentrate. It's just another concert. It's just music, with sleeping naked people, allowing you to accompany their dreams.*

Voice of Doom: *You've been putting people to sleep with your music for years. Nothing new here.*

Voice of Bob (my father): *Now would be a great time for the "Hokey Pokey."*

I swat the voices away—*shew!*—close my eyes and focus on the task ahead. I play the vamp to *Piano del Sol,"* the title track of my album, and let the sound wash over me. Slowly, I wander

Now would be a great time for the "Hokey Pokey."

through the faded light of my past. Through my fingers, I feel the relief of a shade tree on a hot summer day, the golden glow of a cloudless sky in mid-October, the miracle of a clear day in February. For several moments, I even feel young.

I play on and on, caught in my own self-indulgent spell. I don't know if I sound good or bad, but it doesn't matter. I sound like me. Take it or not. My sleeping audience frees me—maybe their nakedness liberates me as well. Together, we've created something magical. Or, maybe, it's just ridiculous. Let's stick with magical. It's as close as I get in this racket.

Five

Don't Eat Pie

January 1981. "Ladies, listen up! It's 'Team Time with Deanna!' Grab your buddy and head to the center of the floor, where we'll meet and greet, dance and prance, and burn away that winter blubber."

Deanna is a thirty-five-year-old exercise instructor and seasoned resident of Queens. I am a twenty-three-year-old out-of-work actor/pianist and a newish New Yorker. I wear a slightly see-through white leotard, a purple polyester sash around my waist, and a very large badge that reads "Elaine Powers Figure Salon Trainee." It is not my finest moment, but I'm grateful to be employed. I've graduated from Chatham College, a gentle but high-minded women's school in Pittsburgh, with a BA in drama. I also have a strong music background. I know a lot about Shakespearean comedies, Greek tragedies, and the circle of fifths but hardly anything about how to get work as a performing artist in New York City.

This is the third job I've had since receiving my diploma. When I moved here eighteen months ago, I landed a fancy-sounding gig as a promotional model at Bergdorf Goodman, where a skinny fashion director wearing a narrow black suit stuffed me into a voluminous Anne Klein evening dress and forced me to spray shoppers with expensive perfume. My most recent round of employment has been a role as a piano-playing stripper in the national touring company of an old-fashioned burlesque show called *Big Bad Burlesque*. Not a bad job, really. I've gotten my Equity card, learned to peel off a corset while playing Chopin, how to cope with weathered burlesque comedians (hint: never steal a laugh from an eighty-year-old top banana), how to crank my hair to skyscraper heights and glue on false eyelashes without blinding myself, and how to save money by sleeping eight actors in a Days Inn motel room meant for two (hint: never room with the top banana—he'll use all the towels).

I've also figured out how to survive on stale Dunkin' Donuts crullers and cold shrimp-fried rice. Dancing (ass shaking disguised as choreography) and road-rat meals (leftover half-eaten Whoppers for breakfast) have left me enviably lanky but one step away from full-fledged scurvy. When I touch my arm, it bruises. For more than a year, I've been counting pennies and looking forward to the day when I can afford food that doesn't come in a white cardboard carton or a greasy paper bag.

Now, a little uncertain about my next shaky steps in a city jam-packed with out-of-work actors skidding in their own greasepaint, I've signed up to work part-time as an instructor at an Elaine Powers Figure Salon. I haven't found an Elaine Powers salon with job openings in Manhattan—those places are already staffed by Bob Fosse rejects, soap opera spit backs, and runway models an inch or two shy of the 5 foot 9 inch minimum, so I've nailed down a position as an instructor at the Flushing, Queens, salon in the shadow of Shea Stadium. In Flushing, accents and waistlines are thicker. Hair and coat colors dazzle. It's a place where, refreshingly, avenues swarm with civilians who want nothing—nothing!—to do with show business. The No. 7 Express train from Grand Central gets me there in no time at all.

During "Team Time with Deanna," I sit on an Elaine Powers weight bench and take notes. I'll be expected to conduct my very own "Team Time with Robin" in the next few days, and there's an Elaine Powers protocol I'll need to follow.

Cats have claws! Dogs have fleas! All I've got are chubby knees!
I'm not dumb! I'm so wise! Pump away these flabby thighs!
Move those arms! Move those feet! How I hate this cellulite!
Pec-tor-als! Stretch and reach! We'll look foxy on the beach.

Remember, it's 1981. "Foxy" is our favorite word. While Deanna and her students recite these rhymes, Donna Summer blares from the Elaine Powers sound system. "She Works Hard for the Money" is the track of choice. The music and the rhymes don't sync, and I feel like I'm caught in an avant-garde nightmare. Deanna, single mother of four sons, resembles an Italian female version of Barney Rubble. She is tiny and rock solid—but no chubby knees. She is a dynamo—during my shift I watch her conduct Team Time every hour on the hour. No matter how much she jumps around, her big Sue Ellen Ewing hair stays in place.

After Deanna's third session, I head back to the front desk—a platform that oversees all the weight machines, vibrating belts, and treadmills. The vibrating belts intrigue me. The clients strap a belt around their problem zones, and the belts shake, shake, shake the fat. Wow.

"Do those things work?" I ask Deanna.

"Nah," she says, evading my eyes. "They make your thighs itch, and that's about it."

"Oh," I say. "Who needs that? Itchy thighs. Blah."

"Right. So, you got a handle on Team Time, now?"

"Yes, I do."

"Good. OK, write this next thing down in your notebook. It's one of our most critical functions, as, like, Elaine Powers role models and instructors."

"OK." I sit with my pen poised and ready to write. I'm good at taking notes. Deanna picks up the microphone. "You turn it on like this," she whispers to me, and shows me a little on-and-off switch. "Write that down. Turn on the microphone."

"OK."

"Ladies, listen up! It's time for your diet tip of the day." The gyrating women step down from their weight machines, treadmills, and useless vibrating belts. They swivel to face Deanna. She is their weight-loss queen of Queens, their calorie-counting pocket pope, their great white hope for slimmer thighs and sleeker silhouettes.

"Are you ready?" she shouts.

"Yeah!" they reply.

"I can't hear you!" she yells.

"Yeah!" they scream.

"What do we wanna do?"

"Lose weight! Lose weight!"

"Louder, louder!"

"Lose weight! Lose weight!"

"OK, ladies, here we go. Your diet tip of the day—drum roll, please!" The ladies beat on the purple padded benches of the weight machines.

"Your diet tip of the day is . . . DON'T EAT PIE!"

A startled silence fills the salon. Then the ladies break into applause. After a few moments, they return to their workouts.

"That's it?" I say to Deanna. "'Don't eat pie' is your diet tip for the day?"

"Yeah," she says. "Good, right?"

"But that's ridiculous," I say. "Everyone knows not to eat pie if they're trying to lose weight. These poor women are paying $11.99 a month—"

"$9.99 a month for the two-year program, $7.99 a month for the five-year plan, and a one-time fee of $499.99 for a life-time membership."

"Right. What a deal. But shouldn't you give them something more than a poem about chubby knees and a diet tip that tells them not to eat pie?"

Deanna glares at me, and I'm really glad she doesn't have one of Barney Rubble's clubs, the thing cavemen carry with them to subdue women and woolly mammoths.

"It's not, like, rocket science," she growls. "Obvious is good."

"Obvious is good," I write in my notebook, which, thirty years later, I dig out of an old carton so I can write this story.

Cathy, a platinum L'Oréal blonde with an inch of black roots, dangling earrings, water-balloon boobs, narrow teenage-boy hips, and lavender tights paces the magenta carpet of the violet-walled Elaine Powers back office. Purple, purple everywhere. Working in this place is like living inside a grape. Cathy (who could be a man—I'm not sure) is our manager, a job that involves chain smoking and convincing the middle-aged female citizens of Flushing that they could look just like her if only they stopped eating pie and forked over $11.99 a month for the next year. Or $499.99 for the lifetime deal.

Cathy has called me into her office to discuss "security" issues at the salon. Deanna accompanies me. We all light up cigarettes. It's 1981. We smoke. No guilt.

"So," Cathy asks Deanna, "did you show Robin the panic button?"

"The panic button?" I ask. "The panic button?"

"You didn't tell her?" says Cathy to Deanna.

"I couldn't," says Deanna. "It's too upsetting."

"What?" I ask.

"Deanna," says Cathy, "if you're going be an Elaine Powers assistant manager someday, you gotta get a grip on these things. Now tell her."

I wonder if the panic button has something to do with pie.

I haven't thought about pie for a couple of years, but now I can't stop conjuring visions of my mom's pumpkin, lemon meringue, pecan, and peach pies. Flaky crusts, whipped cream, the works. I take a drag from my Benson and Hedges Gold 100s cigarette, a luxury I can't afford. I scrimp on meals, but I buy these cigarettes because I like the way the package looks. Classy.

"Terrible," says Deanna. "It's terrible. I'm surprised you didn't hear about it. It was all over the newspapers. It was even on TV."

"It really caused our membership to drop," says Cathy.

"What?" I ask.

"Go ahead," says Cathy, lighting another cigarette. "Spill."

"Well," says Deanna, "it happened in Texas. Five years ago. And people say New York City is dangerous."

"What?" I ask again.

"OK, like, two goons wearing masks busted into one of our Houston salons. They had guns, which later turned out to be toy water pistols, but how could anyone know? Anyway, they made all the ladies strip down to their underwear."

"At least they kept their underwear," says Cathy.

"Yeah, thank God for small favors," says Deanna, "although most of those underpants weren't exactly small."

"Go on," says Cathy.

"I can't," says Deanna. "You tell."

Cathy rolls her eyes and blows a long trail of smoke across the room. "They crowded all of the ladies into a small storage room, more of a closet, really, and then they selected the most, uh, voluptuous women and forced them back out onto the floor."

"They picked the fattest ones," says Deanna.

"Deanna, that's not the way an Elaine Powers instructor talks. Show some respect."

"Sorry," she says, "but it's true. I don't know why we can't say the word fat around here. It's stupid. Fat is fat. F-A-T. So, go ahead with the story."

"Right. The masked men took these stout ladies—"

"Stout? Like that's better than saying fat? Excuse me, but if I ever gain, like, a hundred pounds, call me fat, but don't call me stout."

"Fine. But stout is an approved Elaine Powers word. Anyway, they took the stout ladies and forced them onto the vibrating belt machines, with the belts around their butts. Then they turned on the machines."

"Oh, no," I say.

"You can just imagine how that looked," says Deanna. "All that naked flab, covered by those giant underpants . . . I mean, even a skinny girl on those machines looks like used Jell-O."

"Deanna! That's enough. You wanna tell the end of the story?"

"No way, José," says Deanna. "That's the worst part."

I am ready to resign on my very first day of employment. "Please don't tell me."

"Yes," says Cathy. "They watched the stout ladies on the belts. I guess the shaking of stout butts turned them on. And they did . . . unspeakable things."

"No one was hurt?" I ask, my head spinning.

"No. Upset, of course, but not harmed in any physical way. Sadly, most of them never returned to the salon again."

"Did they ever catch the guys?"

"No. They're still at large. And that's why we have a panic button. If any man comes into the salon for any reason, one of us has to stand by the panic button and be prepared to hit it. Because we don't want a VBI here in Flushing."

"A VBI?" I ask, somewhat terrified.

"A vibrating belt incident," says Deanna, flicking the ash of her cigarette into a lilac ashtray and sighing with disgust.

The following week when I'm alone and closing the salon—Cathy has given me a key because she claims I'm management material—I step onto one of the vibrating belt machines and hook the belt around my butt. I turn on the machine. In the mirror—this place has mirrors everywhere—I catch a glimpse of myself as I shake, waggle, and roll.

Look at that. Turns out I have a lot of fat on my skinny frame. A stout girl is lurking inside me, and I see her, right there in my jiggling reflection. Traumatic, indeed, and no one's even watching. That's it. No more pie for me. I lock up and go home.

A miracle! Four months into my Elaine Powers siege, a music agent calls and offers me a gig at the Newark Airport Holiday Inn, where I'll play the piano five nights a week for turnpike lounge lizards, red-eyed truck drivers, and world-weary flight crews—the worker bees of the transportation industry. I accept the offer.

For a few weeks I do both jobs, conducting Team Time during the day and playing the piano at the Holiday Inn at night. I love my job in Newark—I have a beat-up out-of-tune piano in a smoky bar and my very own hotel room with a bright orange chenille bedspread—no top bananas, bed sharing, or begging for towels. I have a decent paycheck and free meals (featuring egg dishes with melted cheese) in a real restaurant with white tablecloths, and a chance to sunbathe next to a pool with just a thin film of jet fuel floating on the water's surface. From my pool perch I watch as planes take off and land a hundred times a day—sky ships carrying eager passengers to anywhere but here. Sometimes I fall asleep outside with planes disappearing into the clouds over my head. I dream big fat dreams.

Finally, I resign from Elaine Powers and officially launch my career as a New York City pianist. I'm sad about saying good-bye to Cathy and Deanna but happy I've escaped without a VBI. I am sick of the color purple. During my final Team Time, I blast Donna Summer's cassette on the boom box. I work hard for my money, chase away those chubby knees, and wish my clients well.

"You know what?" I say to the ladies. "A little bit of fat is OK. Be fit. Be foxy. Be healthy. Be happy. Listen to music. Dance. And don't worry so much about the pie."

Deanna scowls. Cathy smiles. I exit. Obvious is good.

Six

The Girl Who Curtsied Twice

*L*ondon, November 23, 2017. The Prince of Wales is giving a ball, and so my daughter, Julia, and I are headed to Buckingham Palace, where I'll be playing dinner music tonight for His Royal Highness and 250 of his guests as they celebrate the twentieth anniversary of In Kind Direct, an organization that encourages corporate giving for social good.

Julia and I are wearing our very best sound-check/meet-the-tech-team couture—black stretchy pants with sensible shoes—and have our voluminous ball gowns, golden snakeskin sandals, extra bling, and hair-cranking products crammed into a small trolley bag. This suitcase has seen a lot in its years on the Piano Girl circuit, but tonight takes the royal cake.

Members of my family share a long and celebrated history of playing for royalty and heads of state. We are not exactly court jesters, but we come close.

My Buckingham event is one more gig on a long list of fancy-pants musical soirees. My dad calls us "grinders"—career musicians crushing one gig at a time, most of them in humble places, but some of them decidedly uptown.

Over the decades my drummer dad, bassist husband, and I have played for Lyndon Johnson, Nancy Reagan, George H. W. Bush (come back; all is forgiven), Haitian Dictator Baby Doc

Duvalier (he liked Madonna songs), the Queen of Sweden (a fan of *Cats*, the musical), the president of Brazil (Jobim, of course), Chancellor Angela Merkel (I played a couple of original tunes that she may or may not have appreciated), Vice President Al Gore (big jazz fan), Donald Trump (no obvious musical preference or discernible taste; no surprise), the president of Finland (oddly wanted to tango), Chancellor Helmut Schmidt (who honestly may have missed my performance because he spent most of his time outside smoking), members of the Thai Royal Family (also big jazz fans), various U.S. ambassadors, and (my favorite, mainly because he wore a very special embroidered robe) Crown Prince Sihanouk of Cambodia. I also once played for the king and princess of Oman. The princess liked my version of the Pachelbel Canon in D so much that she gave me a chunk of gold the size of my thumb as a thank-you gift.

Note: sniffer dogs do not like bass cases. Bass cases smell like "jazz."

This evening, the plummy Baglioni Hotel has provided us with a Maserati limousine driven by a Brit-suave guy named Abdul. Traffic slows us down for a minute, but Abdul seems wise to every shortcut in London. We swerve around pedestrians and zoom toward the palace over narrow, Harry Potter-ish lanes. The "backwards" traffic direction in the United Kingdom makes me woozy—every time Abdul turns right, I'm sure we're going to have a head-on smashup with a double-decker bus.

I'm playing at the palace tonight because Robin Boles, director of In Kind Direct, heard my performance at an event in Germany for its sister organization, Innatura (Juliane Kronen, director). Robin, like me, was born and raised in Pittsburgh. Never underestimate a woman who knows the exact location of Kaufmann's clock, the names of the three rivers that form the Golden Triangle, or the origin of the term jagoff (a Pittsburgh insult with Scottish roots, which means, among other things, a thorn in one's side). We bonded. Robin, on behalf of Prince Charles, invited me to perform at the palace.

Both In Kind Direct and Innatura focus on reducing waste by encouraging corporations to donate surplus goods to charities that can use them. A noble cause, on many levels. Tonight's guest list includes generous sponsors of In Kind Direct.

Me? I play the piano for a living and, when I have time, volunteer my musical services to nonprofit organizations creating positive change. I don't have piles of cash to contribute to worthy causes, but I have music.

When Robin booked me at Buckingham Palace—it took eighteen months of careful planning—I asked if I could bring Julia as my assistant. Julia is an aspiring photographer and filmmaker. Sadly, she left her camera back at the hotel tonight—only the royal photographer has permission to document palace events.

"Mom, exactly what am I supposed to do without a camera?" asks Julia. "How should I assist?"

"Pretend to help me. Carry the suitcase and look official. Fix my hair. Make sure I drink enough water and that my bra strap isn't hanging out. Check that I don't have toilet paper stuck to my shoe, lipstick on my teeth, or the back of my skirt tucked in my knickers. You know, the basics."

Mother's assistant: every daughter's worst nightmare. But tonight, there shall be no complaining.

"Do you think Prince Harry will be there?" she effuses. Later this week, he will announce his engagement to the enchanting Meghan, but right now, he's still technically single.

Abdul has instructions to deliver us to the palace service entrance. It figures. Even though I'm in a car fit for a king and have a $3,000 silk-taffeta Ralph Lauren ball skirt in my suitcase (purchased on sale at a Dutch factory outlet for $29.99), I still have to use the back door.

"What?" asks Julia. "We have to go through the peasant door?"

"Yeah," I say. "I'm a musician. Peasant."

"You know what that makes me? Peasant's assistant."

We bid farewell to Abdul and greet a heavily armed guard who checks our names on a list.

"Good evening to you, ladies! Lovely, lovely night, isn't it? I suppose you're here for the gala!" It can't be easy to conduct civilized chitchat while holding a machine gun, but this guy has it down. Very polite, these Londoners. Just don't shoot me—I'm only the piano player.

"Indeed, we are," says Julia, using her official Madonna in London voice. "This is Ms. Robin Goldsby, peasa . . . err, pianist, and I am her executive assistant."

Apparently, Julia gave herself a promotion while no one was looking.

"Very well, then. I'll need to see your passports, ladies, if you please." We fork over our documents. Background checks had been run several weeks ago, so the guards only have to cross-check our IDs with the info on their computers. We also have our photos taken for palace ID badges. My picture is awful; I look like someone coming to mug the royal family, not perform for them. Really, you'd think they'd have better lighting. A portrait of the queen hangs over the guard's desk—a nice touch. Several police officers are suiting up in bulletproof vests as other guards search our bags.

"Thank you for your service!" I shout, because I'm American. I can't think of anything better to say, and I feel a need to babble. A security guard plunders my suitcase, and I'm anxious about him yanking my taffeta ball skirt—also known as the "circus tent"—out of its carefully coiled position. That skirt has a life of its own.

I'm nervous—not about playing the palace piano, but about getting through security. A big part of me—the western Pennsylvania girl who suffers from occasional bouts of impostor syndrome—thinks I don't belong here. I've led a stylish life, but I am, after all, a woman of modest origins. With the assistance of a piano, a great music teacher, and a lot of grit, I've made my way from Pittsburgh to the palace. Banksville to Buckingham. Kennywood to Kensington. Mount Washington to Mountbatten.

Right now, I am about as far as I can get from Kaufmann's clock. Not a jagoff in sight.

"Mom, shall I carry your purse?" asks my executive assistant. "I do believe the event manager is ready to escort us to the sound check."

"Really?" I ask. "We're going in?"

"We're going in."

We follow a handsome event planner named Crowthers up a long set of stairs. This guy radiates star power—he's wearing a James Bond tuxedo, patent evening slippers, and a royal blue silk pocket square with matching socks.

Behind the scenes at Buckingham! We pass a sparkling, state-of-the-art, enormous kitchen with scores of workers preparing for the festivities. I've expected to see Mrs. Patmore and Daisy slaving away in the galley, but the kitchen appears to be staffed by upscale, posh-looking, multiculti Oxford grads.

The palace is huge. No wonder Her Majesty takes her pocketbook with her everywhere she goes—a woman wouldn't want to get lost in this place without taxi fare. We walk forever, up and down, around and around. Eventually, our escort opens a discreet door and—bam—we've arrived.

Julia grabs my hand. "Holy cow, Mom," she says. "Look at this."

We coast into the gallery, a panoramic, portrait-filled corridor with mile-high ceilings, plush brocade sofas, and enormous, polished chandeliers. I assumed Buckingham would have that shabby chic, trampled-by-tourists, slightly musty vibe I know from most European castles, but this place, ancient and modern all at once, is spit shined to the max. I feel like we're walking into the muscular arms of someone else's history.

The ballroom, the venue for this evening's gala dinner, is the location used for both state dinners and investitures. Knighthood! I've been dropped into a real-deal fairy tale. Thick amber light softens the kaleidoscopic effect of the crystal chandeliers. History meets opulence meets Disney.

"Well," says Julia, "I guess I was wrong. Maybe you should have brought that tiara." I actually own a tiara, but my daughter refuses to be seen with me if I wear it.

We meet the stage manager and the sound technician and head to the stage and the grand piano. Julia walks around the ballroom and listens as I play a couple of pieces. The piano sounds warm and bright; the three microphones inside the instrument will ensure proper amplification, even when people are talking during dinner. Or chatting sotto voce, as one does in a palace.

Julia joins me onstage. "Mom, look!" Behind the stage is a throne.

"Is that a real throne?" I ask.

"Mom, it's Buckingham Palace. You think they have fake thrones?"

"Yes, it's real! Pretty cool, right?" the stage manager says. She breaks down the schedule for me: "A porter will take you to a palace bedroom so you can change into your fancy dress. He'll return to fetch you and Julia at 8:30. We want you seated at the piano at 8:40. The guests will come through at 8:50. That's when you start playing. At 9:10, after the guests are seated, HRH will make a short speech from his table. Stay at the piano and resume playing when he finishes. Three courses will be served, and the meal will be finished at 10:15."

"Wow," I say. "That's really efficient."

"Yes," she says. "We're quite good at this."

I want to take this woman home with me and have her run my life.

"Let me continue," she says, glancing at her watch. "After dessert, we will give you a cue to stop playing. There will be an announcement acknowledging you. Stand, take a bow, walk down the center stage steps—facing the audience—and exit to the left. You will be escorted back to your dressing room. Sound good?"

"Wait!" says Julia. "Those steps are steep—and Mom will be wearing a rather, uh, puffy long skirt and heels. I don't want her to have a Jennifer Lawrence moment and take a tumble right in front of HRH."

Julia Goldsby, executive assistant.

"Good thinking," says the stage manager. "I will escort your mum down the stairs."

"Is there a place for Julia to sit during my performance?" I ask.

Julia points to the throne, executively. "Over there would be good."

The stage manager chuckles, royally. She wins. "You may sit in the tech booth. On the other end of the ballroom."

"Great!" says Julia "I'll be with my people."

Our porter escorts us down another long corridor and up an endless spiral staircase. We arrive at our suite and collapse on a couple of overstuffed chairs.

"Look at this!" Julia says. Royal catering has provided a large assortment of pre-event snacks and beverages. Julia turns on the television, and Her Majesty pops up on the screen, next to a little text that says "Welcome to our royal home."

Julia, who now has her stockinged feet up on the coffee table, grabs the remote, flips the channels, and lands on a UK Strongman competition.

"Well," she says. "It doesn't get any better than this. I'm in Buckingham Palace, I've got a bottle of wine, a block of cheese, a greeting from Queen Elizabeth, and a TV show featuring a muscle man who can pull a car with his teeth."

"Jul," I say, "maybe we should unpack and hang up the dresses. They might be wrinkled."

"Go ahead," she says, waving me away. "Just toss my dress on the bed. Man, this cheese is delicious. So cool they have real television in the palace. And Wi-Fi!"

"We only have thirty minutes. Maybe we should think about makeup?"

"You look fine. Don't worry so much. Hey, Mom, they sent gluten-free sandwiches for you. With hummus! I think I'll have one."

"Julia, check this out!" I am looking out the window, down into the center courtyard as the guests step out of their shiny cars. Feathers and fluff and fancy dress; I haven't seen this much white fur since I watched the news coverage of James Brown's funeral.

"Just a minute. Some guy from Reykjavik is picking up a truck with one arm."

"Julia!"

"OK, sorry. Not sorry. These guys are amazing. Do you think Her Majesty watches the Strongman show?"

"She's probably watching it right now."

Our porter picks us up at exactly 8:30. I'm not about to walk the three miles back to the ballroom in heels, so I hand them to Julia and go barefoot. I think "Barefoot in the Palace" would be a great song title. The word "palace" has some interesting rhymes: chalice, malice, Dallas . . .

"Phallus!" I yell.

"Pay attention, Mom. Hold up that skirt," Julia shouts as we start down the spiral staircase. "No accidents, please."

We reach the ballroom. I put on my shoes, head to the stage, sit on the piano bench and, with Julia's help, drape my skirt—the circus tent, big enough to qualify for its own zip code—to the side so that the fabric pools on the floor.

"See you later, Mom! Have fun. You need anything?"

"No, thanks."

"Good!" Julia heads back to the tech booth. The last-minute flurry of crew activity is enough to make me nervous, but basically, I'm chill. I love this. My assistant might be somewhat out of her depth, but even though I'm playing what amounts to a dinner-music gig, I have a porter, a stage manager, a lighting technician, a piano technician, and a sound-design team.

The stage manager approaches. "Five minutes before we start," she says. "I suggest you take this time for yourself to absorb the beauty and history of this room. You don't work in a place like this every day."

I do as I am told and absorb.

The house lights dim; the stage lights flicker and illuminate the piano. The room is completely, unnervingly, quiet.

It doesn't get any better than this. I'm in Buckingham Palace, I've got a bottle of wine, a block of cheese, a greeting from Queen Elizabeth, and a TV show featuring a muscle man who can pull a car with his teeth.

I look over my shoulder at the throne and down at my age-speckled hands. I will turn sixty in three days. When I was a kid, my sister used to drive me around Pittsburgh's Chatham Village on her tricycle. I balanced on the back while she pedaled. I pretended I was the queen and waved at my subjects, the oak trees. A striped lounge chair on our front porch was my throne. Like a lot of little girls of my generation, I thought I could get to Buckingham Palace by wearing the right fairy dress or marrying a prince. But the secret entry to the palace was right on the other side of our porch screen door—an old green piano that I played whenever I wanted to feel less like a princess and more like myself.

Music, it turns out, can be a golden ticket to just about anywhere. It took me fifty years of coaxing reluctant sounds out of unforgiving keys, but for one shining hour, I am here.

The guests arrive. I start my first piece, an original composition of mine called "First Snow." D major. I hope I don't make the royal mistake. I certainly don't want to confuse the aristocracy by playing a flatted fifth. They're very sensitive, or so I've heard.

Professional musicians know that a gig is a gig is a gig. We play the way we play. The only thing that changes, really, is context. As always, I fall into my piano zone. Even though I'm playing solo, I'm not alone—the orchestra invisible has shown up, and everyone I love is here. They're squeezed in next to me on the narrow royal piano bench, jostling for position as I play through my set list.

The hour races by, and the stage manager signals me to stop. I stand, soak up the applause, take my Buckingham bow, do my best to be humble, and extend my hand to the stage manager so I can wobble down the steps without a pratfall. On the last step, my heel catches in the hem of the damn skirt, and I almost careen into a royal banquet waiter carrying a large tray of crème brulée, but I recover in time to avoid an international incident. Pittsburgh will suffer no shame this evening.

I walk through the door as the next performer, Australian baritone Daniel Koek, prepares to go on. I recognize the laser focus in his eyes—he's pumped up and so tense he's ready to snap. Not me. I feel like I've just stepped out of a warm bath.

Julia meets me in the corridor and hugs me. "You sounded great! Nice save on the curtain-call stumble. I thought that waiter was a goner. You might want to rethink that skirt next time you have a high-pressure gig. Hey, can we get some of that crème brulée?"

"Excuse me, Mrs. Goldsby," says an official looking man, in one of those Downton Abbey butler/valet suits. "Lovely music."

"Thank you," I say. I do so love a good costume drama.

"His Royal Highness would like to meet you."

I am tempted to say "get out of town" and punch him on the shoulder—that's what we do in Pittsburgh—but I demur. "Really?"

"Indeed. Please wait here for further instructions."

"Uh-oh," says Julia. "What do you do when you meet the prince? Are there rules?"

The stage manager tracks down a protocol officer for us. He says: "Curtsy. Call him 'Your Royal Highness' the first time, then switch to 'Sir.' Wait for him to extend his hand before you extend yours. That's it. Wait here. Someone will come for you."

We hear Daniel singing "Bring Him Home" from *Les Miserables*. Wow. What a voice! The song seems an appropriate backstage soundtrack as we watch waiters and sommeliers and technicians and dozens of other groomed palace workers buzz from one station to another. I can't pretend to be too cool; I am loving this.

"Did you hear the prince's speech about waste reduction?" Julia asks. "He's really doing something positive for the planet. It's such a simple concept. Take what you have and use it. If you can't use it, donate it to someone who can. No waste." I've done a good job with Julia. If Prince Harry does show up, I will totally sing her praises.

The royal photographer hovers. My legs are stiff from all the sitting, and I'm slightly worried about executing a proper curtsy, but I have confidence that the circus tent skirt will disguise my lack of technique. When HRH shows up, I forgo the "sweep and dip" and opt for a simple hillbilly squat. My Pittsburgh roots have revealed themselves.

HRH and I have a three-minute private conversation about music and sustainability—two subjects that, oddly enough, go hand in hand. I present Julia to him, and suddenly, my cheese-eating, wine-swilling, Strongman-gawking daughter from two hours ago morphs into a picture of elegance as she gracefully nods and curtsies to our host. This child of mine, I think. A strongwoman, a princess. Executive assistant. She can have it all.

"Mom," Julia says, after HRH has departed, "I was so nervous I curtsied twice."

"You curtsied twice?"

"Yes. I don't think he saw the first curtsy, so I did it again. I must have looked like a crazy person."

"Did he notice the second curtsy?"

"Oh, yeah, he noticed. That time I got it right."

We change clothes, freshen up, wrestle the skirt back into the trolley bag, take a few swigs of wine, and slip some royal crackers into our peasant pockets. Our porter takes us back through the labyrinth of rooms and corridors, past the security gate, and just like that, we're on the street—two exhausted women in black stretch pants—looking for a taxi. I can't help noticing that the way out of the palace is much quicker than the way in.

The hulky silhouette of Buckingham looms behind us.

"The golden coach has officially turned back into a pumpkin," says Julia.

"Fine with me," I say. "I like pumpkins."

"Me, too," she says. "Pumpkins are fine with me."

Seven

The Accidental Insult

"Every number you play is better than the next one."

"Your music is so perfect, I can hardly hear it!"

"You've never sounded better."

Thank you. Wait. What?

Ah, the "accidental insult," a comment that forces one to say thank you and consider homicide at the same time. Most of the musicians I know in this racket have developed thick skins for this sort of thing. It's not hard enough to smile and remember three thousand tunes while playing for a chiropractor convention—we must also suffer the slings and arrows, the digs and dings of well-meaning but idiotic customers.

I once played a job at the Manhattan Marriott where members of my audience—attendees at a dental implant conference—had sets of dentures sitting on the cocktail tables next to their piña coladas. One of the dentists said, "You're so good at this piano thing, I couldn't hear a single note." I took a look around the room and decided to let it go.

Eleanor Roosevelt once said, "No one can make you feel inferior without your consent." In general, I agree with Mrs. Roosevelt. Sometimes, though, these accidental insults are so brain twisting that by the time I figure out the slur, the flinger of the barbed words has already left the lounge.

A stout woman with green eye shadow and hair the size of Holland said this to me a month ago: "You have such a great sense of style. We have exactly the same taste. I love the way you dress." Sadly, she wore no bra, a metallic-fringed sweater, leopard-print pants, and a saucer hat with a stuffed pig strapped to the top of it. She leaned on the Steinway to tell me that we could be twins. Miss Chantay sashayed away and left a trail of glitter in her wake.

Or the classic: "I love how you play. Have you ever thought of doing this professionally?" I hear this type of accidental insult often—usually as I am sitting down to play the third set of my fifteenth job of the week. To me this is like asking the technician administering your colonoscopy if he has ever considered charging for his services. *Wow, Dr. Hosen. You're really talented with that nozzle. In fact, you're good enough to turn your hobby into a real job.*

Note: it takes much longer to master an instrument than it does to get a medical degree.

Just last week, an aging rocker with smeared tattoos and saggy-assed pleather pants said, "You're really a good piano player. What do you do for a living?"

"This. I do this," I said.

"Wait. You mean someone actually pays you? Far out."

At the time I was sitting behind a grand piano in a five-star hotel wearing a black cocktail dress and bling at three in the afternoon, greeting each guest with a subtle smile and a sophisticated arpeggio. Maybe I looked like a volunteer—a plush pianist version of the Walmart greeter.

The word "professional" crops up often in an accidental insult. Recently a lovely man told me this: "I heard Martha Argerich play last month at the Cologne Philharmonic Hall, but I like your music better, even though she was way more professional." Perhaps he meant her performance was more structured than my relaxed tinka, tinka style of soothing background piano. She was probably playing some turbo-tempo shoot-me-now Prokofiev or something, and—as we all know—you have to be "professional" to handle that.

In the eighties, my husband was called to sub for another bassist at a midtown concert in Manhattan. The introduction went like this: "Please give a warm round of applause for the wonderful bassist, John Goldsby. Such a professional! He's always the guy we call when the real bassist can't make it."

The accidental insult is not limited to performances. Consider this: a woman I know (who claimed to be a friend) once looked at a published photo of me and said: "You look great in this photo because you're so far away from the camera."

Or this: "Your album cover is *so* pretty. It doesn't even look like you."

And another: "You're so lucky you're not famous. No one in the whole world knows who you are."

The late Dorothy Donegan, a renowned jazz pianist with chops of steel and flying fingers, used to come and listen to me in Manhattan. She said, "You play with an economy of notes. Of course, you have to." Dorothy wore really big red satin under-pants—bloomers actually. Don't ask me how I know this, but I do. I could tell you the story, but the jazz police might arrest me.

Sometimes the insults are real. Consider this slap in the face from a soon-to-be ex-boyfriend who once left his MENSA card on my piano: "What a fabulous job you have. So early in life and you have already ascended to your level of incompetence." He didn't think that I was smart enough to understand the barb. Double insult, no accident. MENSA Man got pretty far with me, but he struck out with that little jab. I can fight back hard when I'm sitting at a piano.

Bob, my dad, who spent decades working with nice people on the *Mister Rogers' Neighborhood* set, is no stranger to the real-world accidental insult. When I was a kid, we spent a summer at Conneaut Lake, where he had a gig playing in a nice restaurant and bar. He fished during the day, performed at night, and grew a beard while we were there. When we returned to Pittsburgh, a woman at our church, Mrs. Rudolph, cornered him in the vestibule after the service.

Mrs. Rudolph: "Welcome back, Bob. You look nice and tan, but I hate that beard."

Bob: "Thank you, Mrs. Rudolph. I like that red dress you have on, but I think you're too fat. Since we're sharing opinions, that is mine."

Go, Bob! I'm not that brave.

And speaking of Bob—we still haven't recovered from the Great Accidental Insult of 2007. Miss Judy Murphy, a senior citizen who boasted a home full of fake Chippendale furniture and a manicured front garden, once lived in my Chatham Village neighborhood in Pittsburgh. She was perfectly nice to my family but, back in the seventies, spent a lot of time on "pet patrol," prowling around our "pet-free" community looking for evidence of people hiding illegal cats in their homes. My mother swore to Miss Murphy that Stripey, the silver tabby who liked to snooze on the sill of our bay window, was a marble statue. Miss Murphy believed her. She may have been a little sozzled—Chatham Village cocktail parties were legendary.

I digress. Decades after all of us had moved out of Chatham Village, and Stripey had gone on to marble cat heaven, Miss Murphy called my musician father to congratulate him on the publication of my first book. By this time Miss Murphy was probably 125 years old.

"Bob," she warbled, "I just loved Robin's book. She is so talented. You know, Bob, you used to have talent, too, but you gave it up for your family."

Even my dad didn't know what to say to that.

Most people have good hearts; they want to say something nice, but it comes out lopsided and loopy. Maybe I'm too sensitive. Or maybe I'm not sensitive enough.

Eight

The Hostess Is on Fire

I change clothes in the wellness area of the five-star hotel where I currently perform—trading my basic-black stretchy sweatpants for a basic-black stretchy evening gown and my Nikes for a pair of golden sandals that have accompanied me on piano gigs for several decades. They are as uncomfortable now as they were when I bought them, but the bling at my toes reminds me, in a good way, of years I'll never recapture and songs I've long forgotten. I'll spend most of the evening sitting on an upholstered piano bench. If I need to make a fast getaway, I can always kick off the sandals and run.

But why would I run? Playing background piano music at an upscale private party offers me a chance to cross into the Piano Girl zone, a tranquil place where the secure borders between *who I am* and *what I do* vanish. I don't always gain entrance to the zone—technical challenges, the bear, and the Voice of Doom often mess with my head—but I try. On evenings when I remain outside the zone, watching the clock and feeling unappreciated, time creeps backwards as I play choruses of songs that never seem to end.

How is it still 8:10? It was 8:10 twenty minutes ago.

I hope to get into the zone tonight. I am playing for a group of Americans traveling through Germany. Because they're connected to the television and radio business, they know about my NPR radio shows and my family links to PBS. About sixty guests will enjoy a four-course fancy dinner while I provide pleasant dinner music. Nice.

I check the Steinway situated in the far corner of the dining room. It's next to a wrought-iron, tree-shaped candelabra. Each branch of the tree holds a small votive candle. Candlelight twinkles in the high-ceilinged, dusky dining room, throwing dancing shards of silver light on the polished ebony piano. I count my blessings, flex my aching toes, and wait for the guests to arrive. I hope there will be snacks on my break; I'm already hungry.

Because I've been doing this for forty years, I know exactly how this evening will unfold. The guests will greet me, applaud politely, have some wine, start chatting, and completely ignore me for the rest of the evening. With the help of the human din and candlelight, I will enter the zone and float through four hours of doing something I love. I will note each food course as it is served, wonder if I'll get something to eat before I faint at the keyboard, and time my music to accompany the flow of the dinner. Right after the main course (medallions of grass-fed something with asparagus) and directly before dessert (a study in mango), things will wind down. At the end of the evening a few well-meaning, lubricated guests will compliment my music, and I will be pleased that someone was listening. My back will protest, but I will play another set for a handful of people lingering over espresso and pralines.

This is how it always goes.

Until it doesn't.

The hostess of the party, a vivacious, curvy Colorado woman named Pat Allen, with a lush head of hair, sweeps into the dining room ahead of her guests. She runs a company called Premier Tours and specializes in planning luxury travel for American companies seeking to reward loyal clients with European elegance. The Excelsior Hotel Ernst is a good match for her high standards.

"Robin!" she says, balancing a glass of champagne in one hand and a handbag in the other. "I am so happy to meet you!

I was a huge fan of Marian McPartland and Mister Rogers and can't believe you knew both of them! We can't wait to hear you play."

American enthusiasm. How I miss it.

Pat is a fast talker, but she's hoarse after shuffling her tour group through various European cities. She sounds a little like Demi Moore on speed. Still, I'm delighted to talk to one of my tribe—something about a straight-ahead American accent warms my heart.

"Thank you for inviting me to play," I say. "It's an honor."

"I'm sorry about my voice," she croaks. "I have been wrangling this bunch for a few days ,and I have the worst case of laryngitis. I love that your father was on *Mister Rogers' Neighborhood* all those years. How cool is that?"

Pat's voice is so far gone that I can only hear every other word. She really needs to stop talking and rest her voice, but she won't take a break.

This particular group of American tourists hails from Louisiana, which leads me to believe they could be conservative Republicans. But I am unsure where Pat sits on the spiked political fence. Because of her allegiance to public television and radio, and her exuberance for all things European, I'm guessing she's batting for my team, but who knows? I am here to play the piano, not give speeches about racism, sexism, and fascism. In fact, I should avoid the "isms" and just sit down at the damn piano and play "As Time Goes By" or something. But Voiceless Pat wants to talk.

She offers me a glass of champagne. Do I say no? Of course not. Never, ever turn down free champagne. As I sip, she says, "The latest election—it's all anyone can talk about. All the Europeans want to know what's happening to America. Not my fault, I tell them."

As Voiceless Pat grows more agitated talking about politics in the United States—and who can blame her, really—she steps back toward the candle tree.

Whoosh! The tips of her big hair catch one of the flickering votive candles, and, as quickly as you can say *"no collusion,"* her hair goes up in flames.

Pat does not feel the heat—she has a lot of hair padding her scalp—and unaware that she's on the verge of igniting the entire dining room, continues to rattle on about the lack of funding for public television. The flames shoot from her skull. She looks like something out of a Harry Potter film. I might be slow to respond to much of what life throws at me, but I am quick in emergency situations. Without missing a beat, I slap her, several times, on the back of her burning head.

"WHY ARE YOU HITTING ME?" Which sounds like: "YY R U ITTIG EEE?"

Pat looks puzzled. Possibly she's stunned that her pianist for the evening—who has yet to play a single note—is accosting her right in the middle of a European luxury hotel.

"You're on fire!" I shout. Then I slap her again.

She tries to say something, but her voice is completely gone, and it sounds like: "H——p—f."

Finally, she smells the burned hair and realizes what has happened.

"Let's blame this on politics," I say.

Her guests, slack-jawed with disbelief and slightly horrified by the sight of their tour guide and party hostess self-immolating before the *amuse bouche* is served, breathe a collective sigh of relief when Pat begins to laugh.

"I always knew I was hot," she rasps.

Either this woman has a really great sense of humor, or she is the world's best hostess—determined to make sure her guests have a good time even if she has to visit a burn unit before they dig into their *poulet* terrine.

"Not bad enough I lost my voice," she shouts, as best she can. "I have to lose my hair, too."

She turns back to me. "How bad is it?" she squeaks.

"Not bad at all," I say. "Here. Sit down on my piano bench. I have a brush in my handbag. I'll patch up your hairdo, *pronto.*"

Whoosh! The tips of Pat's big hair catch one of the flickering votive candles, and, as quickly as you can say "*no collusion,*" her hair goes up in flames.

I brush a few charred chunks from the back of her head. She has a lot of hair. I can hardly see the damage. Lucky for her. If this had happened to me, I'd look like Bruce Willis.

So much for the Piano Girl zone. I am not sure of the protocol for a situation like this. I've seen some weird stuff over the years—a guest who peed in her chair, a dog who howled along to *Phantom of the Opera* tunes, a man with no arms who sat in on my gig and played the piano with his toes—but in my many decades of solo piano jobs, I've never had to slap the hostess to extinguish flames shooting from her head. *Hostess flambé* is new to me.

I glance at my watch.

Ah. 8:10. I should have known. Time to get started.

Nine

Sing

John and I enter the Burgerhaus Forum in Overath, Germany. Tonight, our daughter, Julia, is singing with the Paul Klee High School Choir, a feisty group of kids between the ages of fifteen and nineteen who meet once a week in the evenings to learn new songs, study new harmonies, and tackle new challenges. That's what they tell themselves, anyway. Mainly, for the past two years, they've been having a hell of a lot of fun with music. They call themselves The Singin' Pauls.

The concert is scheduled to begin at 7 p.m. We're fifteen minutes early, and the hall is already full—around five hundred enthusiastic fans have shown up to listen to the choir. I look around and see a smattering of parents and grandparents, but I'm most impressed by the huge number of schoolmates crowding into the venue. Kids cheering for their musical friends! In Germany we don't have school-sponsored athletic competitions. But we have this, and I'm grateful. We root for musicians instead of the athletes. It's a little like having the halftime show without the football game. No linebackers, no pom-poms, no referees. Just music.

But no seats! It's fifteen minutes until showtime, and the joint is already packed. We may have lived in the German countryside for almost nineteen years, but we've maintained a few of our hard-won Manhattan skills—John and I can find a cab, a parking place, or an empty seat in just about any situation. We have good "available space" karma—a talent that comes from squeezing into crowded Times Square subway trains during rush hour.

"Look! There. Front row, left side. Two seats. Go." We advance toward the seats and snag them just in time.

"I don't know," says John as he sets up his dad camera, the video equipment that comes with pride of parenthood. "Julia might not be so thrilled to see us in the first row. Especially since I have the camera."

"What?" I ask. "The only other choice is the very last row. We're American parents. We're supposed to be pushy, remember? We're staying in the front."

At this point I spot Curtis, Julia's brother, right behind us, with a couple of his friends. He's proud of his sister.

Anticipation bounces around the hall. John finishes setting up his Zoom camera, and we're ready to go. The house lights dim. Forty kids march onstage and take their places. All shapes and sizes: Goths and good girls, hippies and Emos, German, Turkish, French, Iranian, Palestinian, and, yes, American. They face the audience. I can't decide if they look old or young. Julia stays out front—she has a solo in the first song. She messes with the microphone cable, then turns around. That's when she sees us in the front row—John with his camera, and me, bursting into tears. Where these tears come from, I have no idea. I could blame it on my mother (she's a champion weeper, and I seem to have inherited this trait from her), menopause, or the whole circle of life thing, which sets me off pretty often these days, but really there's no excuse. It's a high school choir concert, for heaven's sake—a medium-sized group of big kids trying to look cool. That's it. Their sweet, expectant faces are killing me. This is not casual crying with ladylike tears; these are big shoulder-shaking sobs.

Julia laughs when she sees us. Then she rolls her eyes, just a little. Five hundred people are here; she's preparing to sing a solo; her dad, with his goofy grin, is aiming a camera at her; her mother is having a change-of-life breakdown; and she's completely calm. She looks like she's hanging out in a playground with friends. Which, in its own way, is exactly what she's doing.

The audience cheers for the choir before they've even sung a note. Frau Hövel, the maestra, raises her baton. Herr Müller, the codirector of the choir and the accompanist, strikes the first notes on the piano. Forty voices join together, and the room fills with music. Not perfect, but somehow, just right.

Della Henderson Rawsthorne, my paternal grandmother, was an accomplished singer—a contralto—and the musical director at the Haven Heights Methodist Church in Pittsburgh. The church paid her a decent salary to show up once a week for rehearsals, to select the music for Sunday services, and to conduct the choir.

For much of my childhood, I spent Sundays and religious holidays watching her in the choir loft, holding together an aging but enthusiastic throng of warblers, brayers, and chirpers, all of them heaven- and hell-bent on making it through the week's hymns without a misfire, a croak, or one hallelujah too many. Grandma, her deep and powerful voice booming through the sanctuary, covered up a multitude of musical sins with her own contralto valor. Daring and inventive, she led her singers through an inspired repertoire of Methodist music—"Up from the Grave He Arose!" was my favorite—assigning solos to both the strong and the weak, pumping her arm in time to the organ music, plucking notes like daffodils out of her weedy garden of singers.

I admired Grandma's skill and bravery, but the choir itself? High comedy.

I might have been nine years old, but I knew funny when I saw it. Whenever Orville Rudolph—a robust tenor who always sang about a quarter-step sharp—stood up for a solo, my brother, sister, and I would bite our cheeks and turn purple in our attempts to avoid laughing out loud. The "fall on your knees" part of "Oh, Holy Night" rivaled anything we had ever seen or heard on *The Ed Sullivan Show*. We learned to double over in the wooden pew and pretend to tie our shoelaces during the solo sections, our mother clutching her hymnal and glaring at us, our shoulders shaking with silent guffaws. Mom also thought Orville was pretty funny, but at the advanced age of thirty-two, she knew a thing or two about gracious restraint. My dad just raised his eyebrows when Orville hit the high notes, which made us laugh even harder.

I feel kind of bad about it now—really, who were we to giggle at anyone's honest attempt to praise the Lord, or anything else, through music? I hope Orville made it to his own version of choir heaven. I hope he has gotten to sing lots of solos. I also hope, for my grandmother's sake, that they've installed auto-tune in God's control room.

John and I moved to Cologne, Germany, in 1994 when he accepted the solo bass chair with the WDR Big Band. I adapted to the new culture—though learning the language almost killed me—and began playing a solo piano gig at a local castle when I wasn't home making grilled cheese sandwiches for my kids. In a successful attempt to raise bilingual children, we registered them in the local school system. For five years, I was the volunteer choir director of the Paul Klee High School International Choir in Overath, Germany. I slid into the job when my kids were in junior high, and I realized the school didn't have enough music teachers to cover the fifth, sixth, and seventh grade choir. What, no choir? I had little choral experience myself, but I played the piano, I had written a bunch of kids' songs, and I honestly thought, how hard could it be?

Well . . .

Every Wednesday for five years I met with thirty kids, most of them eleven, twelve, or thirteen years old. My own kids were in the mix. We spoke and sang in English, mainly because I didn't want anyone, especially thirty precocious twelve-year-olds, laughing at me singing in German with an American accent. If I wasn't careful, I could sound like Colonel Klink doing Mr. Rogers—or vice versa.

A set of drums sat next to the entrance to the choir room. Here is a fact: it is impossible for a sixth-grade boy to walk past a set of drums without bashing the ride cymbal. Twice. Nothing will stop a boy from doing this.

Each Wednesday, before leaving the house for our five o'clock rehearsal, I took two Tylenol and a hot bath. Preventive medicine. I developed a thick skin, thicker eardrums, and newfound respect for teachers. I worked two hours a week with these kids; I couldn't imagine the constitutions of the brave men and women who showed up Monday through Friday, eight hours at a shot.

"Whatever they're paying these teachers," I said to John, "it's not nearly enough."

"You have an excellent job playing the piano in a castle," John said. "Why are you doing this?"

I didn't have an acceptable answer.

"I have two simple goals," I told John, dodging the question. "First, I want to teach them to clap on two and four." German kids are programmed to clap on one and three, which has the undesired effect of turning everything, even the funkiest piece of music ever written, into a Wagnerian march. "Second," I said, "I want them to sing and say the "th" sound properly. If I can do that, I'll feel like I've accomplished something."

Getting "two and four" wasn't so easy—it took months of backbeat practice—but eventually they nailed it. They started to swing, just a little. The "th" fell into place a bit faster. The "th" sound doesn't exist in the German language, and, most of the time, it ends up sounding like a "z." I wrote a tongue twister for them to practice: "Thelma, the thick-headed thief, had three hundred and thirty-three thousand, three hundred and thirty-three threatening thoughts."

Zelma transformed into Thelma, we found the backbeat, and we were groovin'.

They sang at many concerts, and I watched in complete amazement as these kids—shy, insecure, and standing on the slippery precipice of puberty—learned to take pride in their teamwork. What they lacked in musical ability they made up for in eagerness. One of the "real" music teachers at the school tried to convince me to hold auditions each year—for the sake of quality control—but I refused. Anyone who wanted to sing was welcome.

We found the backbeat, and we were groovin'.

"This isn't about music," I told him. "It's about fun. Singing makes for happy kids. It's almost impossible to sing with a group and be grumpy at the same time. These kids need to have fun. School is serious enough." I'm sure I sounded a little too American for the system, but my class, my rules.

My choir kids never got much beyond two-part harmony, but they were loud, smiling, and full of joy. We had choreography, a healthy amount of "two" and "four" clapping, and a series of soloists with backup singers. During the final year we started to look like a sixth-grade Las Vegas act. Instead of sequins and feathers, we wore red T-shirts. Curtis, my son, would play congas or drums; John, when he was available, would show up and play the bass. Eventually, Julia took over at the piano. The kids hardly needed me for anything at all. They had found each other. Music was their navigation system.

We practiced, we performed, we had a ball. As their leader, I was pretty relaxed. I only had one firm rule: no one was allowed to laugh at anyone else. Never mind Orville and my own sordid past as a laugher; our choir room was a safe place, the sacred ground of creative expression, a space where the kids could be bigger versions of themselves. No laughing, unless we were all doing it together. Orville Rudolph, after all those years, had come back to teach me a lesson.

Five years, a hundred headaches, and twenty concerts later, I reluctantly stepped down. The music faculty had added several new teachers to the staff, my own kids had moved on to the upper classes at the school, and, well, it was time. Not a high school kid alive wants her mother hanging out in the school music room. It just isn't cool.

We made a big splash at our last concert, then kept meeting for the rest of the semester, just to sing and finish the term with style. For the final session, I invited parents and friends for a farewell musical soirée. I thought it would be a good excuse to eat brownies and a nice way to say "auf Wiedersehen." We prepared some tunes from *High School Musical*; a few of my originals, including our big hit, "I Can Speak English," plus "The

Girl from Ipanema" in Portuguese (with the help of a Brazilian choir mom); "Kansas City"; "Seasons of Love"; and, because the kids requested it, "My Heart Will Go On," also known as the dreaded *Titanic* theme.

Five minutes before we were scheduled to start our presentation, Janina, a very pretty and bashful girl who had been with me for two years, came to my side.

"Robin," she whispered, "I am ready."

"Ready for what?" I asked. I had discovered over the years that a kid this age assumes the entire world knows what she's thinking.

"My solo. I am ready to sing a solo."

If Janina had told me she had booked a round-trip ticket to Reno, I would not have been more surprised.

"Really? That's great! Just great! Which song do you want to sing?"

"Titanic," she said. "The second verse. I practiced it."

"You've got it, Janina," I said. "Kids, stay out of Janina's way on the second verse. She's going to sing it solo. Solo!"

They cheered for her.

The soirée was a huge success. We sang and danced and stomped. We got to the last tune of the set, the *Titanic* theme, and I announced that Janina would be the soloist. I saw her mother's jaw drop. We started the song. When it came time for the second verse, Janina stepped forward, with three girls holding her up on each side. Her voice was helium high and tiny, but I swear it was the loudest and proudest thing I've ever heard in my life.

Four years later, here I am, not at the piano, but in the front row, happy to be just a normal parent enjoying the show. Tonight's concert, featuring a generation of kids who will carry the backbeat forward and pronounce every "th" they encounter for the rest of their lives, offers us a little Cold Play, a Beatles tune— "Penny Lane"—"Bohemian Rhapsody," "Stand by Me," "Circle of Life," "Skyfall," and a few trendy songs I've never heard.

Julia and the choir start the evening with a tune called "Happy Ending." The Mama Rose in me wants to quote the musical *Gypsy* and shout, "Sing out, Louise," but the close proximity of the male members of my family keeps me in check. I get control of my sobbing about halfway through the song.

I look around. My sixth-grade choir kids are young adults now, most of them capable of walking past a drum set without hitting the ride cymbal, all of them stretched out and dressed up and ready for anything. A year or two before graduation, these kids face a complicated world, but for now, while they're singing, there's reason to celebrate.

The audience claps along—on the backbeat—and I sit back and watch time roll by, like too many sixteenth notes, my husband beside me, my grown son in the row behind me, my daughter center stage, and Grandma Rawsthorne somewhere in the room. Now I know why I'm crying. When this evening is over, where will the flawed and glorious music go? Poof. I hate when good things disappear.

I hope these kids will hold onto their songs. I hope they'll keep singing for themselves and each other. Look. There, in the second row onstage. It's Janina. She's singing her heart out.

Ten

Astoria

Step lively now!

Back in the eighties, during my busiest years as a Manhattan Piano Girl, I had a subway routine. Late at night I took cabs, but when I played during the daytime, I would finish my last set, grab my coat, fight for an elevator, join the throbbing crowd of Times Square movers, shakers, and sidewalk dwellers, scurry down into the Forty-Ninth Street station, slide onto the RR train, scuffle for a seat, and heave a sigh of relief when I got one. I had a sushi habit during the eighties. Hoping for a wasabi rush, I would often grab takeout tekkamaki from a Seventh Avenue Japanese joint called Iroha and eat it on the subway while cruising past subterranean stops for Carnegie Hall and Bloomingdale's.

The RR train—sometimes called the "Rock and Roll to Astoria"—slithered beneath the plush, posh, privileged pads of the East Side, screeched under the East River, and burst forth onto a sepia-toned mural of outer borough-ness: Queens.

I made my bridge-and-tunnel trip thousands of times in the fifteen years I lived in New York and never tired of the view from Queensboro Plaza, the way the serrated Manhattan skyline taunted the humble Queens horizon. The two parts of my life—where I worked and where I lived—remained separated by a yawning moat of fast-moving, murky water.

At the end of each voyage, I would step off the RR in my low-key Astoria neighborhood, relieved to be a few short blocks from my affordable two-bedroom apartment. It took five minutes to walk home from the train stop. Thirtieth Avenue, a bastion of every possible health-code violation, boasted dozens of entertainment and food-frenzy options—a profound grab bag of multiculti delights.

I always liked Tony's Souvlaki, a Greek restaurant that featured an outdoor, one-armed mannequin wearing a chef's hat and checkered trousers. The dummy waved a skewer of plastic meat with his plastic arm and wore a sign around his neck that said, "Come on in!" Tony's Souvlaki hosted a legendary family of "flying raccoons" living in the restaurant ceiling. When I got lucky, I'd squint into the hanging philodendron and spot the glowing eyes of one of them scoping out my feta cheese and olive platter. I'm still not sure they were raccoons. They might have been airborne rats.

Across the street from Tony's was a Greek nightclub that served hallucinogenic ouzo. I went there once with my husband and a group of musician friends. We drank the famed ouzo (my pal Peter, who is Greek, and should know better, tried to order an ouzo Collins) and listened to a Greek Elvis impersonator singing "Heartbreak Hotel" in 7/4. Or maybe it was 13/4 (an impossible time signature conquered only by Macedonian folk masters or members of the band Rush). Then everyone threw plates. More than that I do not recall.

Astoria pulsed with the odd-meter rhythm of its Greek population, but the bench depth of its diversified community—Indians, Eastern Europeans, Asians—also contributed random swipes of vibrancy to its funky, we're-all-in-this-together vibe. I can trace my family roots back to Plymouth Rock—I've always claimed my ancestors were the lounge act on the *Mayflower*—but in Astoria, I was as foreign as everyone else, a stranger in a strange land, trying to make ends meet while adjusting to life in a city renowned for eating its young.

Happy-Happy Variety, run by a Chinese family, sold take-out Chinese food, an assortment of kneesocks, and flowers. One year, on Mother's Day, I stopped on the way home from my Manhattan brunch gig and bought some dumplings and a big bunch of peonies. I have always loved peonies. They look like petals crossed with clouds.

"Happy-Happy Mutha Day," said Mrs. Chang. "You mutha?"

"No," I said, "I just like peonies."

"No matta. You get penis for Happy, Happy Mutha Day."

"Peonies. You mean peonies!"

"Yeah, yeah. Penis. You like penis! Penis good."

In addition to buying the occasional penis, I ordered a lot of sesame noodles from Happy-Happy. One time the Happy-Happy delivery boy got mugged right outside our apartment door but still managed to ring the bell and deliver our food. Sadly, this was the exact night my husband's parents were visiting. We tipped the bleeding, bedraggled delivery boy—he refused to let us call the police—and sent him off on his mangled bicycle. Then we spent most of the evening trying to assure my in-laws that the mugging was not a nightly occurrence.

"It's safe in Astoria," we proclaimed.

The house next door might well have been a crack den, but that's a story for another time.

Mrs. Chang eventually turned her empire over to her son, Young Chang, who wasn't as bright or enterprising as his mother, but, boy, could he fold laundry. He even pressed my socks—purchased at Happy-Happy Variety before it became Happy-Happy Laundry. They got me coming and going.

I spent a lot of time eating on trains—grazing on New York City delicacies as I "pink-panthered" back and forth to Manhattan gigs. It never occurred to me to cook—I had so many piano jobs that it only made sense to eat while commuting.

Rosie, a Polish woman who worked at a coffee shop right under the elevated train platform in Astoria, made my egg-and-cheese sandwiches every afternoon before I headed into work.

Across the street from Rosie's place was the Keystone Diner, a twenty-four-hour mecca of mediocre cuisine where I could order any of the three million items on the menu at any time of day or night. I imagined their kitchen stretching under the river—all the way to Manhattan—staffed by culinary masters capable of whipping up Greek diner versions of cordon bleu, Belgian waffles, or truffle-stuffed trout at 7 a.m.

I discovered that if I ordered two takeaway baked potatoes from the Keystone, I could stash them in my coat pockets and keep my hands warm on the windy train platform. And once I arrived at my gig, I would hang out in the swank ladies' room and eat my pocket warmers before I started to play. I even carried little packets of salt in my purse—along with golden sandals, an extension cord, and duct tape. It was all very professional.

Also on my block in Astoria was an Indian grocery run by a soft-spoken, elegant man named Sanjay. I liked to buy a delicious Indian dessert called a *gulob*, a word I sometimes got mixed up with gonad, understandable if you've ever seen a gulob (or a gonad). Sanjay also sold frozen Indian TV dinners and made fresh samosas spicy enough to blow off your gulobs. He was my hero.

On my corner was a funeral home run by the LaBrutto family. The LaBrutto brothers—really nice guys—were also in the chiropractor business. Funeral home and chiropractor office—the combination caused me some unease: it somehow seemed like a conflict of interests. Also, having the sound of the word "brute" in the name of a company dedicated to orthopedic adjustments and burial services seemed, at best, like bad marketing.

> *Your crack 'em, we stack 'em.*
> *You squeeze 'em, we freeze 'em.*
> *You stab 'em, we slab 'em.*
> *You kill 'em, we chill 'em.*

Like that.

My Astoria neighborhood was a classic cradle-to-grave community—within one block I had a hospital, a school, a nursing home, and the LaBrutto brothers—ready to align my spine and help me select a casket.

Plus, all those gonads and raccoons.

My fabulous landlords, the handsome Burburan family—originally from Croatia—cushioned me through my serial dating years. Eventually, they sold the house to the Politos, first generation Italian Americans. The Polito family operated a hugely successful office-cleaning company and had amassed a small fortune with hard work and very little English. Charming, cheerful, but a little confused by my lifestyle, the Politos didn't mind the sound of my piano at all hours of the day and night or my cat, Lucky, who occasionally escaped into their part of the house.

"She's a nice-a puppy," Mr. Polito would say, patting the cat on her head.

The Politos grew tomatoes in pots on the concrete driveway. Every year, in the pounding August heat, the entire family would sit in a circle of lawn chairs and puree fresh tomatoes—with an ancient, hand-cranked, tomato squashing machine—to ready them for sauce. The view from my upstairs bedroom window looked like a blood-splattered scene from a Quentin Tarantino film. But the sauce was excellent.

Around the corner from my apartment was a Korean nail salon, called Fancy Finger. I loved Fancy Finger. I would walk in the door, a little bell would ring, and Mrs. Kim, the proprietor, hunched over another client, would yell from behind her surgical mask,

"WELCOME FANCY FINGA. PICK COLOR."

I had always chosen pale beige for my working woman hands and rouge-noir lacquer for my toes. This worked nicely until the final month of my pregnancy. Mrs. Kim refused to paint my toenails a dark color.

"Too much depressing," she said. "Baby pop out, first thing, see devil color. He go back in. No come out. Big scary for baby."

I argued, but she insisted on candy pink for my toes. Big scary for me.

"Nicey color. It say, 'Welcome to world, baby.'"

One afternoon, on my way to a manicure appointment, I dropped off my son at the home of his day-care provider, a Puerto Rican woman named Lisa, who lived two doors down, on the other side of the (alleged) crack house. Lisa had laundered my son's baby blanket and handed it to me at the door. Rather than return home with the blanket and risk being late for my date with Mrs. Kim, I carried it with me and hustled around the corner to Fancy Finger. Just as I passed the LaBrutto chiropractor office, a large Ryder rental truck raced onto the avenue, swerved onto the curb, and almost hit me. The truck squealed to a halt, right across the street from Astoria General Hospital.

I stood there, freaked out and muttering obscenities. The driver—a Jamaican man—leaped out of the truck screaming about his wife. I couldn't understand him, but his hysteria indicated he needed help. He flung open the double back doors of the truck, and there, rolling around like a pea in a barrel, was his wife, moaning, crying, and about to give birth.

I knew nothing about delivering babies—hey, I'm just the piano player—but my own baby was six months old, and I knew a lot about the panic of childbirth, especially, I imagined, if one was flopping around, panty-less and unharnessed, in an empty truck meant to transport dining tables and bookcases.

I stayed calm and told the husband, who was useless, shouting, and flailing his arms in that alpha-male chop-chop motion, to run to the hospital and get help. I climbed into the truck and got the woman on her back. I shoved my son's baby blanket—white with colorful airplane embroidery—under her bottom. I tried to soothe her, but her moans had become screams; and I could see, when she opened her legs, that the baby was coming. Blood. Lots of blood. Not good.

All I wanted was a manicure, and there I was, an unwilling guest star in a pilot episode of *Call the Midwife*.

I glanced up the street and spotted a couple of parked ambulances. Their drivers were probably sitting in the Keystone Diner eating mile-high coconut pie. Frustrating. We were right in front of a damn hospital that boasted dozens of trained medical specialists, we had at least four paramedics within a block's range, and this poor woman was about to push her infant into the trembling hands of a Piano Girl. Big scary for baby.

Finally, the husband came running back to the truck, followed by two workers and a gurney. One of the ambulances, likely summoned by the hospital, turned on its siren and drove the hundred yards to the truck.

We could have done without that siren.

"She's having a baby," I yelled. "NOW! Get a hose or a bucket or some towels or something!"

"We've got this, ma'am," said one of the paramedics—he could have been auditioning for an episode of *Grey's Anatomy*—as he glided me out of the truck and took control. He evaluated the situation and said, in one of those calm, med-tech voices that are the hallmark of EMT professionals:

"Breech. And we're doing this right here."

I stood outside the truck and tried to help keep rubberneckers to a minimum. I really wished I had a piano.

The baby boy—Astoria's newest resident—entered the world ass first. The crowd cheered, and I burst into tears. A paramedic wrapped him in my son's blanket and rushed him into the hospital.

The mother, her eyes squeezed shut against the glare of the Queens sky, chanted, "We are safe. We are safe. We are safe!" The paramedics lifted her onto the gurney and rolled her across the street. The sliding glass doors opened, and she disappeared.

I was already late for work, so I never did get my nails done.

We left New York City in 1994 when my husband the bassist was offered a dream jazz job in Germany. Over the course of fifteen years in Astoria, I had composed several albums of music, made some money, and catapulted myself from chubby-cheeked naïveté to pencil-skirted semi-sophistication. I fell in and out of love, occasionally settled for less than I deserved, and figured out how to get more of what I wanted. I ran the gamut of adult feelings—anguish, hunger, ambition, disappointment, elation, loss. It made sense to leave, but it wasn't easy; Astoria had both grounded me and given me rainbow-colored wings.

The RR train became the N train; the Politos sold the house for a small fortune; the flying raccoons relocated. The Jamaican American baby boy who was born in the back of a truck is now twenty-five years old. From what I've heard, the community gleams with the spit shine of gentrification and has lost some of its ethnic edge. But Astoria will always celebrate diversity and bow to its ouzo roots. The hospital, school, nursing facility, and funeral home remain in place, waiting for the next round of dreamers, doers, and drifters to move in, move out, move on.

Talk to me about immigration, and I will tell you that it makes a neighborhood sing.

Eleven

Magic to Do

*I*t's 1980. Danny Herman, a dancer and acrobat, has pirouetted his way into my heart and become my newest show-biz friend. Not boyfriend; just friend. Last month, the two of us moved from Pittsburgh to New York City and struggled to find work as performers. After a few weeks of pounding the Manhattan pavement in search of a gig, Pittsburgh producer Don Brockett calls both of us and offers us jobs in the national touring company of *Big Bad Burlesque*, a successful off-Broadway show headed to St. Louis.

Back in Pittsburgh, the cast goes through an intense rehearsal period, then we move to St. Louis and spend a few glorious months living at the Chase Park Plaza Hotel, where we perform eight shows a week in a sparkling little theater deep in the hotel's dank underbelly. Danny is our choreographer, dance captain, and lead dancer. I have several roles in the show: I'm a piano-playing stripper, piccolo-toting ballerina, and reluctant dancer. I sing "Hard Hearted Hanna," dance my ass off while braying "Praise the Lord and Pass the Ammunition," and crank out a raunchy version of "Night Train" on an out-of-tune grand piano. We are up to our necks in sequins and Spandex and smell like sweat, hairspray, and eyelash glue.

The theater manager has a pet monkey that sits on his shoulder. Danny is nineteen. I am twenty-three. We are big babies in adult-sized Danskins. Before our first show each night, we dine in an employee cafeteria that features hot dogs and a chalky man with respiratory problems who shuffles around the seating area, chain smokes, and coughs on our food. I'm sure he has been employed by the food and beverage manager to keep performers from eating too much of the free grub.

"Excuse me, Miss," Danny says to the stout, grunting, hairnetted woman perched behind the steam table overseeing an unidentifiable mess in a pot. "Could you please tell me what vegetable you're serving today?"

"That be squash."

We enjoy hearing the hairnet lady, whose name is Winnie, talk about squash. In Winnie's world, any vegetable or fruit is squash. Even the applesauce.

Danny finds out that Winnie owns an apricot poodle. He also discovers that she once worked as a nude toe dancer with Jimmy Durante. How you go from nude toe dancing to squash service is beyond me. There's no business like show business.

We purchase a bottle of Kahlúa and learn to drink after-show White Russians while watching Ernest Angley heal people on television. We hold our hands on the screen while Reverend Angley screams, "Evil spirits come out!"

"Heal me!" I yell. "Make me a dancer!"

"Make me a singer!" Danny says. "Get me out of St. Louis!"

Then we fall back on the bed and laugh.

Danny's hotel room has heating issues. "Robin," he says one morning, his lips powdery blue. "My shampoo is all f-f-f-froze. That's not n-n-n-normal, right?"

Thankfully, Kahlúa does not freeze.

I usually stick to the piano, but in this show I'm also playing comedy roles. Because I'm required to participate in dance numbers, Danny, who always looks out for me, teaches me how to fake it. Swing your arms and smile. I trip over my silver shoes when challenged with anything more ambitious than a single pirouette, but I keep trying. Falling comes naturally to me these days, the result of enthusiastic fake tapping, faulty backstage lighting, and a lazy stage crew that neglects to move large pieces of furniture from key entrance points. I'm black and blue all over. The side of my right thigh is the color of eggplant.

That be squash.

During our run at the Chase Park Plaza, we get roped into performing on a telethon, hosted by Monty Hall of *Let's Make a Deal*. No one tells us who benefits from this telethon, but we don't care because we're excited to be on television.

When go on at two in the morning—a broadcast hour that caters to perverts and demented insomniacs—I wear a flowered bikini and play a medley of "Glow Worm" and "Poor Butter-fly" on the piccolo while the corps de ballet performs behind me. I think we're hilarious, but no one in the studio audience laughs. Danny, sporting a Stars-and-Stripes chorus-boy outfit, is scheduled to tap-dance to "Yankee Doodle Dandy." Five minutes before he goes on, he notices no floor mikes are onstage—a serious problem for a tap dancer on live television. He wants to alert someone, but the floor manager is smoking and flirting with one of our big-haired chorus girls.

"Danny," I say, tapping him on the shoulder with my piccolo, "this is serious. Your ass is on the line. Do something. Talk to Monty."

"I can't talk to Monty Hall about floor mikes," Danny says. "He's a huge star."

"Your ass is on the line, not his."

Danny takes a deep breath, marches right up to Monty Hall, and says, "Mr. Hall, sir, I really love your show and everything, but we have a very big problem. I gotta go out there and tap-dance in five minutes, and there are no floor mikes. It's gonna sound like a silent movie."

"Don't worry about it, kid."

"But Mr. Hall, sir, tap dancing without sound is kind of stu-pid. Do you think you could—"

"Kid, leave me the fuck alone. These tech people are professionals. They'll give you what you need. Get out of my way."

"But my ass is on the line—"

"Out of my way, kid!"

Imagine that. Bullied by the snarling host of *Let's Make a Deal*. I know, Monty is a volunteer like the rest of us, but he shouldn't berate a kid in a sailor suit. What a jerk.

I stand there in my flowered bikini and watch poor Danny on a television monitor—his feet, looking like flag-covered flippers—flapping away with no sound. Is there anything sadder in the history of show business than a teenager—in a stretch-satin patriotic costume—silently tap-dancing to "Yankee Doodle Dandy"?

I think not.

But who am I to judge? I'm wearing false eyelashes, silver heels, and have a piccolo tucked in my bra.

"That Monty Hall is a two-bit nitwit," mutters Danny as he exits stage right and tosses his straw hat on the floor. "My ass was on the line."

When our part of the show concludes, I spend several hours avoiding Byron Allen, the twenty-year-old bright-eyed star of a cheesy TV show called *Real People*. Maybe Byron likes the piccolo, maybe he likes bruised thighs, maybe he just likes blondes, but he chases me all over that damn hotel, knocking on the door of every cast member in an attempt to find me. Danny, still wearing Stars and Stripes, hides me in his shower with the frozen shampoo. At least I have leg warmers; it's cold in the tub.

When we aren't drinking Kahlúa or grappling with B-list celebrities, Danny gives me dance lessons. In return, I help him with his singing, pounding out songs on the piano in an effort to find the perfect audition piece for him once we return to New York. We settle on a song from the musical *Pippin* called "Magic to Do." We won't be in St. Louis forever. We might be having fun, but we believe our squash days are limited, that soon we will take Broadway by storm, that there's more to life than Monty Hall, Ernest Angley, and frozen toiletries.

Manhattan, six months later. I've spent the day doing "promotional modeling" at Macy's for a perfume called Mystere. I wear a black Anne Klein evening gown and a black mask and carry a black basket of black Mystere perfume samples. My job is to sneak up on women shopping in Macy's and slip a sample of Mystere into their handbags, an activity likely to get me arrested, shot, or worse.

But I need the fifteen dollars an hour, so I stalk the sales floors, a masked grim reaper in a couture dress, with Pigpen clouds of patchouli dust wafting around me. In an attempt to avoid alarming unsuspecting shoppers scoping out the sales racks, I lurk in remote areas of the store. Most of the time I hang out in the ladies' room lounge, where I dump my perfume samples in the trash and cover them with paper towels.

The mask is a real drag. It's itchy, I can't see where I'm going, and I keep bumping into terrified shoppers who assume I'm going to mug them. I'm tired. I spent the weekend playing the piano for truckers and flight crews at the Newark Airport Holiday Inn. After my gig on Sunday evening, I drank too many screwdrivers and spent the night with a pilot who looked vaguely like Richard Gere. He adored my rendition of "What I Did for Love."

Later in my Macy's shift, I wander over to the bank of pay phones to check my answering service, an activity that always lifts my spirits. I'm hoping to hear from Danny. He has gone to a Broadway open-call audition today for *A Chorus Line*, and I'm anxious to find out what happened.

"Danny called," says the answering service guy. "He made it through the dance cuts and he has to sing at 3 p.m. Shubert Theatre. 225 West Forty-Fourth Street. He says: 'Please be there to play.'"

Oh, my God. A "cattle call" audition is a nerve jangling, ego shattering, potentially life-altering process invented by the red-tailed demons of the Great White Way. Danny must have plowed his way through five hundred dancers and survived a bunch of dance cuts to make it this far. It is 2:30, but I am only ten blocks away. I make up an excuse about feeling faint, peel off my mask and black gown, throw on my real clothes, jump in a taxi I can't afford, and haul my promotional-modeling ass to the Shubert stage door.

An official-looking clipboard guy stops me. I hate clipboards. Nothing good ever comes from a clipboard.

"I'm here to play the piano for Danny Herman."

"Who's Danny Herman?" asks the clipboard guy.

"He's one of the dancers auditioning today."

"Right. Sweetheart, this is a chorus-boy cattle call. No one brings their own accompanist to a cattle call. We have an accompanist in there. And what's that smell?"

"Perfume. It's called Mystere. It's enchanting, trust me. Look. I'm here for Danny Herman," I say, "and he's not no one. He is my friend, and I'm here to play the piano for him. He needs me. I gotta get in there."

"You got a union card?"

"No. Yes. Not yet. Sort of. Do you count AGVA? I'm from Pittsburgh."

"Christ. Yeah, Danny is on the list. But you're not. Where's your music, anyway?"

"In my head. I've been working with Danny for months on this. He only knows one song. He's an acrobat and flips around a lot while he sings. You know, like side aerials and stuff. He's special. Please. Please. Let me in!"

"How do I know you're not a dancer trying to crash the audition? You look like a dancer."

"Not a dancer! Not a dancer! I'm a piano player. No sane person would ever pretend to be a piano player! And do you really think I'm gonna try and dance in these boots? Please."

"Ack. OK, Horowitz. Go ahead. But if anyone asks, I never saw you."

I enter stage left and squint into the vast space between me and the dancers in the wings on the other side of the stage. I spot Danny and wave. He beckons me to his side, but I'm not sure how to get there without making a spectacle of myself by walking through the interrogation spotlight shining center stage. I decide to cross by sneaking between the mirrored backdrop and the upstage brick wall—the back wall of the theater. No one will see me. A pesky strip of yellow police tape blocks the passageway. I have no idea why it is there, but I crawl under it, get to my feet and scoot sideways through the narrow space—about twelve inches—between the mirrors and the wall. I pause, lean against the wall, and tiptoe so I won't make noise. It's hot back here. And it's really far from one side of the stage to the other.

As I creep along, I hear the voice of Tom Porter, a famous Broadway stage manager, booming over the sound system: "Just a reminder, people—under no circumstance should anyone go anywhere near the upstage mirrors. This is a newly installed mirror system and extremely expensive. One of those panels costs six months of a Broadway salary. Stay away."

Ah. That's the reason for the police tape. They are serious about these mirrors.

But there is no turning back. At the halfway point I see Danny, waiting for me with his hands over his eyes. I'm sure, given my history, he's concerned about me falling, but I've got this. No spinning. No swinging of arms or smiling.

I reach the other side. Danny pulls me out from under the police tape, and I take a deep breath.

"Jesus, Robin. I really thought you were gonna crash through two hundred thousand dollars of stage mirrors. I was prepared to say I didn't know you." I stare at him. "Wow," he says, "you smell good. Enchanting."

"Let's focus. You have to sing. When are you on?"

"I'm number eight. They're on number seven now. This guy sounds pretty good." We listen for a moment as number seven steamrolls his way through a gut-wrenching version of "Being Alive" from the musical *Company*. And the rehearsal pianist, sight-reading a fairly complicated arrangement, nails it. Wow. I'm pretty good with a lead sheet, but when someone hands me one of those piano scores with a gazillion notes, I panic. This guy is a scanner.

Danny, who has spent 90 percent of his life perfecting his dance and acrobatic technique, isn't much of a singer. And I'm not much of an accompanist. Playing Carole King tunes in a hotel lounge has not exactly qualified me for this. But here we are, ready to walk onstage at the Shubert. We are two squeaky-faced Pittsburgh kids on a Broadway mission, fueled by naïveté, hunger, and a genuine belief that we belong on this stage.

To distract from our musical inadequacies, we've come up with an arrangement of "Magic to Do" that features extreme acrobatics. At least once every four bars, Danny flips. Not run-of-the-mill flips, but Flying Zucchini flips that take my breath away and make me wonder if he has bionic knees. No one will pay much attention to the music.

Our Broadway strategy: get the job by flipping.

"You warmed up?"

"As much as I can be."

"You know the drill. Announce yourself and the song and count it off. You can do this."

"Next!" says the stage manager. "Number eight!"

We both seem kind of small in that big space—tiny dancer with Thumbelina on piano.

The stage looks like one giant trapdoor, ready to swallow us whole if we dare to place a misguided foot on its sacred floor-boards. A crappy upright piano stands center stage, facing away from the house, looking forlorn in the cavernous theater. I say hello to the assistant musical director, then sit on the bench with my back to the audience. As I wait for Danny to announce his song, a strong case of impostor syndrome creates sweat circles in the pits of my very best synthetic blouse. It's Danny's audition, but why does it feel like mine?

"What are you singing for us today?" asks an amplified voice from the house.

"Good afternoon, ladies and gentlemen. My name is Danny Herman. I'm from Pittsburgh, and I am very, very happy to be at the Shubert Theatre today auditioning for *A Chorus Line*, one of my all-time favorite musicals."

As opposed to what? Brigadoon? What is he doing? He must be scared. He's stalling. That's it. He's stalling.

"You know, I love the musical *Pippin*. And this particular song, called "Magic to Do" seems like a really good choice for today's audition."

He's babbling. Why is no one stopping him?

"Today I brought my good friend from Pittsburgh with me, Miss Robin Meloy, a wonderful pianist I have known for a very long time. Well, not that long, but many months."

He sounds like the emcee at a Swissvale Moose Club talent show.

"You know, a funny thought occurred to me on the way to the theater today."

I can't stand it a moment longer. I spin around and hiss, "Danny!" He looks at me, and I give him the stank eye, the death ray, the "start singing now" evil stare. I learned this look from my piano teacher. It's very effective.

"Five, six, seven, eight!" he shouts.

I bang out the first chord. Danny flips. We get through the first chorus, and I play a G minor vamp while Danny, suddenly larger than life, soars across the stage. His imperfect vocal melody slices through my flawed, raucous accompaniment. He flies through the Shubert air with the greatest of ease, defying gravity, an upside-down teenage man-boy chasing a Broadway dream one aerial at a time. He finishes the song to a smattering of applause and warmhearted laughter.

The next night, I am in Danny's Fifty-Second Street apartment eating pizza when the phone rings. He has the job.

To celebrate, we go roller-skating at the Roxy, where we hold hands and skate round and round under a giant disco ball. We are dizzy with gypsy love. I do not fall, not even once.

Danny ships out and learns the show with a bus-and-truck company in Boston. Three months later Michael Bennett pulls him out of the line and sends him to Broadway.

I sit in the audience on his opening night and cry.

Nineteen. Danny is only nineteen. I consider his Pittsburgh roots, his emotional and physical sacrifices, and the hardships he has endured to get here. I'm only four years older than he is, but I've been in the business long enough to know that only rarely do the show biz gods bestow a great gig even on a deserving young artist. I tuck Danny's moment away in a place that I can reach when my own spotlight grows dim. Someday my turn will come, but until it does, this gorgeous memory will pull me through.

I wear white gloves so that Danny can spot me in the audience. During the curtain call I jump to my feet and cheer for him, for me, for the bumpy, winding road stretched out before us and behind us. The following weekend I return to my piano gig at the Newark Airport Holiday Inn.

Twelve

Still Life with Grape and Hot Dog

"Good news. We have a songwriting assignment. A chance to make some money," Joe says. He stands next to my piano, a two-day-old turkey leg in his hand, waving it at me like a conductor's baton. As usual, Joe raided my refrigerator the moment he arrived at my Astoria apartment, looking for spit backs and doggie bags—the detritus of a skinny single girl's sad culinary life.

We had planned to work today on a new song—"Eight Miles Home"—for the play Joe is writing about Thomas Jefferson. Joe rocks back and forth on the balls of his feet. He's hyped up, even though exhaustion cloaks his pale blue eyes. Like me, he maintains a patchwork schedule of gigs, bouncing from the Actor's Studio to the television studio to the Madison Avenue restaurant where he serves gourmet morsels to swank East Side guests.

"One of the customers at the restaurant last night—a regular named Judith—knows we write songs together. She's financing a tree project in Israel—one of those forest-in-the-desert things—and she wants a theme song."

"A theme song. About trees in the desert? Cool."

"That's the good news. The bad news is that we have to tie it into world peace and brotherhood."

"Jesus."

"Exactly. She wants 'We Are the World.' But about trees."

It is 1986. I am twenty-eight years old. The sloping lines traversing Joe's sun-faded face tell me that he has at least fifteen years on me. I repeatedly ask how old he is. He refuses to answer.

We met three years ago when we were hired as actors for an industrial training film for a television network, but we really got to know each other when we began writing songs for Joe's Thomas Jefferson project. We're both scuffling to finance our New York City lifestyles. In addition to his burgeoning career as an actor/writer/waiter, Joe is supporting a teenage son and trying to scrape together enough money to buy his downtown studio apartment. I play the piano in several midtown hotels (midday at the Marriott, cocktail hour at the Sheraton, late night at the Hyatt) and grab as much acting work as I can. I date inappropriate men, buy shoes that are too expensive for my Piano Girl budget, and, like so many of my wannabe uptown friends, spend too much time in a salon having my hair painted various shades of gold.

Deep down, I'm really a songwriter. Joe brings me back to the truest part of myself, the part that can start with silence and create, for better or worse, a piece of music. When Joe shows up at my apartment, I know where I'm supposed to be—somewhere in the middle of the second chorus, looking for a bridge. I glance up from the piano and listen to his James Taylor-inspired voice sing the lyric we have crafted and feel dizzy with love, maybe for him, maybe for me, maybe for art. We do not have a romance, but this must count for something.

It takes four or five songwriting sessions, a plate of cold gnocchi, three slices of stale pizza, a few bottles of wine (for me), and half a chicken, but eventually Joe and I come up with a song for the tree project. It's called "If We Believe." We record and submit the demo to Judith. We get the gig, along with a hefty (for us) paycheck. In return, we are expected to show up at a synagogue in Princeton, New Jersey, to present our song to the congregation at a special ceremony.

Several months later, we rent a dark red Toyota and drive to Princeton. Joe will sing, I will play the piano and sing along on the chorus. We practice in the car, puffed up by the prospect of getting paid to do something we love. I'm teetering on the edge of thirty, and Joe has clearly crossed the middle-age superhighway, but we feel like two kids on a road trip, unbreakable, singing a song that will open doors and hearts and pay for a few months of turkey dinners and blonde highlights.

We enter the synagogue. Judith, a large woman wearing small glasses, greets us. I ask about the piano.

"There's no piano," she says. "This is an Orthodox synagogue with restrictions on musical instruments. Sorry. I didn't know. I'm not a member here. You'll have to sing aca-aca-aca . . . ?"

"A cappella?" Joe and I say. Our voices, so strong and confident in the Toyota, now sound squeaky and thin.

"Yeah, that," says Judith. "It will be wonderful. I think the governor is coming. Here: put this on. She hands Joe a yarmulke. "Now go sit down. Here's a program. You're on at the end of the service."

We slide into a pew. "You got a bobby pin or anything?" Joe says. "This thing won't stay put." I dig in my purse, find a paper clip crusted with hair spray and face powder, and use it to clip the yarmulke to a strand of Joe's blond hair. Thomas Jefferson would be proud.

"There."

"Uh-oh," he says, as he reads the program.

"What?" I look around. People stream into the synagogue and take their seats. It's a somber crowd.

"Jesus," he says.

"What?"

"This is a Holocaust memorial service. We are singing to honor the dead and pay tribute to the survivors."

"Joe, we can't sing a song about trees and world peace at a Holocaust remembrance service. What is Judith thinking?"

"I guess she wants a good venue to launch her project? She believes in our song."

"Yeah, but she doesn't have to get up there and sing it on the saddest day of the year. I'm not even a real singer." I wonder if it's too late to bow out. Or sneak out. This service is too meaningful to be marred by a piddling pop song about seeds and branches and strangers far from home. I feel wildly incompetent, out of place, and panicked.

"Joe, what are we going to do?"

Joe puts his weathered hands on either side of my hot face. "Rob," he says, "be strong. Trust yourself."

The service proceeds. The elderly survivors of the Holocaust stand. We pray for them. The rabbi asks the family members of those who perished to also stand. We pray again. Hundreds of people are now on their feet, wounded and sad, but still, somehow, hopeful. It is the most emotional thing I've ever experienced.

Joe leans over and whispers in my ear, "Time for a little music. We're up next."

Tears clog my throat, in that boggy place where songs are born.

"I can't."

Joe grabs my hand. "This isn't about you."

It's not about me. Why haven't I ever thought of that? A composer serves the project; a performer serves the song. It's not about me. And just like that, my fear fizzles. *I can do this.*

The rabbi introduces us and asks the congregation to remain standing during our song.

Joe looks at me, nods, then white knuckles the lectern and begins to sing in a voice so luminous that I forget to feel like an impostor. I sing with him on the chorus. The audience joins us, and our combined voices seem stronger than all the evil in the world. A fleeting musical illusion, but still, I believe.

We finish the song, and I look at Joe. His yarmulke has slipped over one eyebrow, and beads of sweat dot his cheeks. Or maybe they're tears. My heart fills with joy, with relief, with respect. I love this man in a way I can't explain. Or maybe I just love our song.

After the service we meet Judith and her husband, Alex, in the parking lot. They offer to take us to dinner, but it's a Monday night, and their favorite fancy restaurants are closed. The only thing open in the area is an IHOP, which hardly seems fitting after what we've just experienced. Joe, as always, is starving—but Alex, Judith, and I veto the blueberry pancakes and opt to head back to Judith's home, where she will prepare a light meal.

Alex and Judith, speed demons, drive matching Jaguar convertibles. Joe and I pile into our Toyota and drive as fast as we can to keep up with them. Judith has directed us to park outside the gate, on the side of a large circular driveway. She summons us over an intercom, and the gate swings open.

In addition to matching cars, Judith and Alex have matching villas.

'We love each other," she says as she meets us in the foyer. "But we really don't like living together." Every surface of her living room is stacked with huge piles of notebooks, magazines, periodicals, newspapers. I've never seen so much paper in one place. No wonder she wants to plant a forest.

"I don't cook much," Judith says, "but I have some wine and a package of frozen hot dogs."

"Wine sounds great," I shout.

"Hot dogs for me," says Joe. Judith retreats to the kitchen. Alex, a tiny man, has disappeared; he could be hiding behind one of the towers of *New Yorker* magazines. Joe moves a wobbly stack of folders and sits down next to me.

"I'll just put these hot dogs in the microwave," Judith yells from the kitchen.

"Don't eat the hot dogs," I whisper to Joe. "They may have been in that freezer since 1972."

"Rob, we should be polite. If she's taking the trouble to make hot dogs, we should eat the hot dogs."

"No way," I say. I sip a glass of sweet wine. Judith brings Joe a fancy white plate with a gold rim and one hot dog on it.

"Thanks, Judith," he says. "That looks delicious. You have any ketchup?"

I kick him under the table, and a pile of paperbacks tumbles to the ground.

"I don't think so," says Judith, discovering a large plate of half-rotten grapes underneath a periodic journal. "But, here. Have some grapes."

"No, thanks," I say. Joe adds a few grapes to his hot dog plate and cocks his head to study the design. Still Life with Grape and Hot Dog: Princeton, New Jersey.

We talk for a few minutes. Judith thanks us for our song; we thank her for her hospitality. It's time to drive back to the city.

"What an honor to be part of this special evening."

"Better go quickly," she says. "In three minutes the guard dogs will be out. The gate will open automatically for you."

"Guard dogs?" I look behind me and see four Dobermans racing down the driveway. They're practically nipping at our boots as the gate closes behind us. We can hear them snarling on the other side of the fence.

"That was close."

"I don't feel so great," says Joe.

"I told you. Poison hot dogs," I say. "I'll drive."

"Wait, wait!" Judith shouts from the other side of the gate, her voice muffled by the barking Dobermans. "Take the grapes, so you have a snack for the ride home."

"Thank you," we say.

"I'll just leave the bag here on my side of the fence. You can reach through and fetch it. Bye!"

"Let's go, Joe," I say. "The Dobermans are freaking me out."

"What about the grapes?" he asks.

"Leave them. No way I'm going to reach under that fence. Those dogs will rip my arm off. And I have to play for brunch at the Marriott tomorrow."

"Yeah, but they're free grapes."

"They're yesterday's grapes, Joe." But he doesn't hear me. He grabs a stick from the side of the road, and, with the Dobermans growling and snapping at it, manages to pull the bag under the fence.

We drive home, the rotten grapes on the seat between us. We don't say much, and we're certainly not singing.

Years pass. We do not become the next Goffin and King, Lennon and McCartney, or the Bergmans. As so often happens in show business, the slow-moving blob of real life overtakes art. Joe gets a lot of film work, falls in love with a beautiful young dancer named Elizabeth, and marries her. He changes his name to Tobin Bell, revamps his image, moves to the West Coast, and becomes a movie star. I meet the love of my life—a jazz bassist named John—marry him, and have a baby. John and I decide to move to Europe.

In 1994 I see Joe one last time, right before I leave New York. He looks rested and happy. And tan. We discuss projects we'll never work on and songs we'll never write. He eats a salad. A salad!

"I can't remember the key of the tree song," he says.

"D major. You always sound good in D major. It's a hopeful key. Bright."

It's time to go our separate ways. Joe has been more than a friend, less than a romance. We forged an artistic partnership based on vulnerability, old food, and the misguided-but-beautiful belief that a handful of well-crafted songs will connect us forever. Love songs, in a way.

He hugs me good-bye. I will play our music for decades to come. People might move on, but a song? Our songs are forever—aural snapshots of an innocent time; small globes of musical light that roll through my memory and trigger flashes of happiness.

"Be strong," he says to me before we go our separate ways on Seventh Avenue. "Trust yourself."

"It's not about me," I say, repeating the words that got me through the Princeton gig. "I promise to remember that. It's not about me."

"It never was," Joe says. "It was always about the song."

Thirteen

Curves

*C*rescent shapes please me: a sliver of moon, a warm croissant, a freshly manicured fingertip. I enjoy a raised eyebrow, half a smile, a bunch of bananas, the soft spot on the top of my foot where the shoe stops and my skin begins—toe cleavage, I think the fashionistas call it.

A good circle brings me joy: a perfect white plate that holds my not-so-perfect dinner; the silver-blue irises of my daughter's eyes; a symmetrical pancake I've cooked myself; a bagel, unadorned. I love my wedding ring—three circles of gold braided together—*one for you, one for me, one for us*; I cheer for the circle of life, the family circle, the vicious circle (as long as the tail being chased isn't mine). I marvel at the musician's circle of fifths, run circles around myself, come full circle, and circle my wagons when I feel threatened. I circle back to start over and circle forward to find my way back. Loops define my life.

I should mention here that I like to eat pie, my favorite toy as a child was a Spirograph, and I've been known to bribe travelers to bring Pittsburgh's Eat'n Park Smiley Cookies to me on trips to Europe.

Spheres also deserve attention: beach balls and crystal balls, globes (the old-fashioned kind that spin), blueberries, clear glass marbles, iridescent bubbles, an Italian peach, a homegrown tomato in August, emerald-green beads, a hand-painted Christmas bauble splattered with glitter. Snowmen. Pearls. A falling star.

Crescent, round, spherical. Curves dictate my triumphs and failures. Nothing against the straight line—the zipper is truly an efficient invention—but give me a meandering stream, a velvet bow, a cliché rainbow, and I'm hooked. A smudged or muted plot line that takes a subtle twist is one I'll follow with joy. I want a slope (not the slippery kind), a long and winding road (less traveled or not), a twisting path leading to an arched tunnel, a feathery cloud muting the harsh noon light. Give me the curl of a breaking wave, the soft curve of my son's broad shoulders when he returns home, the drape of a girl's hair when it sweeps across her forehead, a baby's clenched fist, the bowed tail of an orange tabby cat, the bent bough of the cherry tree hanging over my skylight.

Shapes show up in sound, too. A guitar, an acoustic bass, a grand piano, a cello—curved instruments that make round sounds when played with grace. I listen to Ravel or Debussy, and I hear life coiling around itself. I fall into the spiral harmonic underpinnings of Maria Schneider's music and travel through an aural serpentine, an oval labyrinth of enchantment. The music I love most makes me feel like I'm inside a Slinky on a steep and narrow staircase, somersaulting over myself, getting where I need to go but taking a scenic route that includes flips, back bends, and an occasional coin-shaped bruise.

A career can take on a rounded shape. As a young artist I tried to travel efficiently from Point A to Point B. I craved logic in my life, but life kept throwing me, yes, curveballs. It took a decade or so, but I realized the logical way to live—the straight-line way—would forever elude me. I discovered that I could have a fulfilling career as long as I took my time, bypassed clogged mainstream intersections, and took a roundabout, more scenic route—one including suspension bridges, tree swings, and Ferris wheels.

My body plays along with the shape of things. Less angular than I used to be, curvy and yielding, I listen to music that bends in the middle—both my meanderings and the melodies of other musicians finding their way back home.

Fourteen

Badass Randy and the Beauty Queens

Chatham Village, 1966. I am eight years old and have recently watched the Miss America pageant—live from Atlantic City!—on television with Grandma Curtis. Grandma, a real shark when it comes to picking winners, says, "Miss California has the best figure, but she blew it in the talent competition. You can't win with baton twirling if you don't have flames. Fire batons score big points with the judges. I'm voting for Miss Michigan—look at her in that white spangled evening gown. Elegant! Brains, beauty, and poise! Never underestimate the importance of poise. And her vocal interpretation of 'June is Bustin' Out All Over' is divine."

Grandma Curtis is almost right. Miss Michigan doesn't win the title, but she gets as far as first runner-up. I am intrigued by the concept of first runner-up. Almost good enough to win but not quite. All of the work, none of the glory. Like the second guy to walk on the moon. What was his name again?

Some months later, my sister, Randy, and I decide to stage our own spectacle—the first annual Miss Chatham Village beauty pageant. Chatham Village, an idyllic National Historic Landmark, a wooded enclave right smack in the middle of Pittsburgh, features colonial brick townhouses surrounding lush green courtyards. Randy and I live in the upper court of the oldest part of Chatham Village, a perfect place for a long runway and a makeshift stage.

We gather a gaggle of our Village girlfriends, including the Marys—Mary Beth Wilson and Mary Helen Joyce; Alyce Amery, Kitty Engstrom, Lisa Hetrick, the Loughney sisters, the Clifford girls. Together we plot and plan the program and send crayon invitations to our parents, who usually spend their summer evenings sitting on front porches sipping drinks and grilling steaks. Chatham Village could be the Pittsburgh setting for a John Cheever story: Wonder Bread-ish, Waspy, and two gin and tonics shy of tennis-white dreamland.

Problem: we need a judge for our pageant. We decide the last thing we want is a parental jury, or, worse yet, a panel of boys. What to do? Randy, seven years old and already a take-charge kind of gal, volunteers for the gig.

"I hate beauty," she says. "I hate swimsuits and evening gowns, and my only talent is chasing my brother with a baseball bat. I might as well be the judge."

We agree. Randy will be the moderator and the jury—Bert Parks and the panel of experts rolled into one cocky little girl.

I think I'm a shoo-in because Randy and I share a bedroom and, on holidays, wear matching outfits with patriotic themes. Randy has become a star in Chatham Village with her portrayal of a wounded soldier in the annual Fourth of July parade. She carries a shredded flag, limps along on a crutch, and wears a ketchup-splattered bandage on her head.

What's this? All of a sudden, all of the pageant contestants are really nice to Randy, even though—as a tomboy—she is a bit of an outlier with this group. She gets extra cookies from our friends, extra rides on the backs of bicycles, extra turns on the Tarzan swing. I am too naive to understand the concept of graft, and the special treatment seems fair to me. After all, Randy has sacrificed her own chances of being Miss Chatham Village by volunteering to run the contest.

It is worth noting that my sister was born with coal black eyes and orange fuzz on her head. It is also worth noting that I have seen her bite a worm in half and that her favorite game is called "Let's Go Die."

The day of the pageant arrives. Our parents collect in the courtyard and sit in assorted lawn chairs. Cocktails in hand, they chatter as Randy, barefoot but wearing one of my dad's bow ties, takes the stage to welcome the audience. She uses a stick wrapped in aluminum foil as a microphone.

Randy begins introducing the contestants.

"Hailing from the lower court, Alyce Amery excels at math and reading. Her hobbies include coloring and going to the library." Alyce takes a long walk down the runway, wearing a frilly pink dress and flip-flops.

"From 610 Pennridge Road, Mary Beth Wilson attends St. Mary of the Mount school. She is a member of Stunt Club and—lucky for us—enjoys singing. Unlike my father, Mary Beth's father works during the day." The concept of being a jazz musician was still a bit hard to grasp at age seven.

It goes on and on like this, with Randy introducing each of the girls competing for the title.

Then she gets to me, last on the list: "Here is Robin, better known as my sister." *That's it? That's all she says? What a gyp!* I march down the runway, remembering what Grandma Curtis says about poise.

Because the pageant takes place fifty feet from our house, we use our living room for quick changes into swimsuit and talent costumes. The screen door squeaks and slams as we run back and forth. Meanwhile, Randy, hardly breaking a sweat, babbles on and on about each of us.

"And now, here is Mary Beth Wilson again, perform-ing her version of 'Down in the Valley.'" From the sidelines, I see three-quarters of the audience blanch—Mary Beth has an impossibly high voice, one that can make your head explode if you didn't come prepared with cotton balls to stuff in your ears. I watch as the assembled parents simultaneously lift their cocktail glasses and take solid, medicinal swigs. But—surprise—Mary Beth has planned a special arrangement of "Down in the Valley"—one that includes cartwheels—twenty-four cart-wheels—we count them. When she reaches the end—way down, down, down in that valley—she modulates to an even higher key, raises her grass-stained hands, and sings the final verse. Wow.

"Thank you, Mary Beth!" says my sister. "A true *highlight*."

"Next up, my sister, Robin, performing a medley of the only two songs she knows."

I smile and stand in the middle of the courtyard with my flute. Poise. I play "When Sunny Gets Blue"—a tune I found in my dad's fake book—then segue into a vocal performance of "This Land Is Your Land," which I sing while twirling the flute. My range isn't as impressive as Mary Beth's—she can go higher than a U-2 spy plane—and sadly, no flames shoot out of my flute. But, somehow, I get by.

Some of the other girls perform splits and back bends. I envy their flexibility, as I have none. Alyce Amery recites a dramatic version of "Gunga Din." Mary Helen does an interpretive dance with seven scarves that borders on inappropriate. Different times.

But we are all fearless. We believe in our beauty, our talent, our intelligence, our poise.

We change into Sunday school dresses—our version of evening gowns—for the final round of the pageant. For music to accompany our final walk down the runway, we hum "The Battle Hymn of the Republic." Again, different times.

The tension builds. Randy has decided in advance to eliminate the runners-up. No finalists. She will select the winner, and that will be that.

We hold hands and glance nervously at each other, just like the real Miss America contestants.

Who will win?

I will win.

I know I will win, but when I look at the other girls, I see the same spark of determination in their eyes and begin to doubt myself. *Maybe the flute twirling wasn't such a great idea. I should have listened to Grandma Curtis and set the tailpiece on fire.*

Suddenly, this isn't as much fun as I thought it would be.

"And the winner is . . . drum roll, please."

The parents in the audience put down their drinks and pound their thighs.

Randy glances at the handcrafted paper crown, bouquet of dandelions, and the crepe paper Miss Chatham Village sash she has stashed on a table next to her.

"And the winner is . . ."

The crowd is literally breathless at this point. Randy, who is really milking it, waits as long as she can to announce the winner before finally declaring:

"Me!"

Randy crowns herself. I stand with the other girls onstage, our mouths hanging open in disbelief, as Randy adjusts the crown, pulls the sash over her head, grabs the bouquet, and sashays—with tremendous poise—down the runway, pausing to wave at our parents and the imaginary press corps lining both sides of the aisle.

Halfway between rage and devastation, we begin to howl. Our parents sit there laughing, which does not make things better, not one bit.

"No fair!" we shout. "No fair!"

"Fair!" says Randy. "You made me the judge, and I picked me."

"You didn't wear a swimsuit or an evening gown. You didn't even have a talent presentation."

"Yep," says Randy, "I was just myself. And I won."

"You can't do that!" Mary Beth says.

"Yes, I can. You know why? Because I'm the judge. I decide. You want to win? You have to be the judge. Any nitwit knows that."

My worm-eating devil sister spins around and takes another turn on the catwalk.

Our parents stand and cheer.

The other girls and I—feeling very much like the Chatham Village idiots—stomp out of the courtyard and go to my house to change clothes. Losers! We are worse than Miss

Michigan—we're not even runners-up. One by one, we slam the screen door in protest. I look out and see Randy, still wearing her crown, signing autographs for the adults. I suppose this time next week she'll be riding on a float in a parade on Grant Street.

"You want to win? You have to be the judge."

Fifty years after the Miss Chatham Village beauty pageant Randy will boast a collection of large snakes that she uses for therapy sessions at a juvenile detention center in Butler County. We don't call her Badass Randy for nothing.

It will take me decades to figure out that my little sister, age seven, was wise beyond her years—smart enough to be the judge instead of the contestant, rebellious enough to make the rules instead of following them, cunning enough to win the top prize without stuffing herself into a swimsuit or Sunday school dress. Badass Randy understood "girl power" before it became a thing. She's not an artist herself—she's a vegan chef and an animal rights activist—but she could write a survival guidebook for freelance musicians. Lesson number one: if you spend time creating a crown, make sure you're the one to wear it.

Fifteen

Varmint on the Roof

*T*hwack. Or is it *thwump*? *Skittle, scratch, scrape, thwop*. It's a
quarter to three, and there's no one in the place except you and
me—*thonk*—and Dumbo? Has a baby elephant crash-landed on
the roof? Thwunk. Bosh. Maybe it's Batman. Sasquatch? A lost
WWII paratrooper? Lord of the Dance? At this time of the night
anything is possible.

I wonder if I should awaken John, my sleeping prince of a
husband. He wears earplugs and misses most predawn rumblings.
'Round midnight, he's in slumber land, oblivious to things that
rattle the rafters in the wee small hours of the morning. I could
wake him, but I know that if I do, he'll go into "rodent red
alert," a state from which he will not emerge until the intruder is
caught and removed from the premises. Not anxious to encour-
age a late-night hunting expedition, I ignore the critter clog
dancing over my head. I retire to the sofa downstairs, leaving
my sleep-diva man tucked in and dreaming of suspicious jazz
chords. What he can't hear won't hurt him. I put a pillow over
my head and hope whatever it is goes away—a time-tested technique for chasing away the heebie-jeebies.

My husband's mission to rid the world of household pests
began in 1964, when, at age six, John rescued his family home
from an invasion of exotic creatures. Snug in his Louisville

bed—this was before he started playing screaming loud rock-and-roll bass guitar and, still sensitive to nighttime noise, began wearing earplugs to go to sleep—he heard varmints eating away the walls, munching on the very foundation of his youth.

Scritch-scratch, scritch-scratch.

"Mother and Daddy," he said with his charming little-boy Louisville accent, "there's something alive in the walls. And it's eating our house!"

Mother and Daddy, whose middle-aged ears couldn't hear what little John heard, brushed off his warning until, at last, little John threw such a big fit that they had to call either an exorcist or an exterminator. They opted for the exterminator. The verdict? Carpenter ants—tiny insects capable of taking down an entire homestead. Little John became a superhero, super hearing being his superpower. He saved the house and reaped the rewards of a grateful family.

The house survived. John used his superpower to pursue a career as a jazz bassist and eventually ended up in New York City. Several decades after the carpenter ant episode, John and I got to know each other while playing at the Grand Hyatt Hotel, next to Grand Central Station in Manhattan. He logged seven hours a night with a jazz trio in a marble lobby filled with fountains, potted palms, and uncomfortable chairs; I played a Steinway five evenings a week in Trumpet's (named after future U.S. President Donald Trump, who at the time was more of a piggy, garden-variety real estate developer than a "very stable genius"). Trumpet's was a cocktail cave that looked like a leather-lined womb. We dealt with a lot of pests on the job—an actual rat lived in the Trumpet's storage closet where I used to hang my coat—but most of them worked in the executive office. Mick Jagger painted with a wide brush when he sang "bite the Big Apple—don't mind the maggots."

Everyone I knew had hideous pest problems.

Oh, the war stories we heard. My friend Patti told me about an army of cockroaches that carried an entire plate of rat poison back to their warrens—only to reappear the next morning, ready for more, more, more. A girl named Nina had a rat the size of a dog fall on her head when the tile ceiling in her bathroom collapsed on her just after she had gotten out of the shower. It's hard for me to imagine anything worse—naked and attacked by a rat-dog. To live in this town you must be tough, tough, tough, tough.

Somehow, our apartment was surprisingly clear of roaches and rodents. Aside from hearing the carpenter ant story about a hundred times—to hear John tell it he saved the entire state of Kentucky and all that came with it, baseball bats, bourbon, and lord knows what else—he had no experience with battling pests except for the kind you'd meet on the gig: a food and beverage guy who once told the trio they couldn't walk on any of the carpeted areas of the lobby, a general manager who refused to make eye contact with any of the male musicians working in the hotel, a human resources director who, at Christmastime, refused to give the jazz musicians a free frozen turkey. The hotel had hundreds of frozen turkeys; they were passing them out like candy.

"These are Christmas gifts for employees," she said, "not for musicians. If we have any leftover frozen turkeys, we will give them to the homeless. Then, if there are still leftovers, we will think about giving one frozen turkey to the trio. You can share."

So, we moved to Germany, where there's a turkey in every pot, even for musicians.

You might say we were asking for it when we built a small home on a piece of wooded property in a village called Wahlscheid, about thirty kilometers outside of Cologne. We moved in with our two kids, overjoyed at having a place of our own. We marveled at the deer, even though they breakfasted on our decorative bushes. The kids caught frogs in the garden and made goo-goo eyes at the hedgehogs. Oh, the birds, the bees, the flora, the fauna, the wild boars—one morning we spotted eight (eight!) of them walking down the slope next to our house. The adult boars were bigger than any member of my family, which is saying something. They weren't aggressive or anything like that; in fact, they were nicely choreographed and even sang on key. Fine. Just passing through, like a well-disciplined chorus line exiting stage left.

This, in contrast to the mouse in the sugar bowl, who descended upon us like a biblical plague. Never mind carnivorous wild pigs: a mouse in the sugar bowl was akin to demonic possession or one of those horror movies where a mouse turns into a clown and starts strangling sorority girls.

I spotted the mouse one morning, flopping around on a white-sugar high, nose deep in the bowl, ass in the air, tail shaking, reenacting the cocaine scene from *Scarface*.

I am strong, I am invincible. But I am, after all, an American blonde, and I can't do much about that. So, I screamed.

John rushed to my side. Rodent red alert! John's eyes glazed over, and he began plotting a trip to the local hardware store to buy every rodent trap available in the German countryside, which is not inconsiderable.

"I don't know," I said, "Julia is not going to like this." Our daughter has always been an animal lover. She has been known to hold funeral ceremonies for drowned wasps. Killing a mouse would have been like whacking a close friend.

"We have to be firm about this," John said to me. "Do you know how dangerous mice are? They can take over. They're worse than clowns. They'll even take bites out of small children while they're sleeping."

I didn't argue, especially when he tried to convince me the mouse might be a rat.

That night at dinner, John, using "the voice"—not the "cool jazz-cat" voice we have all come to love, but the "booming dad" voice he saves for special occasions—told the family about setting the traps and how we had to band together to kill the evil, diseased rodent.

Julia's eyes filled with tears. "Dad," she said, "how could you?"

Never underestimate the power of an eight-year-old girl's protest.

Julia printed out cute photos of country mice, wrote slogans such as *STOP THE MADNESS* and *PLEASE DON'T MUR-DER US* in red crayon on them, and taped the posters to walls all over the house. My daughter, the activist.

John went to Plan B, the "humane" trap.

"We'll get that little rat," he said.

"It's a mouse," I said.

"It could be a small rat. You never know."

The live trap involved peanut butter and a weighted cake pan suspended on a Popsicle stick, which presumably would drop when the mouse took the bait, harmlessly trapping him. As if.

I heard the pan slam in the middle of the night. John slept through it, of course; he was wearing earplugs. I stayed awake with the pillow over my head. The next morning, a look of triumph on his rested face—John drove to the other side of the valley, where he released not one but two mice—they were not rats, but they were tough. The Salamanca brothers of mice. We were saved. Victory for the bass player! As a bonus, we got to hear once again the story of how he rescued the South from the ant army.

For the past week I've been hearing it. Every evening, long after we've fallen asleep, I hear a resounding thump on the roof, followed by a flurry of commotion. The critter must be leaping from one of the old trees near the house. But the closest branch would require Evel Knievel skills to cover the distance. I can't figure it out. On the sly, I ask Julia if she has heard anything.

"Yeah," she says. "It sure sounds big and fat. But don't tell Dad. You know how he gets. The last thing we need around here is another safari."

A couple of times a year since that first mouse episode, we've had visitors. Rodent red alert has become commonplace. But whatever is thumping on the roof is in a different category. We don't need a trap for this thing: we need a counterterrorism unit.

I can't sleep. I keep thinking of my New York friend Nina and that rat-dog crashing through the ceiling and landing on her head. Finally, I have no choice. I tell John. He removes his earplugs, stays up, listens to the racket, and proclaims a full-scale emergency.

He confers with his good friend Hans, a Dutch drummer with pest issues of his own. Hans once tried to get rid of multiple generations of *Siebenschlaefer*—a German rodent that looks a bit like a chipmunk—by blasting jazz-rock fusion through speakers mounted on the rafters in his attic. John and Hans, experts in jazz and critters, determine that our roof dweller is a *Marder*, an American martin, which is a member of the dreaded weasel family. Just what we need—*ein deutsches Wiesel*.

We hear from neighbors that this particular weasel has been chewing on brake cables of parked cars down the street. He has also massacred and eaten the pet bunnies living next door to us. Julia's friend Maryam is still heartbroken. She didn't even have a carcass to bury: the weasel ate it all. Julia nicely arranged a small memorial service.

"No more Mr. Nice Guy," says John, using "the voice." "This is a dangerous situation. That weasel gets under the shingles and into the walls of the house, we're in big trouble." *With a capital T, and that rhymes with P, and that stands for Protected Species.* In this part of Germany, we have to be nice to the weasel. The weasel is our friend.

We buy an expensive device called a *Wiesel-Schreck*, which claims to make a constant high-pitched squeal—unappealing to members of the weasel family.

Doesn't work. Perhaps the weasel, like the bassist, is also wearing earplugs.

Following Hans's advice, John buys a pricey live trap that looks big enough to catch one of the neighborhood toddlers. I spy John setting the trap with a cheese-topped cracker and an olive. Looks like a weasel cocktail party.

Doesn't work. The crackers and olives are gone, but the trap remains empty. I suggest a pitcher of martinis.

We drink the martinis ourselves, call the *Baummeister*, and spend hundreds of euros having him trim back branches close to the house.

Doesn't work. The thumps at night grow louder as the weasel leaps from even greater distances. We have a rogue member of the Flying Wallendas living on our roof.

We consult with a home improvement center *Schädlingsexperte*—the pest expert. He tells us there's no legal way to get rid of a German weasel. Then he takes us aside, lowers his voice, and tells us to wait for a full moon, drink some schnapps. "You're American. Go out on the roof with a shotgun," he whispers. "Sit there until he shows up. Then blow the weasel to smithereens when he's not looking."

This won't work for obvious reasons. In contrast to so many of our fellow Americans, we don't own a gun, and it's not like we could borrow one from a neighbor—we don't know a single German who collects firearms. We don't like schnapps, we're afraid of heights, and we're skeptical about spending a winter night—even with moonlight—perched on a steep and slippery roof with a lethal weapon. That seems a bit twentieth century.

Meanwhile, John should be preparing for his new trio recording, aptly titled *The Innkeeper's Gun*. I'm supposed to be writing a book called *Waltz of the Asparagus People*. Instead, we are on weasel watch. For more than a month, the weasel on the roof dominates our conversations. We're obsessed with the weasel. In addition to Ritz crackers and cheese, the weasel also likes to eat wiring, plastic tubes, and insulation. I have a nightmare that he breaks into the house, eats my iMac, all of my groceries, and kidnaps the children.

Then, one night, it all stops. The weasel is gone. No more thumps or thwacks at three in the morning. I don't think the weasel is finished with us, but he has evidently gotten bored with Project Goldsby and moved on to the next thing. I can't say I miss him, but, as an artist, I sort of respect him.

"Robin, we have a '*situation*,'" John says, a few months later. I've learned to dread these words.

"What?" I ask. "*What?*"

"There's something frozen in the rain barrel. And it looks like a human head."

"No more Mr. Nice Guy," says John, using "the voice." "This is a dangerous situation. That weasel gets under the shingles and into the walls of the house, we're in big trouble."

"*What?* How is that even possible?" There was a lid on that barrel—we've always kept it tied down with cables and weighted with bricks. A small hole in the lid allowed rainwater from the roof of the garden shed to drip into the barrel—a perfect system for collecting water for the garden, not necessarily an ideal place to store heads. "Nothing could have gotten in there," I say, trying not to panic.

"Someone opened it and put the head—or something that looks like a head—in there. The lid was off. Here, look. I took a photo—"

"Nooooo!" I scream. The last thing I want to see is a photo of a frozen human head in my rain barrel. I swat John's camera away from me before the image burns itself onto my brain. "Just tell me what it looks like."

"Well," he says. "It has gray hair and pointy teeth and blood-shot beady eyes."

"That could be anyone," I say. "Or—"

"You know what?" John says, as he studies the photo. "It could be an animal. Maybe some poor critter chewed through the cables, knocked the bricks on the ground, dislodged the lid, and dove into the water barrel. He drowned, and then the water froze. What an awful way to die."

Silence.

"The weasel?" I ask.

"The weasel," he says. "Brick throwing. Cable chewing. Death-defying leaps. Think about it. This situation has *der Wiesel* all over it."

"What are you going to do?" I ask.

"Don't know," says John. "He's frozen solid in there right now—I'd have to use an ax to get him out. Looks like one of those exhibits at the Museum of Natural History. Look at the photo—"

"Nooooo! You're sure it's the weasel and not a human head? I mean, maybe we should call the police or something."

"Nope," John says as he continues to look at the photo. "Not a human head. It's a frozen dead weasel—*ein gefrorenes totes Wiesel.*

We just have to wait for the weather to warm up so I can hack him out. But don't tell Julia. She'll want to have a weasel burial. And, sorry, but I just don't feel like singing 'Amazing Grace' for a weasel."

John sends the photo to Hans.

I think about the weasel a lot. He was nasty: killing those bunnies, making little girls cry, destroying brake cables on cars, and keeping entire families awake at night. But, you know, he was acting in character, just being a weasel. He was likely living here before we moved in, hanging out with the mice, the frogs, and the wild boars. We might have served a nice cheese, olive, and cable buffet, but we didn't exactly drag out the welcome wagon for him. I feel a little sad about his gruesome demise. I still haven't seen the photo.

So, we go on: man (and reluctant woman) versus nature. A couple of musicians, trying to create something meaningful out of the mess of the day—raising kids, cooking dinners, practicing, writing, setting live traps, practicing some more, listening for noise in the walls and thumps on the roof, and trying to get some sleep.

The weasel reminds us of several bothersome but endearing jazz guys we once knew—skilled players who bugged us for gigs, called at inopportune times, showed up at our home, drank our vodka, ate our salty snacks, and moved on when nothing was left to pilfer. It was just who they were.

I hope the wild boars come back up the hill someday.

Sixteen

The Mister Rogers' Songbook

On February 27, 2003, America lost one of its national heroes. For more than three decades Fred Rogers, of *Mister Rogers' Neighborhood,* taught parents and children about joy and sadness, life and death, about being different and fitting in. "You are special," he sang to us, without a tad of irony or skepticism.

"It's '*you*' I like."

Because my father played percussion on the Mister Rogers' program (Fred never called it a "show," it was always a "program") for thirty-five years, I had the honor of knowing both Fred and his spirited wife, Joanne. Along with pianist Johnny Costa and bassist Carl McVicker, Dad logged hundreds of hours at the studio, playing vibes and drums for Fred and his family of puppets and "Neighborhood" regulars (Neighbor Aber, Handyman Negri, Chef Brockett, and Mr. McFeely among them). The Neighborhood, a popular hangout for famous musicians such as Tony Bennett, Wynton Marsalis, and Yo-Yo Ma, was also populated by real men who drove bulldozers, real women who worked in graham cracker factories, and real nine-year-old boys in very real wheelchairs. Fred's true gift was the ability to make every one of these people feel loved, respected, and unique. He used music to orchestrate his message of radical kindness.

In Fred's universe, we were all special. We were all, as Fred liked to say, "fancy on the inside."

People often ask what Fred was "really" like off camera, hoping, I guess, to hear that he was too good to be true. He wasn't. The television Mister Rogers mirrored the real-life Mister Rogers. Talk to any of the musicians, administrators, and technicians who worked for him over the years—Fred was Fred. I got to visit with him once or twice a year—sometimes at the studio, sometimes at the annual picnic he hosted for his employees' families, sometimes at his "Crooked House" on Nantucket Island. He always remembered the tiniest details of our previous conversations. His genuine curiosity about my piano world made me feel, for lack of a better word, *safe*.

Fred possessed a wacky sense of humor and a true love for all things whimsical. Most of us lose our childlike sense of wonder as we grow up—he clung to his innocence and treasured it until the end, sort of like his well-worn cardigan sweater. He found an inner quality that worked for him, and he stuck with it. Lucky for us.

"You make people feel good with your music," Fred said to me once, words of gold for someone like me who makes a living playing cocktail piano. "What a wonderful feeling that must be for you. Isn't the piano a marvelous thing?"

Fred understood, perhaps better than anyone, that playing made me happy, even if no one in particular seemed to be listening. Fred played the piano to express his own feelings. He recognized that music, along with its challenges and frustrations, can bring comfort to those of us who play.

Like many young adults, I had conflicts with most authority figures in my life, but Fred was different, because I never felt judged by him. I always knew he would accept me, accept my music, without hypercritical assessment. He loved that I played the piano, he loved that it made me feel good to connect to the world through music, and he related to my need to belong. He listened to me. Really listened. Whenever I spoke with Fred, I was the only person in the room for him.

Even though I live in Germany, I don't have to travel far to hear Fred's voice. I often stream a *Mister Rogers' Neighborhood* episode and fall into a melodic time tunnel. Fred left behind a billion notes, a dizzying number of beautiful thoughts transposed into song, and a musical tapestry woven with the fragile threads of optimism and inspiration. Watching *Mister Rogers' Neighborhood* reminds me that each supportive person in a young person's life—teacher, parent, or TV star—has the potential to spark the artistic flame that lives in every child's heart.

I am still waiting for someone, *anyone* on television, to fill his sneakers. Come back, Fred. We miss you. All of us, more than ever, need to feel special again.

In early 1968, pianist Johnny Costa called my dad to appear on *Mister Rogers' Neighborhood*. At that early point in the show's long run, the music budget only included funds for Costa on piano—but whenever the producers scraped together enough bread, they added bass and drums to the mix. Fred Rogers loved musicians—the more, the merrier.

A couple of other drummers had auditioned for the gig. A renowned player named Johnny Vincent stumbled over his lines again and again whenever he was asked to appear on camera, once calling the royal puppet, King Friday, "Your Magistrate" instead of "Your Majesty." Vincent lost the gig, not because he couldn't play—he was a killer musician—but because he couldn't handle talking to a crown-wearing puppet in a Liberace-inspired fake ermine cape, and the producer couldn't justify the expense of extra takes just because the drummer flubbed his lines ten times in a row.

Dad, who played as nicely as the tongue-tied Johnny Vincent, happened to be a skilled on-camera presence. He also had a percussion storage closet at home, jammed with temple blocks, a marimba, vibes, various types of cowbells, glockenspiels, bird whistles, even a stump fiddle. If you're producing a kid's television show, call the guy with the fun sound effects. Dad got the gig.

"No one thought much of the program back in 1968," Dad says. "In fact, some of the local musicians made fun of me for taking a kids' show. They didn't understand that Fred and Johnny Costa were dead serious about keeping the musical standard high—they wanted kids to hear sophisticated jazz."

Costa—arguably one of the best jazz players in the world—took the Mister Rogers' gig because he wanted to stay in Pittsburgh (he had been offered the nationally televised *Mike Douglas Show* in Philadelphia but turned it down), and his salary would be exactly enough to pay for his kid's tuition at Bethany College. Fred and Johnny were at opposite ends of the personality spectrum, but Fred, who knew musical brilliance when he heard it, accepted Johnny's diva antics and occasional off-color comments. Most important, Fred stayed cool about Johnny playing the way he wanted to play—Costa often sounded very much like his friend and colleague Art Tatum, the greatest of the great, a pianist whose harmonic style might have been considered too complex for small children. But Fred gave Johnny the freedom to really play, and in doing so, elevated everything about the program. Good became excellent; excellent became legendary.

Half a century after my father's first appearance on the program, Dad is still asked if Fred's off-camera personality was anything like the kind, gentle, public persona that several generations of children experienced.

"Yeah," Dad says. "Fred was the real deal. I knew it from the moment I met him."

On that first day in 1968, Dad drove to the program's original studio, located on the University of Pittsburgh campus, unloaded his drums, and went to park the car. When he returned, Fred Rogers greeted him at the door.

"Welcome, Bobby," Fred said. "Let me help you with the drums." He picked up a large tom-tom case and a smaller bongo case and carried them into the studio.

"At that point I thought *this guy must be OK*," Dad tells me. "I mean, who does that? He was the star of the show, and he offered to carry my bongos."

Both Fred and Johnny Costa were perfectionists. Fred's style brought a sense of calm to the studio neighborhood, but sessions with Costa were harrowing and full of surprises.

Dad called the band the Kamikaze Trio. He and bassist Carl McVicker never knew what Costa would do next—he had a habit of switching keys at the last minute, causing low-level panic for his experienced sidemen. In the shoestring budget world of public television, the trio was usually not offered more than one chance to get it right. Sink or swim.

"What key is this in?" Dad would ask, mallets hovering over his vibes, as they prepared to record improvised music with complicated changes, live on tape. "What key, what key?"

"Only God knows the key, Bobby," Costa often said, seconds before launching into one of his Ravel-influenced improvisations on one of Fred's melodies. "Only God knows."

Dad and Carl would hang on, finish the take, and silently congratulate each other with a subtle "yeah, man" nod. Costa once kissed his own hands a dozen times, raised them to the sky, and accepted praise from heaven.

Like Fred Rogers, Costa knew when he was on point.

"How about that?" Costa would say to Fred, Bobby, and Carl after pulling one more musical miracle out of his piano. "How about that? It's a beautiful fucking day in the neighborhood."

On a sparkling July morning—another beautiful day in the neighborhood—three broad-shouldered men gently boosted a nine-foot concert grand from a fourth-floor apartment window onto a towering platform. Swaddled in thick blankets, the Steinway D waited for the next part of its voyage to begin. The workers cautiously slid the piano onto a set of pipes that extended from the scaffolding while a crane operator attached the rope coiled around the instrument to a large metal hook. After much double-checking, the crane jumped to life, lifting the Steinway into a beam of sunlight. The piano seemed to hover over the street, pausing for just a moment, and then—with an almost human air of self-determination—it swooped to the earth below, one thin crane cable determining whether it would live to play another Chopin nocturne or end up as a pile of rubble on the Pittsburgh nightly news.

Joanne Rogers, then a seventy-nine-year-old concert pianist who had spent much of her adult life playing this piano, stood in the imposing space once occupied by the instrument and took a deep breath. She hurried down to the front of the building and watched as the movers loaded the piano into a truck. The time had come to say good-bye.

"I thought at one point, this is crazy, why am I doing this?" said Joanne from her home, six weeks after the piano's departure. "I guess maybe we have those feelings about every big thing we do in life. We want to back out at the last second."

Joanne's honest words would have made her husband proud. She was married to Fred for fifty years. Mr. and Mrs. Rogers celebrated their golden wedding anniversary at the White House in 2002, on the day Fred was awarded the Presidential Medal of Freedom. A year later, her husband was gone.

Almost five years after his death, Joanne had decided to donate Fred's Steinway D—not the piano used on the program, but the instrument upon which he had composed many of the neighborhood tunes—"Won't You Be My Neighbor?," "The Clown in Me," "You Can Never Go Down the Drain"—to the Fred Rogers Center for Early Learning and Children's Media at Saint Vincent College in Latrobe, Pennsylvania, the town where Fred was born and raised. In a way, the piano was going home. But first, it would travel to the Steinway Restoration Center in New York City, where master technician Chris Arena supervised a total restoration of the piano's interior and exterior. The work was completed in time for the spring 2008 opening of the Fred Rogers Center.

"The idea to donate the piano to the center suddenly came to me," said Joanne, who followed through on her promise in spite of last-minute jitters. "It was a very practical decision, and yet I got very excited at the same time."

Two years before Fred died, Archabbot Douglas R. Nowicki of Saint Vincent Archabbey had begun planning the center with Fred. According to a statement compiled by its board of advisers, "the mission of the Fred Rogers Center is to advance the fields of early learning and children's media by acting as a catalyst for communication, collaboration, and creative change." These are fancy words to describe the philosophy of a man whose remarkable career was launched by the purest of musical beginnings.

Fred's beautiful journey began with a piano.

"When he was a child," says Joanne, "he would go to the piano to express all of his feelings: mad, glad, and sad all came right out through his fingers."

In the early 1940s, in a scene out of every piano student's wildest fantasies, Fred's parents took him to Mellor's Music Store in downtown Pittsburgh. Fred, thirteen at the time and blessed by a supportive and enthusiastic family of means, was given his choice of instruments. He selected the Steinway D. The piano, manufactured in 1920, had been played for two decades by famous concert artists passing through the city. Shortly after taking possession of the instrument, Fred, inspired by standards in the Great American Songbook, developed a strong interest in songwriting.

When I asked Joanne if her husband had cited any mentors, she said, without missing a beat, "Why yes! Jack Lawrence!" Mr. Lawrence, born in 1912 and inducted into the Songwriters Hall of Fame in 1975, had penned an astonishing number of popular songs that became standards, including "Beyond the Sea" (a huge hit for Bobby Darin), "Tenderly" (hits for both Sarah Vaughan and Rosemary Clooney), and "All or Nothing at All" (a Sinatra classic).

In his book *The World According to Mister Rogers*, Fred talks about his meeting with Mr. Lawrence: "I took him four or five songs that I had written, and I thought he'd introduce me to Tin Pan Alley and it would be the beginning of my career. After I played he said, 'you have very nice songs. Come back when you have a barrelful.'"

Taking Lawrence's words to heart, teenage Fred Rogers devoted himself to the art and craft of songwriting. Sitting at his piano, he began shaping many of the ideas that would later become Mister Rogers classics. "The more I wrote the better the songs became, and the more those songs expressed what was real within me."

Authenticity was a big deal to Fred—he knew children had a laser-like sense of what was honest and what was fake. He chose themes such as anger, divorce, love, death, and fear of going down the drain with the bathwater. He tackled topics kids cared about, and they trusted his songs.

"Fred was a very disciplined writer," said Joanne, who met him while she was studying classical piano performance at Rollins College in Florida. "He had a composition teacher there who taught him the necessity of having a time every day specifically for writing. You go and you just do it. You sit there until you can."

Joanne's practice schedule and Fred's devotion to his writing meant that the Rogers family needed instruments everywhere they went. Joanne enjoyed practicing for her concerts on one of the big pianos at home in Pittsburgh, but Fred accomplished some of his best work on Nantucket Island, where the Rogers family owns a lopsided Madaket beachfront cottage called The Crooked House.

"His piano there, a tiny thing, was from a company called Grand," said Joanne. "So the piano was referred to as his 'grand' piano. You know, the music was in his head; he didn't need a big fabulous piano to compose: he always had a sense of what the piece would sound like."

In their Pittsburgh home, next to Fred's Steinway D, Joanne also kept a Bechstein C, a slightly smaller concert instrument with a softer, easier-to-play action. For the previous thirty years Joanne, a former student of Ernst von Dohnanyi, had performed two-piano concerts and recitals with her good friend Jeannine Morrison. She and Jeannine frequently practiced side by side on the grand pianos in the Rogers's living room. "Fred's Steinway was the piano I loved to play the most when I had a lot of practicing to do to get ready for a concert. It had a firmer touch than the Bechstein. Fred and I played both pianos, but when Fred was working, he liked to play his Steinway. He would almost purr when he played that piano. He connected with it."

A good instrument can bring out the best in any composer. Pianos have personalities. Taste matters, but so does touch—a good match between player and instrument relies on both physical and emotional chemistry. The very instrument I adore might hinder another player, or the other way around. Steinways tend to fight back, but I love that; the tension gives me a feeling of control. I never played Fred's D, but I bet I would have loved it. A spectacular instrument has no wrong notes.

Millions of children who have listened to *Mister Rogers' Neighborhood* over the years have been enchanted by the lush sounds of the television studio's Steinway B, a smaller instrument than the one Fred played at home. Every so often Fred played on the program, but most of the time he left the pianistic heavy lifting to Costa. This piano, signed by John Steinway, holds the honor of being heard by more children than any other piano in television history. The raffish Costa—Fred's musical director for thirty years—arranged Fred's tunes and peppered Mister Rogers' easy-going neighborhood with fiery dashes of swinging jazz, performed live for every program.

"Sophistication was built into Fred's compositions, and Johnny always knew how to find the right chords to enhance that," said Joanne. Lovely surprises came from Fred's collaboration with Costa—childlike melodies that seemed to dance through a maze of mature harmonic underpinnings. Those elements, mingled with the poetry of Fred's lyrics and the thrill of Costa's playing, created a magical partnership. When Costa died in 1996, pianist and arranger Michael Moricz stepped in as musical director, taking over Costa's duties and gracing the neighborhood with his own creative brilliance and musical charm.

Fred insisted on a stellar jazz trio for the program—including bassist Carl McVicker and percussionist Bob Rawsthorne (my dad)—and he taped memorable segments with other piano giants such as André Watts, Van Cliburn, and Ellis Marsalis. By avoiding obvious commercial choices, he hit on a simple truth: that children, when given the opportunity to hear excellent music, will listen. "Fred provided children with music they ought to be hearing," said Joanne. "He always knew he was giving them the best."

Fred never lost faith in the power of musical expression. Recalling her husband's final weeks, Joanne said, "When he returned from the hospital, he walked straight to the piano and sat down. That's what he wanted to do. And he would go every day to the piano and play. He did this until he was completely bedridden. I think he was improvising—his way of composing—until the end."

The restored Steinway was eventually given a place of honor in the atrium at the Fred Rogers Center—a fitting tribute to a human being whose evolution from young man to television legend began with a piano, a soaring imagination, and the desire to give shape to his feelings through song.

When the piano is played—by hands large and small—Joanne Rogers hopes visitors to the center will remember that Fred's music has carried millions of children to the proud heights of self-recognition. Check out the swinging trio playing an improvised take of "It's Such a Good Feeling" at the close of every program, or the twisting harmonies of "When the Day Turns into Night," maybe one of the saddest and, yet, most hopeful songs ever written.

Fred Rogers taught me a lot about being a decent human being, but I learned even more from him about the art and business of making music: show up, express yourself honestly, treat your fellow artists with respect, never play down to your audience, and remember that someone is always listening.

I've always liked this Fred Rogers quote about "Tree, Tree, Tree," a hauntingly simple song from the *Mister Rogers' Songbook*: "This is a song that may be good to sing before you go to sleep.

It's easy to sing if you can say *tree, tree, tree* and *we love you, yes, we do.* Some people even like to make up their own words for it."

One heartfelt song: that's often all it takes to make a person feel good. In his lifetime, Fred Rogers wrote a barrelful of them.

Seventeen

The Magnolia Sessions

"Hey, Momma, I want to write a song for you," says Curtis, my nineteen-year-old son.

"For me?"

"Yeah, for you. You know—for your new recording. I'll compose it. You play it."

Curtis is eating ramen noodles—the massive consumption of which seems to be a rite of passage for most boys his age—while constantly checking his phone for text messages, Facebook alerts, check-ins from his pals at the university, and e-mails from his boss at the language center where he teaches English. It seems impossible that with all his ramen-slurping, techno-toy-fidgeting, and learning-teaching multitasking, he could find time to compose a piano piece.

But I'm not about to turn down the chance to work with my almost-adult child on a musical project. We see each other far too little these days. We clog dance in widening circles around each other and prepare for the day he moves out. It could be tomorrow, next year, or next decade. The uncertainty makes us both a little cranky.

"Look, Curtis, I'm recording in January. It's already November. If you want to compose something for me, I'll be happy to consider it, but it has to be finished soon so I can get it into my fingers before the first studio date. And no hip-hop. Hip-hop solo piano won't work for me."

"OK, Momma," he says, rinsing out his ramen bowl and heading down into the music room. "I've got an idea. Let's see what happens. Oh, by the way, if I compose this and you record it, I get money, right?"

"Yes. But it will take a long time before GEMA and BMI royalties kick in."

"How long?" he asks. "I need to buy some new shoes."

"A year," I say. "Maybe longer."

"Really?" he says.

"Yep. Welcome to the music business. You want new shoes? You really have to plan ahead."

Two days after his initial trip to the basement music room, Curtis emerges, flushed and nimble-fingered, ready to perform his piece for me. "Are you ready?" he says.

"Sure," I say.

"It's in F minor."

"OK," I say. "I like F minor. F minor is good."

He sits at my 1964 Baldwin grand—a gift from my grandfather—and rips into the composition. I'm right in the middle of hacking onions for lentil soup, but I stop mid-chop, because, frankly, what he's playing is beautiful, rhythmically influenced by his jazz-guy father, but leaning unabashedly in my contemporary classical direction. It's the best gift he has ever given me. Because of the speed, and because his hands are so much larger than mine, I know it won't be easy to learn. But now I'm on a mission.

"What's it called?" I ask.

"I like the name 'Mirage,'" he says. "You know, when you think you see something, but it's not really there."

"Perfect."

"What's up, Momma?" he asks. "Are you crying?"

"No, no, no. Onions."

"OK."

"OK," I say, wiping my hands on a dishcloth. "Show me how it goes."

And he does.

I prepare like crazy for my recording sessions—even with several solo piano albums under my skirt, I'm not the type of musician who can mosey into a studio and wait for magic to happen without doing my homework. My creative process has never included dewdrops, angel voices, spiritual transformations, or sparkling moments of enlightenment. Where, oh where, are those lovely muses in flowing white robes? The ones with lilting accents and fluttering wings who might drop into my consciousness and gently guide me through my projects? I have never met these fantasy ladies, but I hear they're out there somewhere, probably perusing the flowing robe department at Bergdorf Goodman. If you run into one of them, send her my way.

My recording process has to be carefully plotted and mapped out, which makes it less like magic and more like work. I've learned to respect my method, the same way I respect other slightly scary things I adore—fierce and foamy waves in an unsettled sea, a bowl of fiery chili peppers, a frosted bottle of really good vodka. I proceed with caution. I practice and pound the music to a pulp, hating it just a little before I begin to truly love it. And then I fall in love.

When the melodies and rhythmic patterns are so ingrained that nothing trips me up—I ruffle the edges and resuscitate the stuff back to life, head to the studio, and hope for the best. Sometimes, when I'm calm, I scatter my musical thoughts like stardust onto the keys; sometimes it's more like sawdust. No big deal—I brush away the detritus and start over. Unlike real life, the "take over" option in a studio is always available. This comforts me. The piano zone is just a little bit gilded like that.

In 1994, I recorded my first album, *Somewhere in Time.* My dear friend Robin Spielberg had brokered a record deal for me with a fledgling record label called Evergreen Music. I didn't think I was up to the task, but she yanked me into

Nola Recording Studios (in the old Steinway building on Fifty-Seventh Street in Manhattan) and sat me down at Erroll Garner's Steinway B. Erroll was a fellow Pittsburgher, and I imagined his legendary fingers on the piano, playing his signature tune, "Misty." This did nothing to calm my nerves. I had been playing in Manhattan piano lounges for eleven years, so I knew I was ready, but still, my knees knocked together, my hands began to sweat, my heart felt like a metronome turned up to tempo *terror.* I wanted to sound perfect, a concept that now makes me laugh. Back then, at age thirty-five, it wasn't so funny. Perfect was perfect, and that was that.

We recorded about twenty tracks that day. In six hours. Spielberg wore the producer's hat; she had the lights in the studio turned down low, tea candles on a nearby table, the temperature in the room set at just the right level. In the end, I felt at home, just like I was in a cocktail lounge—minus the bowls of smoked almonds and tables of chattering orthopedic shoe salesmen.

She talked to me between takes—in a way that only a best friend can—and convinced me to play just for her. We soldiered through and got it in the can. No magic—just trust and a lot of hard work. I kept waiting for the ladies in the flowing robes, but they didn't show up; and as it turned out, we didn't need them. Spielberg and I toasted each other with Diet Coke and Fig Newtons. Then she bought me an egg salad sandwich, we cried, I moved to Germany, and my music career was punted like a football to the other side of the Atlantic. I arrived in Europe just in time to catch it and run. The album, released about two years before everyone and her sister had a recording to her name, helped establish my musical street cred and launched me as a pianist suitable for gigs in castles, villas, and embassies.

My dad always said to me, "The key to sounding good is to know when you don't." I like that. Stay focused, stay real, and remember your limitations. And forget about sounding perfect.

Since that day in 1994, I've learned to treasure every imperfect minute in the studio. No more anxiety attacks. No more second-guessing or losing sleep. I still have moments of indecision and confusion—all artists do—but I don't let them slap me down. Or if they do, I slap them back. Many voices crowd into my mental control room during recording sessions—some of them judgmental, some of them kind and supportive, others philosophical or whimsical or wacky. I hear my parents, my best friends, my piano teacher ("curve those fingers!"), my kids

("what's for dinner?"). In between bouts of intense playing and concentrated listening I hear the roar, the cheers, the boos and hisses, of my personal crowd. If you were beamed into the studio during one of these sessions, you might think I look lonely—there's something melancholy about a middle-aged woman sitting at a very large piano in a darkened room—but honestly, an invisible party is going on in here. Have a drink. Pull up a chair. Tell me what you think. Everyone else does.

On the day I'm scheduled to record Curtis's "Mirage" for my *Magnolia* album, Curtis and I arrive at Topaz Studios in Cologne, Germany. I've asked Curtis to sit in the producer's chair for this session. As any mother will tell you, our children—one way or another—produce our lives from the moment they're born, so today shouldn't be any different.

He folds his lanky body into a chair in the control room, and we wait for Hans Giese, the piano technician, to finish his work. Reinhard Kobialka, the sound technician, chats easily with Curtis about how he has miked the piano and how the recording will proceed.

When Hans finishes tweaking the last few notes, I head into the main room and sit at the Steinway. I feel happy here. I've been recording on this instrument for so many years—my hands feel at home. The keys are warm. I play a few scales, a few arpeggios, a few chord progressions. Then, after Reinhard checks the levels of his many microphones, I start to record Curtis's piece.

I'm here at the piano, Curtis is in the control room, and a thick wall of glass separates us. I close my eyes to play, but my eyelids won't block the slideshow in my mind. As I move through the piece, I see all nineteen years of him, from babbling baby boy, to sullen eight-year-old with skinned knees, to sultry hip-hop teenager, to now, when he is actually producing a track on my new record, a composition he wrote. A feeling of calm drops over me. and I have the sensation that everything in my life—my children, my marriage, my music—all of it is turning out OK.

When I'm a wobbly—but hopefully hip—old lady in a lavender lace dress, I'll look back at my audio scrapbooks and be reminded of the things that counted enough to make me run to the piano and play. My records are, in a way, public musical diaries—finger paintings of small moments I want to remember. I feel like my albums aren't really "released" into the world so much as they break out and escape the boundaries of my control, gallop into the distance, and leave me empty-handed but with plenty of freedom to move on. I guess they're a little like children that way.

The music I'm playing is fast, but it can't sound hectic. "Mirage" needs to flow, like brook water on a spring day; like magnolia petals in a sudden breeze. The song should sound like a nineteen-year-old's idea of the future—unexpected, forward moving, optimistic. As Curtis has said, the piece should sound like we're seeing something that isn't really there.

I finish playing and glance at my son in the control room. He smiles, nods, and says quietly into my headphones: "Let's try it again, Momma. One more time."

Fucking producers.

Eighteen

Enough

*I*n the early eighties, I was living alone in New York City, wondering if it was remotely possible to "have it all." Judith, my long-suffering therapist, said to me, "A career, marriage, and family? You *can* have it all. You just can't have it all at the same time."

Discouraging words in 1984, especially because I didn't have anything, let alone everything. I was divorced, dating two wonderful but flawed guys—one of them married, a compulsive gambler, and twenty-three years my senior; the other sneaky, smart, and movie-star handsome. I almost married the handsome guy for his decorating sense and real estate perks (Nantucket beachfront home plus a Chelsea loft and rent-controlled Village apartment), but I found out that while he was seeing me, he was also sneaking around and dating a man-boy named Steve.

My so-called career consisted of dashing from one five-star Manhattan hotel to another, playing the piano for chiropractor conventions and drunken delegates to the Toy Fair and occasionally being cast in an off-off-awful Broadway show, with a script written by someone just as depressed as I was. I tried to have it all; instead, I had nothing, except for a closet full of black evening gowns and a nice cat named Lucky.

New York City, back then, was an artistic hamster wheel for people like me. The more we suffered, the better we fared, at least in our own minds. None of it mattered, because no one cared. Round and round we sauntered, gritting our teeth, drinking overpriced white wine, and assuring each other that we were having *so much fun*.

Three decades later, I'm shocked to find I do have it all—in a circus juggler, European plate-spinner kind of way. A musical marriage to the world's best (and least-flawed) guy, two brave and funny kids, and, yes, a career. In many ways, Judith was right all those years ago—a woman's life is one of compartmentalization. Most working mothers wear so many hats we could work as quick-change artists for the finest London milliner. Over the course of one day, we might be chefs, taxi drivers, glamor girls, math experts, IT queens, bartenders, craft masters, gardeners, toilet cleaners, laundry mavens, and soothers of broken spirits (sometimes our own). And that's just in our down time, before we've started whipping up the crème brulée, toasting the goat cheese for the roasted beet salad, and heading to the office—in my case, a grand piano nestled into a cocktail lounge or grand European castle.

Judith the therapist wasn't quite right—occasionally it *is* possible, maybe just for one ephemeral moment, for various components of a tumultuous life to collide and morph into a genuine feeling of roundness that produces a gorgeous *boom* of affirmation in all the important categories: family, career, art, personal values. Let me tell you about one of these epiphanies.

Mountains. Alps, actually. And a lake. My flight from Düsseldorf circles the airport and prepares to land. From my airplane porthole, Geneva, Switzerland, looks like a well-endowed woman so certain of her powerful beauty that she only needs to strike a pose to soak up admiring stares. The words to Duke Ellington's "Sophisticated Lady" float through my mind—"smoking, drinking, never thinking . . ." I don't know if lyricist Mitchell Parish ever visited Geneva, but I like to think he did.

I am headed to the United Nations—the *Palais des Nations*—to perform a song I was commissioned to write with my daughter, Julia. The piece, called "Maybe It's You," is the theme song for the NGO Beijing +20 UNECE Regional Review, an international forum on the status of women. Seven hundred influential and politically active women will attend. At the closing ceremony I will play our song on the piano for them. And my daughter will sing. She wrote the music; I penned the lyric.

I'm familiar with the United Nations in New York, and I thought the Geneva branch would pale in comparison—sort of the European hillbilly cousin to the real thing. But when my train arrives outside the *Palais,* I am stunned by the magnitude and beauty of the grounds. Julia, my famed rodent's rights activist and future executive assistant, has been a UN intern for the past week and runs outside the gate to greet me. For the past five months she has been serving as a youth ambassador for FAWCO (Federation of American Women's Clubs Overseas), a UN-accredited nongovernmental organization. Her star is rising, and I haven't seen much of her.

We wrote the song back in May, before she left on her travels. Julia is eighteen. Wearing a chic outfit she bought at Swiss Zara—the "UN intern look" she calls it—she bounds across the big square where we've arranged to meet and escorts me through a security gauntlet to get inside to the general meeting.

We hold hands as we walk a long distance from the entrance to the main hall. I try to catch up on everything I've missed about her. But the UN, with its audacious history, high ceilings, and glorious artwork, puts our personal conversation on hold. We stride through resplendent corridors, appropriately awe-struck.

"Act/Advance/Achieve/Women's Rights"—music will be the tiniest part of the equation. This is a serious conference on human rights for women and girls. We'll learn about slavery, genital mutilation, the sale of girls for marriage, domestic violence; we'll learn about our lack of reproductive rights, lack of equal education, lack of gender equality in the workplace. We'll learn about how much we're lacking when it comes to human rights. And we'll learn about the heroes trying to change things for the better, step by step.

"Look, Mom. Look at the way we're walking. You can't help it. When you're in here, you start walking like you're important. Sort of like the principal of my high school, except faster. I call it the '*important walk.*'"

I know exactly what she means. It's silly. I have been here for about twelve minutes, and I already feel important, that the world respects my opinion. I haven't played a note or said anything at all, but because they let me through the front door, I find that my head is higher, my shoulders are back. I am taller. We enter the Plenary Hall. Seven hundred women, wearing earpieces, sit at desks and listen to a panel discussion called Women's Rights: A Power to Create Change. I grab an earpiece and listen in.

The palpable energy spits and crackles in the hall. It's contagious, and waves of inspiration wash over me. It's astounding that our theme song will be part of this forum. Half of me feels overwhelmed, a little freaked out by the scale of the event; the other half feels *ready*. I feel *important,* and as I will learn over the next three days, far too many women and girls in the world never get the chance to feel important. But that's the point of this conference: we're important. We count. Every single one of us.

"Isn't this the best thing ever?" Julia asks.

I can't answer because I am fighting back tears. That's what feeling important can do to a fifty-seven-year-old woman.

I've lived a privileged first-world, hamster-wheel life, but still, I've been waiting a long time for this. It is one thing to be acknowledged by my family and friends for being a good mom, or to hear the applause of a generous audience after a successful concert. It's quite another to know that the world's policy makers are *listening* to the concerns of mothers, working women, and girls. My concerns. My daughter's concerns. Whether the world community will act on our concerns remains to be seen. But at least they're taking notes. It's a start.

A perfect Steinway B was delivered to the UN the day before the conference began. It now sits in the front of the Plenary Hall, close to the speaker's dais. The participants' desks surround the piano in a "U" shape. We are scheduled to meet with the head technician at 12:30 for a sound check while the conference attendees are having lunch.

I'm worried about the sound situation—it's a huge room and a technical nightmare. Every single desk has a headset and controls that allow the listener to switch from English to French to Spanish to Russian. It's an amazing system and an amusing distraction when bored: *wow, wonder how Julia sounds in Russian.* How they are going to get around this for our song concerns me. Oddly, I don't even see a microphone, but it's the United Nations, so they must know what they're doing.

The IT coordinator, Valerie, meets us at the appointed time. Smart and funny, she is also beautiful—a tall woman with long white hair and no makeup. She's both Bohemian and elegant. But right now, she has bad news, which she delivers in a Bohemian, yet elegant, way.

"There is no microphone," she says.

"Seriously?" I reply. I just had assumed one would be on the way, or at least a headset or whatever diplomats in Sweden use.

She calls the head technician to the floor. After much shrugging of shoulders and use of the word *compliqué*, I begin to understand that we are screwed. I suggest that we bring in an outside sound crew. Valerie is willing, but the union technician won't allow it. "A security nightmare," he says. Plus, the outside system would cause feedback on the seven hundred earpieces at the individual desks. I imagine the sound of seven hundred earpieces squealing all at once. It has the potential of being an avant-garde masterpiece, but not the kind of thing that would go over with this group.

One would think this might have come up in pre-conference technical planning, but for whatever reason it didn't. *Merde.* I know a losing battle when I hear one, especially when it's in French, so I smile and say, "We'll make it work."

"We will?" asks Julia. "How?"

"You'll have to sing acoustically. No amplification."

"For seven hundred people? Mom! Are you nuts?"

"*Oui.*"

"Well, that's a stupid idea," she says. "But I can do it. I'll have to channel Aretha or something."

I am very proud of my daughter right now. More so than even before. This is the Matterhorn of motherly pride. As the snarky sound guy sneaks away, Valerie apologizes a thousand times. We assure her that we will make the best of the situation.

"Of course," she says. "This is what women know how to do. *We make things work.*"

We do a sound check, even though we have nothing to check. The room is very bouncy and bright, and performing unplugged might actually work. Anyway, we have no choice. If everyone listens, we'll be heard—and that's sort of the theme for the entire week. I wonder if the interpreters in the booth upstairs will translate Julia's words as she performs. I wonder if they will sing along, and if so, in what language.

Julia and I are staying outside Geneva in the lakeside villa of former FAWCO president Kathleen Simon, along with eight other FAWCO members and Kathleen's good-humored husband, Andrew. Ten women staying in one residence, all of whom need to eat breakfast, shower, and dress for the day so we can leave at 7:30 sharp.

The *whoosh* of blow-dryers, the gurgle of a designer coffee machine, the mingled scents of L'Oréal hairspray and Jo Malone perfume greet me as I round the corner into Kathleen's designer kitchen. The irony of this scene—a gaggle of privileged women lining up for organic morning beverages so they can adequately hydrate themselves before a dead serious meeting about the perils of being a woman in sub-Saharan Africa—does not escape me. We are white-privilege poster gals, decked out in cashmere and silk, off for a day of talk about saving our less fortunate sisters. Maybe guilt has guided us here. Maybe we are saving ourselves.

Reeling from the previous day's roundtable discussions—
Women and Poverty, The Girl Child, Human Rights and
Migrant Women, Violence against Women—we're ready to
head to the UN for more, more, more. Julia and I are dressed
for our performance at noon. We're wearing coordinated black
and white dresses, and I'm hoping no one says we look like the
Olsen twins.

I'm nervous about technical issues—is it really possible to
sing acoustically for seven hundred people? Julia is worried
about her panty hose, which seem to be slipping down. Crotch
sag—any woman will tell you, it's a major drag. All this women's
rights stuff is important, indeed, but really, someone needs to
invent suspenders to hold up our tights.

Oh, wait—maybe we should just wear pants.

The Plenary Hall has no backstage —the space isn't set up
for theatrical events or concerts (*UN, The Musical*)—so we sit at
a front-row desk, close to the Steinway, and wait for our cue to
perform. We whisper back and forth to each other as the former
president of Finland gives a speech. I admit it: I'm a little nervous. I've played my share of state dinners and royal banquets,
but this is different.

"Are you drinking enough water?" I ask Julia, who complained about a sore throat this morning, no doubt the result of
the stadium singing she did yesterday at the non-sound check.

"*Oui,*" she says.

"Are you warmed up?"

"*Oui.*"

"Do you remember the form of the song?"

"*Oui, oui, oui.*"

"Don't forget the third verse."

"Mom."

"And to repeat the refrain three times at the end."

"Mom, I am fine. Calm down. I just wish my tights would
stay up. They're halfway down my butt. This is making me nuts.
I should have worn pants."

Right.

Nyaradzayi Gumbonzvanda, CSW (Commission on the Status of Women) Geneva president, winds up the conference with a lovely speech about diversity. I have practiced saying her name over the past three days, and now I can do it without stuttering. Nyaradzayi commands attention; she is strong and funny and controls this huge crowd with her rich voice and compelling speech. She calls several women to the stage—a ninety-year-old delegate, a woman with a disability who is in a wheelchair, a female member of the Roma community, a Muslim woman, a Jewish woman, a token man, and then—big surprise to me— Julia, who at eighteen, is the youngest delegate at the conference. She is also the tallest, although that doesn't count. There Julia stands, front and center, smiling and representing her generation. For what must be the twentieth time since this conference started, I cry. And this is unfortunate timing, because we are on, *now.*

Simone Ovart, forum cochair, moderates this part of the ceremony and begins to introduce us in French. I wipe the mascara smudges off my cheeks and listen. I had provided a brief description of the two of us in English, which was successfully translated into French. I sit at the Steinway, attempting to understand Madame Ovart—I don't have a headset at the piano, so I can only hear the French, a very elegant way to be introduced. She finishes her brief words about me and tucks into Julia's introduction. I glance at the FAWCO delegation sitting several rows back, listening—with their earpieces—to the simultaneous English translation of the French translation of the original English version. *C'est compliqué.*

The FAWCO women burst out laughing at something they've heard. Later I will find out that the translator said that Julia "*received her PhD at the age of eighteen.*" Wow. Dr. Julia. And she can sing, too! I glance over at her, and she looks completely relaxed. She looks focused. She also looks like she is trying very hard not to tug on her panty hose.

I take a breath and play an A major triad—an axis of wonder in a working mom's world. Dr. Julia and I are safe with this audience. They carry us as far as we need to go, which isn't too far, because we're only performing one song, but still, I'm glad they're along for the ride. I play the piano, because that's my job, but I listen to my daughter have her moment of importance, because that's my job, too. I am a musician; I am a mother; I am a human being who cares about the status of women everywhere.

And today I get to be all of these things at once. I *can* have it all at the same time. If it only happens once in my lifetime, this is plenty.

> *You are brave,*
> *You are fighting for a change,*
> *You'll save,*
> *The life you want to live—*
> *Maybe it's you . . .*

By the end of the song, Julia has most of the women on their feet, clapping and singing along. The applause rings out and will echo in my heart for weeks to come. We hug dozens of our sisters and grab our coats. We're still doing the "important walk."

Nineteen

Wake Up, Santa!

*I*n 1972 I won the coveted role of the talking Christmas tree at South Hills Village in Pittsburgh, Pennsylvania, a classic suburban shopping mall whose other highlights were fast-food french fries, soft pretzels, and Florsheim shoes.

I called myself "Tanya Baum" and spoke with a *Hogan's Heroes* German accent. The kids were a little scared of me—I was a blabbering Christmas tree, after all—but I cracked myself up, which I had discovered was the secret to success in just about any job.

I made twenty-five bucks for crawling inside the tree suit and yelling seasonal greetings at kids for a couple of hours. My Tanya was a little nasty, she had a slight prison matron edge to her, softened by her coat of fake blue spruce and tinsel. I flicked her lights on and off with hand controls. By looking through the angel on the top of Tanya's head, I could see how much I was scaring everyone.

I got the gig because my dad was the bandleader of a jazz-comedy group called The Steel City Stompers, a popular trio in Pittsburgh with Dad on drums, Ray Defade on saxophone, and pianist Bookie Brown. All three of them sang.

For years, Dad ran the McDonald's sponsored Wake Up, Santa breakfast at South Hills Village. Wake Up, Santa became popular after several failed attempts at having Daredevil Santa skydive into the mall parking lot, an annual disaster that once culminated in Santa crash-landing in a tree next to a gas station two miles down the road, where he was rescued by a crane, untangled from his parachute, and transported to the hospital by ambulance. Daredevil Santa wasn't very good at judging wind currents. Or maybe it was Rudolph's fault—when all else fails, blame the damn reindeer. The shopping mall officials decided it was safer to place Santa in a comfy bed onstage inside the mall, with Dad's band, Tanya Baum, and hundreds of Egg McMuffin-stuffed screaming children yelling for Santa to get the hell up. Apparently, nothing says Christmas quite like a snoring Santa refusing to wake up for the holidays.

Santa was played by a stout guy named Tony, who, during the rest of the year, worked as a manager of the shopping mall Baskin-Robbins ice-cream shop. A few years into the Santa gig, Tony started hitting the booze, and who could blame him? As a matter of fact, so did Bookie, the pianist in Dad's band. Bookie, who eventually joined that elite group of juiced-up stride piano players in the sky, had a really LOUD voice. We called him the "acoustic miracle," because his voice could penetrate any crowd without amplification. With a deep and guttural timbre, he growled his way through songs, announcements, and the occasional prayer. Dad had to turn Bookie's microphone volume down to minus two when Bookie was drinking, because you could never be sure what he might blurt or bray across the room. Even Bookie's whisper had legs.

At one of our annual Wake Up, Santa events, after we jumped on Santa's bed, played a trumpet in his ear, slapped him in the face with a wet washrag (a child's suggestion), smacked him in the stomach with a pillow (another child's suggestion—the kids never suggested anything gentle), and tickled his feet with reindeer antlers, Bookie raised his hand—and his voice—and said he had an idea.

"Yes, Grandpa Bookie?" asked Dad with a palpable amount of exasperation and trepidation. "What's your idea?"

Bookie, it seemed, had been imbibing with Santa at the local derelict bar down the road. Prebreakfast holiday cheer. Who needs eggnog when you can have your Maker's Mark, straight up?

"SANTA, YOU ASSHOLE!" slurred Bookie, in a stentorian tone. "If you don't wake up, we're gonna shoot you with the reindeer gun."

Keep in mind—this was Pittsburgh in 1972.

Dad, sharp-witted but slightly hard of hearing from years of slamming the drums, put down his microphone, looked right into my angel-head eyes, raised one eyebrow, and asked, "Did Bookie just say what I think he said? Did he just call Santa an asshole and threaten to use a reindeer gun?"

"*Jawohl!*" said my Tanya Baum, because I took pride in my ability to stay in character. "*Die Rentierpistole!*" Dad and Ray were horrified, even though most of the parents and kids in the audience laughed. Nervous laughter, but laughter, nonetheless.

"Jesus Christ," muttered Dad. "OK, kids, never mind Grandpa Bookie—now it's time for 'Deck the Halls.' Bookie, get back to the piano! NOW! Stick out your tongue on the fa-la-la part. And look, kids! Grandpa Bookie is gonna wear the elf hat. Maybe that will wake up Santa."

This was the last year we played for the Wake Up, Santa breakfast. Not because Grandpa Bookie called Santa an asshole and threatened to shoot him, but because my father, at one point in the show, made fun of the McDonald's breakfast buffet—"all you can eat for two dollars. One bite, and that's all you can eat"—and insulted the scary, big-lipped floppy-footed Ronald McDonald clown, played by a local bartender unironically named Jerry Error. In his day job, Jerry often poured bourbon for Grandpa Bookie and Santa.

"Check out Ronald McDonald," said Dad to the kids after a rousing rendition of "Jingle Bells," pointing at Jerry Error, who kept tripping over his clown shoes while trying to perform some kind of holiday jig. "South Hills Village must be missing its idiot."

"*Jawohl!*" I yelled. "Merry Christmas!"

Tanya Baum was the sanest part of that show.

More than forty-five years later I wonder if Santa is still at the mall—sleeping off an early morning bourbon buzz, oblivious to the innocent but violent threats of little kids and the earsplitting rants of tipsy piano players. The jesting, jabs, and slapstick brutality seemed slightly amusing in 1972. By 2021 these shenanigans cease to be funny, especially if Santa, the pianist, or an outraged, unhinged parent—or a child for that matter—might actually be packing heat.

I'm sure the live music is gone, even if Ronald McDonald is still stomping around. Maybe the mall has gone back to the skydiving Santa theme, just to keep things edgy. Or maybe Santa now sits in a throne, and kids come to perch on his lap while nymphs (or are they elves?) in red velveteen miniskirts and thigh-high white boots dance to Mariah Carey Christmas songs blaring from speakers covered in plastic holly. Or maybe they blast Santa out of a cannon—I've read about places doing that. That's one way to wake up Santa, even if he's drunk.

Pittsburgh, I came to discover, did not have a monopoly on Christmas insanity.

Thirty years after Wake Up, Santa, my daughter, Julia, was enrolled at a Montessori kindergarten in Germany, and every Christmas, the parents at the kindergarten performed a holiday play for the kids—a civilized, child-friendly policy that took pressure off the youngsters and placed it squarely on the sloped shoulders of the parents (moms). Appalled by the lack of suitable holiday plays for kids—most of the material in circulation was scary, religious, or inappropriately both—I sagely decided to write a musical. Come on, Germany—let's have some holiday fun! Good tidings and cheer!

I needed to attract other parents (moms) to take part in the musical, so my cast of characters included a bunch of wacky fairies, because fairies are cute, entertaining, and provide multiple costume opportunities for those of us longing to relive our prom queen days. I also had access to an adorable rabbit costume with floppy ears, so I added a giant bunny to the cast, along with a narrator dressed as a tree. Tanya Baum, it would seem, was now part of my DNA.

We had several children with disabilities at the kindergarten, so I put the head fairy in a wheelchair, because it seemed like the Christian thing to do. Fairies and a rabbit may not have been traditionally Christian, but they screamed "enchanted forest," which is very German. I'm not Christian or German, but I know a thing or two about playing to the crowd.

I needed a plot. Remembering my days with drunk Santa at the Pittsburgh shopping mall, I decided a snoring, sleeping fairy might be a good starting point. I named her Fatigue. The plot: Fatigue's fairy sisters—Faxana, Flip, Faloona, and (my favorite) Farteena—spend thirty minutes trying to wake her so they can all fly home together for the winter holidays. They tickle her, yell, use magic wands that don't work, and try to shock her awake with the smell of a dead fish. Nothing works. Finally, a giant, orphaned rabbit named Hobo joins them and wakes up Fatigue with a kiss on the nose. They sing a song and invite Hobo home with them for the holidays. The end.

Basically, *Hobo and the Forest Fairies* was a fancy-dress, bourbon-free version of Wake Up, Santa.

Amazingly, like our disabled lead fairy, the show itself had wheels. Over the course of several years, it was produced as a radio play by Germany's largest radio/television conglomerate, then released as an audio CD, and eventually staged as an annual holiday musical at a German castle. What started out as a slapdash shoestring budget musical for a bunch of really cute kids turned into a small fairy empire.

The live, professional production of the show debuted in 2009 at Schlosshotel Lerbach, where I was also the house pianist and artistic director of a concert series. To keep costs down and maintain control over my script, I cast myself as Flip the Fairy, a Barbie blonde with good intentions and a brain the size of a cranberry. I wore a prom gown, lavender rubber boots, and a huge wig that made me look more like a country and western has-been than a fairy.

Julia, who had grown into a relaxed, well-adjusted teenager—in spite of her wand-toting mother—played Fatigue, the snoring, sleeping fairy. My biggest concern during the five-year run of the musical was that she would literally fall asleep onstage. Each year she seemed to skate closer to the edge as the novelty of playing the snoring fairy wore off.

The show, of course, was in German. *Wach auf!* means wake up. But my American accent made *wach auf* sound like fuck off, not a phrase most parents want to hear in a children's musical.

"Fuck off!" I yelled at our sleeping Fatigue during one of our dress rehearsals. "Fuck off!"

"Mom!" Julia said, sitting up and using her stern teenager voice. "I know you're really into your role and everything, but you can't yell 'fuck off' in a play for five-year-olds."

Our musical director (the tree) needed to put on his tree suit in front of the kids, because, understandably, the kids freaked out if a mighty oak entered the room and began singing a sensitive ballad. My shrill, slightly sharp, Beverly Sills version of "Silent Night" and the cartwheeling giant rabbit caused more than one child to burst into tears. But the kids loved the magic wands—one of the wands was a *Star Wars* laser sword—and they flipped over the huge rubber fish and stuffed alligator. And they particularly loved Fatigue, who was already asleep onstage, snoring away, when the kids entered the theater. Some of the kids poked at her and wondered out loud if she might be dead. Julia was actually quite a good actress.

We had hecklers, and worse. One time a kid in the audience gave me the finger and bit me on the knee during our rendition of the "Stank Fish Tango." Another time a little girl—who had eaten too many of the complimentary butter cookies—exited stage left and threw up directly in our entrance/exit path. Sometimes the kids hooted and hollered; sometimes they remained eerily silent.

After each performance our motley crew of fairies—Faxanna, Flip, Flop, Faloona, and Farteena—stood in the castle hall and greeted our guests, most of them the same age that Julia was when I wrote the play for her kindergarten. Our run, which lasted long enough to get my daughter through high school without hating me, ended in 2014 when the castle closed. Good timing—my sixtieth birthday was looming, and I was a bit long in the tooth for a fairy costume. I enjoyed tulle as much as the next gal, but the Dolly Parton wig was like having a squirrel on my head and did nothing to help my hot flashes. Also, I had my career and reputation to consider. The fairy thing was taking over. And I really didn't want to be known as Robin Goldsby, menopausal fairy.

Now I look back on that show as both harrowing and full of joy—an American holiday tradition that I swiped and reinvented for myself and my daughter because I didn't much like the existing models. Festivus for the rest of us!

I cried when I got rid of the costumes. I had seven sets of feather wings and nowhere to fly, so out they went, along with the lavender rain boots. But I saved the rubber fish, because I figured "Stank Fish Tango" might one day find a place in my act. You never know. Two years after our last performance, a German mother told me wistfully, "Farteena was my favorite fairy. I think of her so often. What a beautiful name."

There is no stopping Christmas.

"Robin," says Mr. B, the food and beverage manager of the five-star hotel where I currently play the piano. "We have a big problem. Santa is stuck in the snow."

It's December 2017. I am huddled, freezing, in my parked car in Honrath, waiting for the RB25 train to arrive and whisk me off to Excelsior Hotel Ernst. I'm scheduled to play teatime piano for a group of civilized adults. In another area of the hotel, thirty excited kids and their parents are arriving for a children's tea with Santa. But Santa, defying all odds, is stuck in the snow.

"How is that even possible?" I yell. "He's Santa! He can't get stuck in the snow!"

"I don't know," says Mr. B. "It makes no sense. But he's stuck. Can't get his car out to get to the train."

I happen to know that the actor playing Santa, a corpulent celebrity named Manfred, lives in my neighborhood, and I am not stuck in the snow, so how can he be stuck in the snow? I don't want to get Santa in trouble, so I say nothing. Besides, maybe he really *is* stuck; I live in the valley, and he lives high on the hill, two apparently different ecosystems. Sometimes it's downright tropical in the valley when the hill people are scraping ice off their windshields.

"Do you have any ideas?" asks Mr. B. "We have all these kids coming, and they are going to be very disappointed if Santa doesn't show up. We certainly can't tell them Santa is stuck in the snow."

Just when I thought I was out, they pull me back in.

"Who has the Santa suit?" I ask.

"We have it here at the hotel."

"Good. I know what to do. Move the piano into the ballroom and find an employee to play Santa."

"No one wants to play Santa," he says. "They are shy. Plus, they are all too skinny."

"Get Patrick the waiter," I say. "He has acting training."

"But he is the skinniest of all of them."

"Doesn't matter. We can stuff him. We also need a bed or a large chair. Someplace onstage where he can sleep."

Obviously, my entire life revolves around one plot.

On the train ride into town—about thirty minutes—I plan the program. My husband sends me music—over my phone—to a dozen German children's Christmas songs, all of which, like most Bob Dylan tunes, have three chords and four hundred verses. I stop at the Christmas market and pick up a couple of elf hats, race into the hotel, get Mr. B to print out the music so I can actually see it, and assemble the skeptical banquet team for a panicked talk-through. I tell them that the emergency Santa (Patrick) will be asleep on his giant chair and that we, with the help of the kids, will spend thirty minutes singing and trying to wake him up in time for Christmas.

Apparently, nothing says Christmas quite like a snoring Santa refusing to wake up for the holidays.

Ten minutes till showtime. I can hear the kids buzzing and jostling for position on the other side of the door.

Movie-star handsome Patrick, my emergency Santa, might be slightly hungover from the night before, but he's more than willing to help. Plucked from obscurity to step in for the stuck

Santa, Patrick, in his skinny black jeans, looks like he stepped out of a Prada advertisement. Or at least he does until he puts on the red suit. The banquet director stuffs numerous pillows into his jacket and adjusts his fluffy white beard.

"You can do this Patrick," I say, switching to a "firm director voice." "We are going to sing the Santa song, and then you stagger by the window and yawn, like you can hardly manage to carry that big ass sack of toys. This is no time for subtlety. You are exhausted. Wiped out. Can barely keep your damn eyes open. Enter the room, stumble over to the Santa throne, and fall asleep. Snore into the microphone as loudly as you can. We will spend the next thirty minutes trying to wake you. It might get rough—kids can be brutal—but stay asleep no matter what. Until the kiss. Then you wake up."

Patrick tries to sip coffee through his Santa beard and stares at me like I have reindeer poo on my head.

"You sure this is going to work? I mean, have you done this before?" he asks.

I place my hands on his shoulders, look into his twinkling eyes, and say, "Trust me, Patrick. I've been in the 'Wake Up, Santa' business for forty-five years. It never fails. '*Wach auf, Santa!*'"

"Ha!" says Patrick. "With your accent it sounds like 'fuck off, Santa.'"

"Exactly," I say. "Go with it."

The kids enter the room. I put on my elf hat and play the piano. They sing along and eat cookies. I play the Santa song, and Patrick, the world's skinniest Santa, wobbles, teeters, and lurches past the window.

"Oh, no," I say to the kids. "Santa looks *very* tired. I wonder what could be wrong?"

Right on cue, the ballroom door creaks open, and Patrick, going for gold with his portrayal of a drained and weary Santa, moans and crawls—crawls!—to the stage, dragging his overloaded bundle of toys behind him.

Best emergency Santa ever.

Wach auf!

Along with a couple of banquet waiters, I drag Santa into his chair. He snores like a drunken elf. We do everything we can think of to wake him. We sing. We yell. We tempt him with over-priced macarons and tap on his head with pinecones from the expensive centerpieces. We get parents to do the reindeer dance. Volunteers from the audience don the elf hat and jostle Santa to no avail. I really wish I had thought to bring the rubber fish.

Finally, after we reach the thirty-minute mark—the longest half hour of my life—I suggest a kiss, and a sweet little boy puts on the hat. Smooch! Santa wakes up. The children cheer. This might be a decidedly upscale group of privileged European children, but, really, at this moment they seem identical to their Pittsburgh shopping mall and Montessori kindergarten colleagues.

Kids are kids. Fun is fun.

Ho, ho, ho. Santa might have gotten stuck in the snow, but emergency Santa, one pillow shy of a proper jelly belly, has saved the day. After the show, Patrick returns to his glass-polishing post in the kitchen, I return to my Steinway in the posh lounge, and the kids, high on chocolate and sugared tea, head into the winter wonderland, clutching swag bags of candy and small toys.

On his way out, the little boy who kissed Santa asks my permission to keep his cheap, felt elf hat.

"Of course," I say. "It's yours—the holiday chapeau! You saved Christmas for all of us."

"Look," he says, pointing outside. "It's snowing! Santa is going to have a great trip around the globe this year. He loves snow!"

"Yes," I say. "Let's hope he doesn't get stuck."

"Don't be ridiculous," says the boy. "Santa would never get stuck in the snow."

Twenty

Beach Song

I love the ocean. The most musical of Earth's components, its rhythmic pulse floods my soul with hope, quenches my desire for a wider perspective, and washes away the grit and grime of a landlocked life. I've spent time on beaches all over the world, not because I'm a Birkin-toting, stiletto-heeled jet-setter with beachside chateaus in Malibu and St. Tropez, but because I'm the daughter of a musician, I'm married to a musician, and I'm a musician myself. Music, for most of my life, has provided me with prepaid tickets to the destinations of my dreams. Coastal concerts, harbor happenings, beach bashes, seaside shindigs— we've played for them all. Short of being the world's oldest *Baywatch* lifeguard, I can't think of any better way to finance my addiction to saltwater and sand.

In 1966 my father played the drums in a Dixieland band for a Teamster convention in Miami Beach, Florida. He took us along for a two-week vacation. I ate frogs' legs at an outdoor luau at the Americana Hotel—frogs' legs, it turns out, really do taste like chicken—with a picture of Jimmy Hoffa projected (eight stories high) on a wall of the hotel. My dad's band wore red-and-white striped shirts and straw hats. I liked the tuba player, because, you know, tuba players are likable.

"Who is this Jimmy Hoffa?" I asked my dad.

"He's the boss," said my dad. "He's the reason we're here."

So, I became a big Jimmy Hoffa fan. After all, he got me to Miami.

During the day I hung out on the beach with my brother and sister. Because we spent so much time underwater, my mother dressed us in matching neon tank suits so she could see our behinds on the surface of the bright blue sea. After two days of this, even my eyeballs were sunburned, and I had to go to dinner in the fancy hotel wearing eye patches. Fearful of looking like a pirate, I placed my mother's big black sunglasses over the patches—a *"Jackie Kennedy meets Bluebeard"* look that I thought would pass for Miami Beach chic. I was nine years old.

Due to temporary blindness, I could not enjoy the Fourth of July fireworks that night. It didn't matter—all I cared about was getting back into the water the next day. My sister, Badass Randy, and I played a game called "Let's Go Die" at water's edge. We held hands as the waves broke over us, determined to cling to each other no matter what. We rolled back and forth, as sand scraped our private parts and salt stung our eyes. We laughed and held on tight. A lifeguard yelled at us for pretending we were drowning, but we were actually perfecting our synchronized swimming skills. Some might have called it synchronized drowning.

My father caught a fish while we were flipping over each other in the water and threw it at us. It tangled in my hair. I developed fear of fish and spent the next few decades terrified of underwater critters.

A few years later, in 1969, Dad booked a summer jazz job in a resort area a few hours away from home. We spent three months in a lakeside cottage next to Conneaut Lake, a dark blue body of water in western Pennsylvania. Not an ocean, but it might as well have been. I spent my days on a sand-covered pier, swimming back and forth to a raft anchored twenty meters away. Speedboats churned the water and rocked the raft, and my sister and I smeared ourselves with baby oil and iodine so we could tan faster. By August, I resembled a rotisserie chicken with strong triceps. My hair turned silver. I hoped that Davy Galla-gher, the bronze lifeguard who looked like Ivy League Tarzan, would notice me. He did not. But a boy named Timmy Catcher caught me. We danced around each other and played splash games in the lake. Despite rumors of snapping turtles, I learned to waterski and got pretty good at it, except for one instance when my hair got caught in a tow rope, and I almost drowned.

I did worry about those snapping turtles.

In the evenings, I brushed pier sand out of my hair and strung tiny love beads into necklaces that no one would ever wear. Timmy Catcher kissed me. Just once.

By my eighteenth birthday, after watching my dad sing for his family's supper in one vacation paradise after another, I figured out that I, too, could visit the world's most beautiful oceanside resorts and probably have even more fun if I played my own gigs. In 1976 I arrived on Nantucket Island with a dozen suitcases, packed mostly with books and bikinis. Two weeks before Memo-rial Day, I landed a job playing the piano in a bar. What a thing! I spent the summer on a New England beach and got paid to play the piano. During the day, I basked in the sun on beaches called Madaket or Dionis or Nobadeer. As far as I was concerned, any beach named by Indians was the real deal. At night I put on a glittery tube top and a long skirt and played Carole King songs. I was wave-tossed, sun-kissed, and boy crazy. A swain named Joe stole my heart and taught me how to surf fish.

I was the only female member of the Kamikaze Water Ski Club, a Nantucket Yacht Club subgroup founded by the stoned teenage children of various titans of industry. I worried about sharks and other fish with large teeth. This motivated me to avoid falling while waterskiing. I perfected a one-ski beach land-ing after I spotted a sand shark swimming too close to shore.

My favorite bikini was white.

By the end of my first summer, the subtle pulse of the waves synced with my own rhythm. I was hooked on music and salt-water. The sand shark never got me.

I returned to my Nantucket piano job every summer for many years. The romance with Joe the swain faded, but my love affair with the island hung tight. The rhythm of the waves seemed like an external heartbeat, nature's metronome, an urgent throb that counterpoints human instinct.

I traveled now and then to Haiti, where I played American-style cocktail lounge piano for upscale guests at a swanky but suspicious five-star hotel. The Third World piano bar, tucked into the corner of a disco that regularly blared merengue, was patronized by military thugs, New York garment-district guys who owned factories in Port-au-Prince, gray-faced gamblers fresh from the casino next door, and lost souls who showed up after spending hours at the Barbancourt rum distillery. Baby Doc was still in office, and the atmosphere felt tense, the resort air smug and sticky. When I was lucky, I got a lift to Ibo Beach. The road to Ibo was lined with potholes, rocks, scrambling chickens, and artists attempting to sell colorful paintings for a dollar or two. It made me sad.

After an hour-long dusty ride in an old Cadillac, I would take an *African Queen* boat to Ibo Island—a slice of sun-drenched wonder in a ravaged country, a place where I could stare at the sea and imagine I lived in a fair world. The sand was sugar white and soft.

A jellyfish stung me, and a Haitian woman treated the sting with vinegar and shaving cream. It burned, but not for long.

I ate too many mangoes.

I flew from my Third World gig in Haiti to a private island populated by rich Republicans and wild turkeys. Between piano sessions at Bloody Mary brunches and daily performances at *happy, happy, happy hour* whiskey tastings, I walked pristine beaches, stared at sparkling water, and tried to figure out who I was. I belonged on a beach, but maybe not this one.

In 1991, after being fired from my seven-year piano engagement at the Marriott Marquis in Manhattan and replaced by a fake piano—management had figured out they could install a player piano and a tuxedo-clad mannequin to sit there and look like a stuffed musician—I flew to Hawaii with my husband, John. In my opinion any time you lose a gig, especially if you're replaced by a dummy, a Hawaiian vacation is in order. Kauai seemed a little distant, but my sister had offered us a place to stay. I cashed in my American Airlines' frequent-flyer miles (all those gigs in Haiti) so we could fly first-class for free.

The Kauai beaches, manicured but still rough around the edges, reminded me of everything I'd been missing. My husband and I slid down a steep hillside to visit Secret Beach, where huge boulders interrupted long stretches of white sand. We did secret things on Secret Beach. Then we almost killed ourselves climbing back up the hill. We hung out at a Princeville resort and drank martinis while a jazz trio played, and swore that one day one of us would land a gig there.

I attempted to overcome my fear of snorkeling when I watched small children and old people frolic in shallow water, chattering about the colorful varmints that swam among us. I hated knowing that living things were in the water with me, but it was time to overcome fear of fish and get with the program. I donned a mask and flippers and forced myself to enjoy the *"lovely"* residents of the sea as they glided past me.

I hate this. I do. Oh, look. Electric blue, bright yellow, there's one with stripes. Isn't this fun? What if I see a stingray? Or a shark? Or, God forbid, an eel?

Something that looked like Karl Lagerfeld with gills drifted under my right hand.

Very nice. God, I hate this. Look there—a group of tiny orange fish with spikes. Are they following me? Do they bite? Are there piranha in Hawaii?

While my rigid body tried to enjoy the underwater fin fashion show, a huge dog—I found out later it was a Great Dane named Junior—jumped into the surf and began swimming toward me. When Junior swam into my line of vision, I panicked, lost all sense of reason, and knew for certain I was being attacked by a monster dogfish. I took one look at his choppers and churning paws and knew I was about to die one of those long, slow, *Jaws* kind of deaths, where my body would fly into the air, the ocean's froth would turn bright red from carnage, and everybody would scream and vomit. I forgot how to swim and tried to run out of the water on my flippers. Junior continued to have fun.

My husband and Randy laughed for hours. I swore I would never snorkel again.

Badass Randy made a bra out of coconut shells and invented a dance we called the "Big Butt Hula." My dad penned the lyrics. We sang this song for years: "She lives in a grass hut, she's stuck in a deep rut, she's dancing the big butt hula." It became a family hit, almost as good as "Stank Fish Tango."

We moved to Europe in 1994. Our kids both learned to swim at an early age and, in spite of our son's dislike of sand, we've taken occasional seaside vacations whenever we can afford it, or whenever someone pays us to go. Sometimes, I'm the one playing; sometimes, it's John. Porto, Essaouira, Cape Town—we've scalded our feet traversing the dunes of Grand Canary Island and have taught the kids how to body surf in the freezing North Sea on the Belgian coast. We've encouraged them not to stare at topless sunbathers on the Côte d'Azur and to wear sturdy swim shoes when navigating the rocky shores of Cornwall. We've also encouraged them to see the world through music—it's fine to pay for your own holiday but much better to be the recipient of a generous hotel owner's deep pockets and desire to keep you comfortable when you're not behind the piano or the bass.

Carrying on with the Piano Girl tradition of performing in exchange for a cultural adventure, the kids have—on their own—visited some of the world's most impressive beaches while taking part in educational trips, volunteer opportunities, or music exchange groups. They have played the piano in Tel Aviv, worked in a percussion section in South Africa, and made music videos in Mykonos. They've walked on beaches I've never seen, beaches that will live in their memories, not mine.

Slathered in sunscreen and decades past my best bikini years, I remember sitting on the sand and watching my kids when they were little, holding hands and leaping through the surf into deeper and deeper water. I remember the game I once played with my sister: "*never let go, no matter what.*"

Respect the water, dive under the waves, and when you're older, wiser, and more tired than you want to be, remember there's magic at the beach. Let music take you there. Fall in love a few times. Get a suntan. Feel the salt in your eyes. Encounter a dogfish. You might avoid the frogs' legs buffet, but by all means, do secret things on a stretch of sand where the roar of the water is louder than the sound of any piano. Music, if you learn to swim and overcome your fear of sharks, will take you, like the tide, to beaches both exotic and familiar.

Twenty-One

I Am Not Tom Wolfe

I am not Tom Wolfe, although I do own a white suit. But today, for my appearance at Book Expo America in New York City, a gigantic industry trade show, I am wearing a pink dress, purchased this morning during a panicked twenty-minute shopping spree at Anthropologie. What does an author *wear*, anyway? I've got the *Piano Girl* wardrobe covered, but I can't very well sport a black evening gown at eleven in the morning. Tom Wolfe stands next to me in the greenroom area for featured authors about to take the stage, and he's wearing "*the suit*." He looks just as he appears on his book jackets—eccentric, a little arrogant, foppish. I'm bonding with him, even though he has cast nary an eye in my direction. His agent, his publisher, and two or three other well-dressed minions hover nearby. Perhaps one of them keeps the suit clean.

I don't have an entourage or a minion with me, but I do have lovely Nina by my side. Nina is the publicist for Backbeat Books, publisher of *Piano Girl*.

Book Expo America is held at the Javits Center, a convention hall with bad fluorescent lighting, rock-hard floors, and acres of space for publishers to hawk the newest additions to their catalogs. Because *Piano Girl* has been awarded a *Publishers Weekly* starred review, I've been invited to take part in the traditional

Autograph Circle, a name that brings to mind large gatherings of businessmen playing African hand drums. I'm not far off—a lot of chest thumping is going on here today. The Autograph Circle, as far as I can tell, offers an efficient way for publishers to create buzz. It also gives conference attendees a chance to score free books from their favorite authors. I'm flattered to be in the small group of authors selected for this event but a little concerned about the setup. As a debut author, I'm hardly anyone's favorite anything.

Writers sit behind podiums next to stacks of their books. A long empty aisle stretches out in front of each author. When the bell rings—*ping!*—a gate opens, and loyal fans swoop down each aisle. One at a time, they meet the favored author and collect the coveted book, along with the author's signature. A fine system, assuming one *has* loyal fans.

"Nina, no one knows me. This is my first book. It's about playing the piano in hotel bars. The people who might know me are currently circling the Marriott Marquis bar, slurping down strawberry tequila drinks, knocking back martinis, and eating pretzel nubs. Who will be in my line? No one!"

"Don't be silly," Nina says. "There's a lot of buzz about your book. I know about buzz. And besides, that pink dress is, like, perfect. You might want to check your lipstick, though. It's getting cakey. But really, I love the dress."

"No match for the white suit," I say.

"I know," she says. "Isn't Tom just dreamy?"

We've got *Piano Girl* books piled high on a table. I can't imagine who will want them. Maybe the people I wrote about? Tempest Storm, the Gay Baron, Hans the International Tenor, Grandpa Bookie Brown, Roy Boy? They're busy, dead, or too drunk to care.

Tom Wolfe has sold millions of books. I've yet to sell my first copy. And what's all this nonsense about *buzz, buzz, buzz?* As far as I can tell, the only buzz we've created occurred yesterday afternoon, when Backbeat hired a bartender to stand in front of the *Piano Girl* display and serve happy hour Blue Hawaiian cocktails to anyone willing to talk to me. People lined up for the blue drinks, not for the book, but, hey, buzz is buzz. Maybe they should have gotten me a Steinway B.

Today, for the Autograph Circle, we're missing the cocktails. No bartender, no buzz, no crowd. At least not in my line.

The bell rings—*ping!*—and the gates open. Fans flood into Tom Wolfe's aisle—a mad dash down the lane to the man in the ice-cream suit. For a second I think a riot might break out as fans jostle and shove to get to the front of Tom's line.

"Nina," I say. "There is no one in my line. *No one.* I told you this was a bad idea. We need the bartender."

"We could only afford the bartender for one day. And we're giving away free books. Isn't that enough?"

"Evidently not."

"Look, don't panic. Sit there and smile," Nina says. "I'll think of something."

Nina "Buzz" Lesowitz always thinks of something; she's beyond resourceful. But today, I'm doubtful. Hundreds of people propel themselves—human scud missiles—toward various authors. But my lane looks like Death Valley, a parched canyon of solitude.

Wait! A solitary figure ambles down the aisle toward my desk. Waddles, actually. Is she limping?

"Look!" says Nina. "A fan! *See?* You have a fan!"

The aisle stretches a good twenty-five yards. I have to squint to see my fan. The woman draws closer. I'd recognize that walk anywhere.

"Nina, that's no fan."

"Of course, it is," says Nina.

"No, it's not," I say. "That's Sue."

"Sue who?"

"*Sue,* that's who. She's in *Piano Girl.* The college student with rigatoni stains on her sweatshirt? The philosophy major? I didn't write very nice things about her."

"Who cares," says Nina. "Sue is in your line. We love Sue! Sue is our best friend. Sue is your fan."

"Nina, she might be here to kill me. Look, she's got that Kathy Bates *Misery* gleam in her eyes. She might have a baseball bat in her NPR tote bag."

"*Misery* was a *great* film."

"Nina! What should I do?" Sue is gaining ground, and she might be packing heat. I look like a stuffed author—a fan-less target, a literary bulls-eye. Maybe if I remain very still, Sue will think I'm either a memoir-writing taxidermy specimen or made of wax. Maybe she'll walk away.

"Stay here and talk to our friend Sue while I recruit some more fans."

I'm scared to stay here by myself. And I don't think it's possible to *recruit* fans. Either they're fans or they're not, right? But Nina has fled into the crowd, poaching fans from other authors and bribing them to step over to my aisle. Take a walk on the wild side. What's she promising them? Drinks? Cash? Sexual favors? I almost don't care. A few of my accidental fans begin to trickle toward me. But first I must deal with Sue.

"Welcome, Sue! Wow, what a delight to see you."

"Hello, Robin."

"So! Sue! It has been, how long?"

"Twenty-six and a half years. Loved *Piano Girl*. I got an advance copy," she says. Her eyes shift back and forth. I wonder what she has in that tote bag. I envision a chain saw or an ice pick. Maybe a bloodied sledgehammer.

"Oh. *Really?* Thank you. Love your sweater."

"Will you sign this for me?"

"Sure. So, what brings you to Book Expo America?"

"I'm a publisher," she says. "Science books."

"Wow. Science books." Yesterday's rigatoni-stained college student is today's purveyor of chemistry textbooks. There's a lesson to be learned here, but I don't know what it is. I wonder what kind of drinks they're distributing upstairs at the science booth.

"Next!" yells Nina, who has returned from fan foraging. She practically pushes Sue out of the way. Having coerced a dozen

Tom Wolfe fans into my line, she sets about trying to make me look busy and successful.

"Nice to see you, Sue," I say. Sue turns around and clumps down the exit aisle. I feel like I'm in Walmart. *Clean-up, aisle four!*

"Step right up," says Nina, somehow managing to combine California élan with circus-barker barking.

"Meet Robin Goldsby."

"Hello!" I say, perhaps a tad too enthusiastically, to the next man in line. "Would you like the book personalized, or with just a signature?" Nina told me earlier that most fans prefer a simple signature, so they can give the book away later or sell it online.

"Don't care," says the man. "I'm your friend Robin Spielberg's brother-in-law. She told me if I didn't show up in your line, she would never talk to me again. I really wanted Tom Wolfe's book, but I'll settle for yours."

"Next!" yells Nina.

It's Harlan Ellis, my New York City music agent.

"Nina said you needed fans," he says. "I was trying to get the Wolfe book, and she yanked me over here. Just *pretend* I'm a fan and sign the damn book. I'll hang out until the line fills up." I have lots of reasons to adore Harlan. This is just another one.

"Next!"

After Harlan leaves, I meet and greet a good thirty people, most of them disappointed spit backs from Tom Wolfe's line. Tom's new book is called *I Am Charlotte Simmons*. My book should be called *I Am Not*.

"Next!"

I sign; I smile at strangers and hand each one of them a copy of *Piano Girl*. I don't know whether to be happy or sad as I watch tiny pieces of my musical story escaping, one note at a time, into a crowded and noisy world. Happy seems like the better choice.

Twenty-Two

Song for My Daughter

*L*ife can be one long love song, a musical scrapbook of your greatest hits, a jumble of waltzes and nocturnes, hip-hop moments, and two-part inventions that weave melodies in your head with harmonies in your heart.

Life can also be one long dirge, a monotone drone without shape or nuance, a thin and reedy voice drifting over swampy waters and the five o'clock shadow of parched fields, sad and sorry and soulless.

You're twenty-one years old.

Here's the thing—you're the composer. You're also the conductor, the *Maestra*. At this point in your life, with teachers and parents and colleagues and friends all telling you what to do and where to go, you probably don't feel like you're in charge of anything.

But you are.

You get to choose your life song.

You, as a strong young woman living with the comforts of the modern world, can pluck the best notes, the finest sounds, from your musical garden. You can string notes together any way you like. They can be cliché and smooth—a daisy chain of simplicity—or rough and raging, as thorny and complicated as the world around you. The notes, when linked together, will lead you somewhere or nowhere, far away or back home, to the hardened soil of foreign lands or the soft chairs of familiar rooms. All of these places will be safe, because you own them; they will be part of your soundscape.

Like generations of women before you, you will encounter swollen, oily men with grabby hands and bloated egos. You will walk into seemingly harmless situations—petal-strewn pastures that turn into minefields capable of shredding your confidence and obliterating your self-esteem. When you're not treated well, speak up. Do not play the shame/ blame game. Shout out the name of the offender and move on. Let punctuated shrieks of anger and survival be part of your life's soundtrack.

Eleanor Roosevelt said it best: "no one can make you feel inferior without your consent."

Expect respect in every aspect of your life. You are not a princess. You are a queen. Off with the metaphorical head of anyone who flunks the human dignity test!

Move on. Can I say that often enough? No.

Move on.

I promise you this: Good guys *do* roam the earth—you will meet them, and they will acknowledge and appreciate your wisdom and strength. Accept no less.

You will succeed; you will fail. You will laugh and cry. You will fall in and out of love. You will stumble in the haze of romance, dance on the toes of an unsuspecting partner, and shield your tired eyes from loss and loneliness. You will study and work and then study some more. You will have babies or not. You will learn to say yes; you will learn to say no. You will speak up and sit down, stand tall and stop short. You will figure out what you want; you'll decide what you need. You will learn to say good-bye.

When you are old, say, fifty or so, you will shout, "This is my song!" Some will sing along. Some will plead indifference. Others will think you're crazy. At this point in your life, and you can trust me on this, you won't care; you'll just be proud to have a song worth singing.

Is there any place better than where you are right now?

You're ready to pick up the conductor's baton, poised to deliver the downbeat, prepared to guide your orchestra through a musical score full of highs and lows, crescendos and diminuendos, full stops, repeat signs, and codas. Anything might happen.

Go for it, *Maestra*. Find your song. Be fierce. The music waits, just for you.

Twenty-Three

The Krankenhaus *Blues*

The right side of my abdomen throbs. It's not a stabbing pain, but more of a low-grade annoyance I've been living with for the past three days. I'm functioning—I even played twelve hours of piano gigs over the weekend, but I can't stand up straight without feeling like a family of five is throwing a grill party in my intestinal tract. Right now, they're tossing more coals on the fire.

Our doctor's office is a five-minute walk from home. Hobbling over to see her is no big deal, assuming I can still hobble. I call at 8 a.m., and she sees me at 8:30. After a minimal amount of belly tapping and prodding—this woman could have a career as a conga player—she tells me she suspects appendicitis and insists I go immediately to the hospital, or the *Krankenhaus*, as it's called here in Germany.

I love the word *Krankenhaus*. It's right up there with *Kaiserschnitt* (C-section) and *Dudelsack* (bagpipes) on my list of German words that sound exactly right.

"Should I call the *Krankenwagen*?" the good doctor asks.

"No," I say, "my husband is home. He'll take me. He drives faster than a *Krankenwagen* anyway."

"OK, but don't waste any time. You need to go immediately."

I leave her office and, glancing over my shoulder to make sure the doctor isn't looking, head into the local grocery store.

My son will leave for a semester abroad in California in a few days, and his friends will throw a farewell party for him tomorrow. It's a German tradition for the honoree to take a cake or some sort of treat with him to the shindig. Curtis has requested my brownies.

"What did the doctor say?" asks John when I arrive home with a sack of eggs and dark chocolate.

"Not good. She thinks it's my appendix. I've got to go to the *Krankenhaus* right away. But first I have to bake these brownies for Curtis."

"Really? You have appendicitis and you're going to waste an hour baking brownies?"

"I've had this pain for three days. I played four piano gigs feeling like this, one of which included the world's longest Lionel Richie medley. Another hour won't make a difference."

I have been baking brownies for both Curtis and Julia for more than twenty years. I'm not much of a baker, but my brownies are the *shiznit*, as the kids like to say. Julia, the younger of the two, has already left home for nine months; right now, she is in Seoul, Korea. Now it's time for Curtis to jump on the empty-nest express. Knowing my son will be gone in just a few days, this final culinary favor takes on new meaning.

I'm a fool—risking peritonitis for a Betty Crocker moment, but I'm hardly the first mother to bake a cake for her son when she's not feeling up to par. My sister once baked a vegan coconut cream pie for her son's birthday while recovering from a hernia operation. I have another friend who made three-dozen artisanal cupcakes (with rainbow-sparkle icing) while attached to a heart monitor. Of course, her son was three, not twenty-one, but still. You never get over this mother thing. Or at least I hope you don't.

Here's what I figure: your nest can't be empty if your plate is full. Bake the damn brownies. Show the love. Melt the chocolate.

"I could bake the brownies," says John.

"Yeah, you could," I say, "but this is my job."

I start the brownie batter. My appendix doesn't burst while melting the butter or beating the eggs. The scent of dark chocolate wafts through the house while I pack an overnight bag. I take the brownies out of the oven.

I've baked a good batch.

At the *Krankenhaus*, I answer a bunch of questions and go through a battery of tests, the results of which prove inconclusive. No elevated white blood cell count, no fever, no sign of anything dangerous during the ultrasound procedure, which goes on forever and hurts like hell. But the pain persists, and my lower abdomen is rigid and bloated, even though I did not eat any of the brownies, I swear. I see three or four different doctors, starting with the emergency room resident and moving my way up to the chief of surgery. Together they decide to check me into the *Krankenhaus* for a few days of starvation, bothersome tests, and, possibly, an appendectomy. Our insurance entitles me to a private room, but the *Krankenhaus* is full today, so I have to take what I can get. What I get is a double room with a triple-sized woman named Patrizia Parrott. Pat is enormous, the size of one of those unfortunate people you see on American reality TV shows.

Because of Patrizia's double-wide hospital bed, my humble single-wide has been shoved to one side of the suite, right up against the washroom door. I notice a crane next to Pat's night table, and I panic a little when I spot the potty-chair, parked conveniently next to the dining table. The feng shui masters would not be pleased.

Pat sighs and groans and crams *Brötchen* into her mouth, all the while issuing instructions to the overworked aide and flipping through the channels on the TV suspended over the two beds.

"Well," whispers John, "this is everyone's worst roommate nightmare."

I try to stay chipper, but I've been here for five minutes, and the racket coming from Pat's side of the room rattles me—coughing and belching and other unmentionable sounds. Good thing I brought my noise-canceling headphones.

"I kind of feel sorry for you," says John.

I glare at him, because I feel sorry for me, too.

It occurs to me that the last place anyone should have a roommate is in a hospital. Humans do not exhibit their best qualities when faced with failing health. Who decided that having two sick people three feet away from each other would be a wise idea? Mister Rogers or the Dalai Lama could be in the next bed, and I would still be cranky about sharing my space.

"Try not to talk to Patrizia," John whispers, in English. We are out in the corridor while Pat has a sponge bath. "Trust me on this. She seems kind of bossy. If she gets a chance, she'll start giving you orders. Look how she treats these poor nurses. Put on your headphones. You can always smile at her."

He has a point. I have no desire to spend the next few days as Pat's nimble bitch. Or changing her channels. And I am terrified of Pat's potty-chair. And the crane.

On the other hand, maybe I should help out a bit. I'm not really sick. I feel a bit like a *Krankenhaus* fraud. Aside from the dull throb in my right side, there's not much wrong with me at all. Maybe I shouldn't be here. If I check out now, I can play my gig tomorrow night.

"So, do you need anything?" John asks, just as Pat, finished with her bath, demands more bologna from the woman working the dinner wagon.

"I'm really hungry," I say. A rolling buffet on a cart rolls right past me.

"Sorry, honey," says the food Frau, checking her chart. "Nothing for you but tea and water."

Pat requests another *Brötchen*, this time with Nutella. I'm not sure what's wrong with her, but it's certainly not her appetite.

"Young man," Patrizia Parrott says to John in German, "can you open the window for me?"

John, polite as always, opens the window and then scoots out of the room before he receives further instructions. I say good-night to Patrizia Parrott, open my book, and prepare for a long night.

Sometime around two in the morning Pat begins chomping on cookies and chips she has stashed in a locker next to her bed. I can't see her very well, but I can hear her; the crinkling of bags, the rattle of packages, the tentative chewing and sputtering one associates with illicit junk food consumption. I can't lie flat with my bulky noise-canceling headphones, and I don't have any ear-plugs, so I accept my fate and lie there in a semi-hallucinogenic state. It wouldn't be so bad if I weren't so hungry. I smell Twix bars and salt-and-vinegar chips and consider breaking my silence and asking for a tiny bite of something, anything. I'm a healthy eater, but I'm bored, I'm famished, and I'm sleeping two feet from a woman with a serious eating disorder and a very large clandestine stash of junk food. *Come on, Pat, toss a bag of Cheetos in my direction.*

The last time I was in a hospital was to give birth, two decades ago. I drift in and out of sleep and wonder if I've become one of those half-crazy, washed-up moms who gets sick to distract herself from an "empty nest," a term I've come to loathe. Maybe I'm not really sick. Maybe I'm making myself sick because I'm worried sick. It has never occurred to me that I might actually miss my kids when they leave; I've always thought I might become more of who I used to be once they were gone. Perhaps that's the problem. Better to check into the hospital than tune into my own dread.

Maybe that pain in my side stems from the pain in my heart. Maybe the act of saying good-bye to my adult children has jumbled my well-being.

The waving hand, the failing heart, the empty nest, the bursting appendix.

Edna St. Vincent Millay could have dined on this for decades.

If only I could dine right now. I try to ignore Pat's crunching sounds, close my eyes, and drift into a hunger-fueled sleep.

The next morning: no water, no tea, no justice. Pat eats the German version of a Denny's lumberjack special while I gaze longingly at my empty water pitcher. I'm scheduled for an ultrasound and CT at ten.

The German word for appendix is *Blinddarm*. *Blind* is blind. *Darm* translates to "intestine." The blind intestine.

T'was blind, but now I see . . .

Herr Dr. Stanayotolopolous, who has an extension on his name tag to accommodate the extra letters in his name, performs the procedure. He pokes around for twenty minutes while I wonder if ultrasound gel can be used for erotic purposes. He asks me to hold my breath about a dozen times. This makes me dizzy.

"He is very hard to find," he says.

"Who is?"

"The appendix. *Der Blinddarm*."

Appropriate that something shaped like a *Blinddarm* should carry a masculine article.

In an effort to impress Dr. Stanayotolopolous with my knowledge of all things Greek, I tell him I once lived in Astoria, Queens. He grunts in response. I shall keep my opinions about spanakopita and baklava to myself. Why can't I stop thinking about food?

"Ah! There he is!" Dr. Stanayotolopolous swivels the screen around so I can see the swirled mess. Somewhere in all that fuzzy stuff is my appendix.

"He is subacute," he says.

I like this term, subacute. It describes my mood.

"So, this means surgery?" I ask.

"No. There are new studies. The British Medical Journal says 50 percent of subacute appendicitis patients will heal on their own."

"And the other 50 percent?"

"They need the operation."

"So, what do I do?"

"Talk to the surgeon."

He walks away, leaving the nurse to de-gel me.

"Can I eat something now?" I ask.

"Probably," she says. "But only broth and other clear liquids. They might operate tomorrow."

Time for Pat to use that potty-chair. To get there she needs the crane. It's like watching a slow-motion accident unfold—I can't turn away. The crane, an electrical human-hoisting system attached to a heavy anchor, has a harness that goes around Pat's midsection. The machine whirs as Pat begins to levitate, an activity that does not please her.

As the crane heaves Pat to an upright position, I wonder how many Oreos a woman has to eat before she notices she needs a winch to help her stand up.

"Lunch!"

Pat, sniping and groaning as the crane transports her to her final destination—the potty-chair—scolds the nurse for not finishing the procedure before lunchtime. My pity for Pat evaporates when I hear her insult one of the workers.

"We're having goulash today," Pat yells, suspended midair. Both Peter Pan and Divine come to mind. "I need to use the toilet before it gets cold."

"We'll warm the toilet seat for you," says the nurse.

"No. The goulash—warm the goulash," says Pat. The nurse prepares to lower her onto the potty-chair.

"Lunch, Frau Goldsby!" says the food Frau.

Rather than eat while Pat uses the potty-chair—I have to draw a line somewhere—I decide to take my chances with the Marlboro gang in the lounge. The food Frau follows me with her cart.

"Here you go, dear," she says. "I know you're on a vegan diet, so we prepared special broth just for you."

My mouth waters at the thought of food. I'm tired of my bad attitude. Maybe the food will help. Broth. Ahhhh, liquid gold. I haven't eaten for thirty-six hours, and I shake with anticipation as I remove the lid from the bowl.

It's chicken broth.

"But this is chicken!" I say.

"Yes," she says, beaming with pride. "Vegan chicken broth! We took all the chicken meat and skin out of it. It's just the broth. It's vegan."

She's a pleasant woman with happy eyes, and I'm too exhausted to argue with her, plus the smoke drifting in from the terrace nauseates me. Some lunch this is. Vegan chicken broth with a hint of nicotine. I used to be a smoker, but that doesn't stop me from casting a scornful glance at the patients puffing away on the balcony attached to the lounge. Every time the door opens, a blast of freezing air and a cloud of smoke hit me. If you are in your pajamas, in a wheelchair, and attached to an IV pole, you probably shouldn't be lighting up.

What's the matter with me? I don't like myself today. I'm angry, out of sorts, and taking it out on stout stealth-eaters and gray-faced smokers. I need a drink. I wander the hallway for thirty minutes yearning for vodka—that's a clear liquid, right? I settle for a cup of chamomile tea.

"There's a hair in my veal parmesan!" yells Pat.

Two days go by.

The food Frau, the aides, the nurses, the crane expert, and the potty-chair woman treat Pat with respect, although I catch them muttering to themselves when they turn away from her. I'm growing less tolerant of Pat by the hour. If I were in charge of that crane and had the likes of Pat screaming at me about keeping her lunch warm, I'd be tempted to leave her hanging there, with a plate of *schnitzel* just out of reach.

I maintain my silence, put on my headphones, and try to come to terms with my lack of compassion for a woman who is clearly in a wretched situation. How can she live like this? Maybe she's lonely and fills herself with food to chase away the emptiness. Does she have grown children? Is her empty nest lined with candy wrappers? Did she ever have a nest at all? How did she end up here, and how will she ever go home? Maybe Pat was once middle-aged, semi-vibrant, reasonably thin, with kids who needed her. Maybe Pat used to be like me. Maybe I'm turning into Pat. Maybe you start with appendicitis and, before you know it, you need a crane. Maybe I am losing my mind. If I could just eat something, I'd feel better. Everything in this room revolves around food, and I'm still not allowed to eat.

Patrizia Parrott yells, "I need a cookie!" I am tempted to shout *Polly wanna cracker?*, but I resist. That would be cruel.

"More pudding!" she shouts.

My daughter Skypes from Korea to see how I'm doing. My son calls from home to thank me for the brownies. My husband drops off some instant miso powder for my next broth meal. I'm grateful for any contact at all with my misplaced real life. I'm dizzy from hunger. I still have a pain in my side. I want to go home.

The head surgeon, after reviewing test results, schedules surgery for the morning. I'm too weak to argue, and at this point, I'm actually looking forward to anesthesia. Five hours— an entire morning—without Pat. And after surgery, I'll be able to eat. Who needs this stupid appendix anyway?

Pat rips open a *Beefi*, the local version of jerky. I will *not* call her Fat Pat. I will not.

I call several piano players to cover my jobs for the next few weeks.

When the nurse asks if I want a sleeping pill, I shout out a resounding "yes." Tonight I dream of food and departing children and cranes.

I awaken the next morning feeling lightheaded and a little strange. It takes me a few minutes to realize that the pain in my side is gone. I press on my stomach, and there's nothing—not a stab or a stitch or a spasm. Hallelujah.

John arrives at the crack of dawn, just in time to watch Pat inhale her daily loaf of bread. The surgical team squeezes into the room and surrounds my bed. It's a teaching hospital, so a half dozen doctors and trainees gather around my belly. I feel like a Thanksgiving turkey or an Easter ham.

"How are you today?" asks the surgeon.

"The pain is gone," I say.

"Your stomach is no longer rigid. This feels like the stomach of a completely different patient."

It does not escape me that, for the first time in many years, I have an audience of six young men staring at my naked torso with admiration. Maybe the starvation diet served its purpose.

The surgeon presses harder and invites another doctor to have a poke. I sense Pat's judgmental eye on me as the doctors confer. I hear Pat chewing. A privacy curtain is in the center of the room, but Pat's double-wide puts her way past the center mark. Even if we pulled the curtain, she would still be on my side. I feel like her head is in my lap.

"No surgery," he says. "The inflammation is gone. You need more tests, Frau Goldsby, just to rule out anything else, but you can schedule those next week, as an outpatient."

Dr. Stanayotolopolous was right. I healed, on my own, motivated by desperation, hunger, and the ever-present smell of Doritos coming from Pat's side of the room.

"Can I go home?" I squeak. "Can I eat? Please?"

"Yes. Have some breakfast, wait an hour, and see how you're feeling. Then you can leave."

I pull down my nightgown while John rushes out to find the food Frau. The doctors file out, consulting their clipboards. So much for my audience.

Now that I'm leaving, it seems safe to talk to Pat. I feel guilty for not being kinder to her. I had a chance to be compassionate, but, caught up in my Hunger Games drama, I blew it.

"So, I'll pack my things," I say to Pat. "It was nice meeting you. I hope you feel better soon."

"You're not the only one going home," Pat says, between bites of apple. "I'll be leaving the day after tomorrow. My son is coming to fetch me."

"How many children do you have?" I ask.

"Three. They don't live around here. They are good boys. They visit when they can. Two of them are doctors. The third is a lawyer. He's the baby. He's thirty-six. They kept me very busy when they were little."

"Do you miss them?" I ask.

"I never stop missing them," she says. "I carry them with me, everywhere I go. Maybe that's why I weigh so much." She laughs, just a little. "Here. Take an apple with you. You might get hungry on the ride home."

"Thanks," I say.

"You were a good roommate," she says. "You were quiet. I like that. I need my rest. The last woman who was here never shut up."

The suite fills with the sound of Pat's labored breathing. I feel unbearably sad. For her. For me. For every mother in the world who bakes farewell brownies for a departing child; for every super-mom has-been who eats too much, smokes too much, drinks too much, hoping to fill empty space; for every woman who refeathers her nest, restructures her days, reimagines her life—not because she wants to, but because her options have dwindled.

Little birds fly away. That's the way it works.

Maybe if I eat something, I'll feel better.

Twenty-Four

Picture Perfect

Most musicians, in spite of our occasional "back-to-nature" urges, want to look as good as we can, especially when a hot-handed social-media expert with a cell phone camera is lurking in the wings.

Like so many of my friends, I waltzed into my mature soft-focus years just when the world decided it absolutely needed harshly lit candid photos of all of us. It's bad enough dealing with wrinkles and chins and roots and flab, but it's far worse for those of us in a business that necessitates maintaining a "public face." I play a concert and "flash" goes the camera. I play for a wedding, and I show up in a dozen home videos, many of which end up on YouTube. I pose, I pose, I play. It's stupid. I have enough to worry about trying to hit the right keys and make emotional sense out of my compositions.

Do I need to worry about the hideous angle of the camera pointed at me, held by a Taiwanese tourist whom I will never see again? At this point in my life, do I really need to be concerned about back fat and batwings?

I realize this is a taboo subject. The world is going to hell in a handbasket, and I'm worried about how I look in an iPhone photo? I'm not the only one. Pretty much every woman I know—skinny, stout, lifted, tattooed, coiffed, buff, chilled, or uptight—thinks about how she looks, probably a little too much. Maybe even a lot too much. Even the deepest of us occasionally wades in shallow water.

Professional photos are also a source of psychological stress. In the past month I've survived two photo sessions, each one intended to help promote a new project. I worked with two great photographers, Andreas Biesenbach and *Piano Girl* media director Julia Goldsby, but still, I did not walk willingly into the light. Filled with dread, I complained about the sessions for about a month in advance.

"This, Robin, is an uptown problem," said my actor friend Peg. She has an intelligent sense of humor, soulful eyes, and a wide, quirky smile. She is beautiful. I would paint her if I had that kind of talent. "Complaining about having your picture taken at our age is sort of like crying because you got too many flowers for your fiftieth birthday."

She has a point. I'm happy people still take my picture. I'm not so happy that I worry about it.

My pianist pal Robin Spielberg says she would gladly stop thinking about her appearance if she had a normal job that didn't mandate new glossy photos every few years. The lovely Ms. Spielberg, with raven hair, green eyes, an hourglass figure, and a husband who takes gorgeous photos of her, worries just as much as I do, even though, most days, she looks as if she slipped out of a beauty and style blog. We joke about being successful and well-known enough to demand looking as put together as possible, but not quite famous enough to call in Madonna's A team of cosmetic surgeons or her daily spackle squad. Not that we want those things. Or do we?

Actors, musicians, and artists aren't the only women who strive to look good (or at least not fat) in photos. I know prominent businesswomen, doctors, United Nations representatives, judges, lawyers, teachers, and stay-at-home moms who battle the vanity monster. I know teenagers who stand in front of the mirror and practice poses. I know grandmothers who have perfected the art of using the selfie pole. I know really powerful women—women who take down organized crime syndicates, battle the NRA, and bench-press hundreds of pounds—who cower at the idea of having an up-to-date passport photo taken.

Why worry about a silly photo session? It's not like we don't have anything else to think about. We are raising families, raising hell, redecorating our dining rooms, making scientific break-throughs, writing novels, helping to coordinate refugee relief. We are ruling on critical legal matters, planting herb gardens, planning philanthropic events, delivering our children to college, and mending broken hearts. We are repairing skinned knees, vis-iting autoimmune specialists, balancing hormones, and trying to save the world with a plant-based diet. We are practicing hard, living disciplined Fitbit lives, and getting better at what we do. We are creating music.

Do we really care if our gray hair is showing? Or if we look jowly in the reunion photo?

Uh, yes.

Too bad we can't post 4-D scans of our working brains and full hearts instead of pictures of our laminated smiles and sooty-lashed eyes. Scans that would show kindness and strength and resolve. Humor and resilience. Rage. Is it possible to photograph a woman's unbreakable spirit?

Less silicone, more sass. Less filler, more fight. Not that there's anything wrong with filler. If it's what you want, go for it.

In the meantime, here's my marketing advice to the budding musician: Book a good photographer and a stylist. Their photos will compensate for the hideous casual shots that seem to show up on social media. It's money well spent. Once the photogra-pher sends you the finished photos—if she's smart, she'll send you the touched-up versions, and you'll think she's brilliant, and you're a tad more polished than you imagined—you can take a deep breath, feel a little foolish about the whole thing, and go back to practicing scales. You can have a cocktail and a club sandwich and discuss politics and your children and the melting world with your friends. You can post your photo everywhere and bask in the afterglow of everyone's warm comments. "Wow," they'll say. "Wow. You haven't changed a bit."

But I know better. You've changed a lot since the last time you had your picture taken.

If you don't like your new photo, I suggest taking the Carole Delgado approach. Throw the picture in a drawer and don't look at it for ten years. Take it out. You'll see so much more than an airbrushed face. You'll see a younger you, picture perfect, wind-blown and beautiful in all your naïveté, ready to take on the world. A woman with a song worth singing.

If only you had known back then how good you looked.

Twenty-Five

Love Note to a German Castle

*I*t's New Year's Eve, 2014. I'm playing the piano at Schloss-hotel Lerbach. I've been performing here for almost fourteen years. Tonight will be the last time—the castle, in its current incarnation as a hotel, will close its doors to the public after this evening's celebration. Three weeks ago, just fourteen days before Christmas, eighty hotel workers, me included, lost their jobs. But there's a party going on here right now. Our guests—titans of industry, beautiful people with nothing to prove, lovers, families, and boisterous buffoons gather in the main hall.

Parts of Lerbach are almost eight hundred years old. Some of the guests seem equally ancient. Tonight looks like the German version of *Downton Abbey*, with an unusually high percentage of women playing the Maggie Smith role. Draped in mink and satin and sequins and silk, they glide from one end of the hall to the other, clinking glasses, sipping champagne, and nibbling on mysterious gourmet tidbits. The black-and-white granite floor serves as a five-star chessboard for their social strategies. My colleagues, professional and gracious right to the end, coast along with them. We have a silent pact among us—it might be the end of an era, but we're going out with style.

I observe my young coworkers from my seat at the grand piano as they smile and nod and make nice with guests they have

Fashionistas and fops, foolhardy fellows on the fast track to fame drift through the castle lobby like glamorous dust particles suspended in moonlight.

known for years. It's difficult to see the evening unfold without wondering why in the world such a beautiful place is closing.

"A little quail and tomato mousse, Frau Falswick-Weiss?" a tuxedo-clad server asks a corpulent woman wearing emerald green velvet.

"Why not?" she says, as she pops a ruby-red square into her ruby-red mouth. "One last time."

The owners of the castle and the current hotel management company could not come to terms on a lease renewal. That's the diplomatic version of why we're forced to close. My version? The negotiations were a big game of chicken, and everyone lost. But what do I know? I'm a pianist, not Donald Trump, and although I played the piano at his hotel for a while, there weren't many teaching moments about conflict resolution, unless you count the time that I played an ill-conceived medley of *Moonlight Sonata* and "In the Mood" while Billy Martin (the drinky, often fractious, fired-and-hired manager of the New York Yankees) got into a fistfight with George Steinbrenner (the despotic owner of the team, convicted felon, and Richard Nixon crony). I played as well as I could, but they still wouldn't stop punching each other. That was the day I learned that some problems cannot be solved by Beethoven or Glenn Miller.

Even the food seems to sparkle tonight. Shimmering dresses, jewelry, crystal, and candlelight twinkle in the golden glow of the Murano glass chandeliers. At the same time, a haze descends over the lobby. Has the ghost of Lerbach returned to remind us that the end is near? No, it's just the midnight dance band—Upper Class, featuring Go-Go—warming up the smoke machine.

In a few hours we'll say good-bye. *It's just a gig* I tell myself over and over and over again. *Nothing more, nothing less.* But still, I will miss the absurd people in this noble place and this plush cushion of elegance that has softened my middle-aged landing in a foreign country. I slip into my next song, a piece I wrote called "December," and try not to look back.

I'm not sure when I fell in love with Lerbach. It started as an infatuation—an impulse decision to go back to work after swearing off hotel piano gigs forever. But one fateful night—five years after my last gig on the Manhattan Piano Girl circuit—I went with John to his trio concert performance at Schloss Lerbach. I walked into the main hall of the castle, saw the grand piano sitting there, took one look at the guests, the fireplace, the winding staircase, and the shaft of light slanting through the tall windows, and I was smitten. "Well. Maybe I could play *here*," I said to John. He introduced me to the director, and a year later—*poof*—I landed the job. Seems like yesterday or a million years ago; I can't decide.

Right from the start, Lerbach proved itself different from any gig I've ever had. If you play a solo piano job in a hotel, you have a lot of time to observe what makes the place tick (or, in some cases, tock). After a few years of playing every weekend at Lerbach, I figured out its secret: *respect*.

In such a small house, the employees really knew each other. We worked well together and treasured our various contributions. Piano music created a warm and welcoming atmosphere in the main hall. I knew it; so did everyone else. The director of the hotel was in the lobby with me every night. He heard me play; he saw me work. I wasn't just another expense on his balance sheet; I was part of his team, making an artistic statement that attracted customers. Because I had the respect of my peers, I began to trust myself more and doubt myself less.

Little by little I got sucked in—the place became a second home to me. Working in a five-star hotel means creating elegance—candlelight, food too pretty to eat, wine no one will ever forget, and the music that helps them remember.

I sit at the piano tonight, and faces from the past fourteen years flash through my mind—a Ken Burns slideshow of my extended castle family. I will never forget our elegant maître, Monsieur Thomann, pushing the stinky French-cheese wagon through the lobby every evening at 8:15—the only man I've known who looks good in a pink suit; Rawi, the Sri Lankan valet, arranging flowers on my piano every weekend, using leftover petals from the arrangements of departing brides; lovely Andrea, raising the bar for graciousness and good humor during her many years at the castle; Sabine, the front-desk manager, asking me to name one of the black Ninja swans swimming on the little lake in the castle park; Dieter Müller, world-renowned chef, taking time during the busy weekend dinner service to cook for dogs waiting for their owners behind the front desk; three sommeliers—the flashiest guys in the hotel industry—Silvio Nitzsche, Thomas Sommer, and Peter Müller—teaching me that every good Riesling, just like every good song, should tell a story; Benedikt Jaschke, who worked with me to initiate both a children's Christmas program and a concert series—turning the castle into a cultural sanctuary for the residents of Bergisch Gladbach; Christian Siegling, Christina Esser, Thomas Tritschler, Nils Henkel—the housekeepers, the service staff, the banquet team, the kitchen guys and gals, the many apprentices who have been trained at the castle over the years—I raise a glass to all of you.

We've greeted married couples from around the block and married couples from Oslo and Israel and Russia and Spain.

Wandering gourmets, galloping gourmands, and staggering oenophiles; fashionistas and fops, foolhardy fellows on the fast track to fame; intellectuals and artists, poets and painters, interpretive dancers and Brazilian football stars—celebrities of all sorts, including has-beens and wannabes, have drifted through the Lerbach lobby like glamorous dust particles suspended in moonlight. Tonight is no exception.

I've adored all of them, even the half-blind Lamborghini-driving wine enthusiast who used to make me play "Fly Me to the Moon" while he sat at the piano and wept.

I marveled at the white-haired professor who routinely checked two women into the hotel at the same time (three separate rooms) and kept them a secret from each other, turning the hotel into a Moliere-inspired, door-slamming French farce.

I felt a particular fondness for Frau V., a woman in her eighties whose husband had been dead for twenty years. She arrived at the castle every Christmas and carried a silver-framed photo of him that she would place on my piano so he could be part of the celebration. Frau V., bejeweled, beloved, and bewildered, had a beehive hair-do so high that one of my colleagues thought her husband might still be alive and hiding *there*. I admired the Arabian princess who stayed with us for months and presented me with a chunk of gold when she left.

I've written many stories about Lerbach in my *Piano Girl* books—favorites include the tale of Herr Klingball, the ninety-year-old who wanted to hear nothing but the *Titanic* theme; the diva bride who replaced my picture on the cover of my CD with a photo of herself, then distributed the CD to eighty of her closest friends; Uncle Wilhelm and his two-hour speech; the relentless wheelchair guy and the piano crash that almost took off my leg; the attack of the Indian runner duck on the Lerbach pond; the Valentine's Day visit from Buttercup Blondeau (perhaps not her real name), one of Germany's most infamous porn stars. I'll miss all of them.

It kills me to say good-bye to the piano at the castle—over the course of a decade and a half, a woman can really get attached to her instrument. I'm on the Steinway Artist Roster, but very few hotels can actually afford a Steinway. Yamaha, with a sales force that rivals the Green Bay Packers' offensive line, has infiltrated almost every hotel I've worked in over the years. Generally, they are solid pianos. My Lerbach Yamaha C5 is a winner. It sits next to an open fireplace, unfazed by heat and blasts of cold air coming from three different directions. It has been shoved and jostled on a regular basis when moved from the main hall into our banquet and concert room.

In an episode I call the Barenboim bounce, the poor Yamaha was dropped on the staircase when eleven kitchen workers attempted to carry it upstairs and into a suite for the Maestro Barenboim the day before he arrived at the castle. The Maestro's manager wanted nothing to do with the Yamaha and had a Steinway delivered to his suite. Back down came the Yamaha.

The piano, I am told, only bounced once, but still, that's about a thousand pounds hitting the floor. Battle scars in the hotel business are common—we all have them. Aside from a chunk of wood missing from the piano's casing (artfully disguised with a few deft strokes of black magic marker), the piano survived the bounce, just like the rest of us. The carpet on the staircase did not fare as well.

Many powerful musicians have played this workhorse piano. Still, I think of it as mine. And it's not. I've played well over two thousand jobs here, but the piano doesn't belong to me. I have kept it tuned and pimped and well turned out. When tonight is over, I'll probably never see it or play it again. As hard as I'm trying to remain stoic, my eyes well up when I think about leaving it behind. My fingerprints are on this piano.

It's just a piano.
It's just a gig.
Right.

"You'll lose every gig you ever have," my father said to me in 1976, when I began my career as a hotel pianist. "Don't take it personally."

Ultimately, he was right. Over the years I have been replaced by the food and beverage director's girlfriend, a table for two that fit nicely in the corner where the piano once stood, and, after seven years of playing at the Marriott Marquis, by a player piano and a mannequin that looked like a crash-test dummy in a tuxedo. I'm still not over that one.

Call me paranoid, but I have never felt any amount of job security on any gig I've had. I take some comfort in knowing I wasn't fired or replaced at Lerbach—I closed the joint. I'm going down with the ship, just like one of those *Titanic* musicians. Good thing I know the song. My heart will go on, and all that.

I look around the room on this festive night. The fake glee and forced fun wear me down. I am fifty-seven years old. Part of me thinks that this could be my swan song, as far as the hotel *Piano Girl* thing goes. I play concerts, compose music, make recordings, and write books. Maybe that's enough. I claim my fourteen years at Lerbach as a victory—it's almost unheard of to have a freelance piano engagement last so long. Part of me wants to jump up and yell, "Hallelujah, I'm outta here!" Part of me is determined to find another job that will be just as good, or better. Part of me wants to take a nap—saying good-bye can be exhausting, especially when you're trying not to cry. Part of me wants to collect all these different parts of me and glue them back together in a new and unusual way. Piano Girl jigsaw. That could be fun.

At 11:15 I play my last song, "Somewhere in Time," which, according to my "journal"—a slapdash, inconsistent collection of notes that covers significant Piano Girl events over the decades—happens to be the very first song I played at this hotel way back in 2001. I have no idea how many songs are in my mental "book." I'm intentionally disorganized that way; I have an evolving repertoire that suits my mood, the location, the clientele. On a background music gig, I never work from a set list—I always go in cold and see what happens. Sometimes I forget what I know, and a guest will request something I used to play a million years ago. When that happens, I rely on muscle memory, blind faith, and the reassurance that if I get lost halfway through, I can always play the bridge to "Blue Moon"—it works for everything.

I am secretly hoping for dozens of white roses, a standing ovation, a gold medal, or a Purple Heart, but no one presents me with anything. I hear chatter and clinking glasses. In a way, it's exactly like my first job here. I've come full circle. As I've learned over the course of my career—first gigs and last gigs don't matter much. It's what happens in between that counts.

I close the fallboard over the keys and place my hands on the polished ebony, almost overwhelmed by a feeling of gratitude—to the piano, my colleagues, our guests, and the bizarre magic we've made together. *Look! Just look at what we've created!* It took me a long time to find truth in my music, but this place—in all its wacky wonder—encouraged me to do just that. A funny thing happens when you accept truth and beauty in yourself—all of a sudden you see it all around you, wherever you go.

Two weeks ago, when I told my daughter Lerbach was closing, she burst into tears.

"They can't close," she said. "I grew up there."

"Me, too," I said.

Upper Class—featuring Go-Go—takes over. They are the opposite of me. Go-Go—an Eastern European fashion model with a green sequined gown, a halo of hair, and a slinky voice that slices through Donna Summer's greatest hits—dazzles us with slightly funky disco tunes as we count down to midnight. The smoke machine amps up; the guests start doing the rich-person lizard dance. My husband is waiting outside for me in the circular driveway, engine revved, anxious to whisk me away before the fireworks start.

I grab a permanent marker and sign the inside of the piano. *Robin Meloy Goldsby*, I write. *2001–2015*. An act of vandalism perhaps, but maybe someone, even if it's just the ghost of Lerbach, will see my name and remember the music. Maybe not.

I touch the piano one last time, put on my coat, open the door, and walk to the car.

It's just a gig. It's just a gig. It's just a gig.

As we drive through the park, I look out the window to get one last glance at Schloss Lerbach. A thick veil of fog has dropped over the castle, and I can't see a thing. It doesn't matter. I'll always remember what was there.

"Great run," says John. "Next."

Twenty-Six

Last Train to Clarksville

I stand on the train platform and wait for the 5:54 to Honrath, the train station near the village where I live. Rays of late summer sun cast crooked shadows on the determined faces of commuters. We're at the main train station in Cologne, Germany, and all of us are trying our best to get home. Students in jeans, musicians with guitar and trombone cases, office workers in Esprit mix-and-match suits, and senior shoppers lugging cloth bags of discounted groceries—we crowd around information boards, benches, and vending machines. We are Germany's middle-class, daytime travelers waiting to be whisked from the city to another place.

A robust man with a rosy face sells bratwurst and *Brötchen* to those who have skipped lunch or are thinking about skipping dinner. I have been eating all day, but still, my stomach growls at the smell of the grilled pork. I don't eat meat—so I ask for a plain piece of bread. The *Brötchen* is a crusty roll, white and carb laden, but delicious. In Germany, even the train station bread meets the highest culinary standards.

I met my friends Christina and Christina for coffee today. They are willowy blondes, both of them twenty-five years younger than I. Our paths have crossed because they have hired me to play the piano for various events. Christina One has a new baby; Christina Two has a new career; I have an odd feeling that I am morphing into their Great Aunt Edna—a nutty and slightly eccentric older woman, reasonably well-preserved, but, like the September sun poking through the smudged glass ceiling of the train station, maybe trying a little too hard to keep on shining. I love my circle of young friends—I have about six good pals who are in their thirties—but they are just so, well, young. They still have menstrual cramps and waistlines and instant-recall memories. Some of them even have mothers my age. Not one of them, as far as I know, actually has a Great Aunt Edna.

I rip off a piece of bread and glance at the automated board overhead. Good. My train is coming. The S25 to Honrath—right on time. How I love rail transportation in Europe!

Moving more slowly than usual, the long red train creeps into the station. I chew my *Brötchen* as the lead car, the one housing the engineer, edges past me. The engineer, let's call him Axel, leans out the window. Axel is hot. Axel knows he's hot. Axel is literally hot, too—sweaty and dirty and just a tad unshaven, and he smiles in my direction. Whoa. Smile is not the correct word. He leers in my direction. Shouldn't he be watching the track? I turn around to see where he's looking—must be a college girl in short shorts, or a super-model wannabe, or an Eastern European pole dancer in thigh-high boots—but I stand in a cluster of forlorn looking teenage boys and men in dark suits. The brakes of the train squeal. I turn back around and face Axel. He grins at me again, runs his eyes up and down my body, and does a funny thing with his tongue. He points at me and nods. Oh! I don't know what to do. As a happily married fifty-five-year-old woman, I'm out of practice with nasty flirting.

I'm so flustered that I salute Axel with my half-eaten *Brötchen*, a gesture that immediately makes me a strong candidate for Desperate Woman of the Year. Saluting with a *Brötchen*? The heat rises in my face as I step onto the train.

I sink into my seat. What in the world was that? I guess I don't look so bad today. *Quick, what am I wearing?* White linen pants, tennis shoes, and a black T-shirt. I have breadcrumbs on my T-shirt, but still, it must be a pretty hip outfit. Axel is like, what? Twenty-eight? I wonder what would happen if I went up to his cockpit (is that what they call the engine car of a train?) and knocked on the door. Not to jump on him or anything, just to ask him personally why the hell he glad-eyed me. I've spent more than a decade being ignored by guys like Axel, and I'm curious why today, of all days, I'm a target.

My fantasy conversation goes like this:

"Was it the linen pants? Or the Brötchen *crumbs?"*

"I love mature women," he replies. "And you, with those adorable little Ecco sneakers in just the right shade of taupe? You, baby, turn me on."

"Oh, thank you, Axel," I say, feeling a little shy but not the least bit tempted by him.

"You're so youthful, so full of vitality," Axel says. "Your face isn't falling down at all. You're hot."

"Me? I'm hot?"

"You. You're hot."

Never mind that Axel would be speaking German—guys who look like Axel don't speak English—his words would be poetic and warm. He would be polite in a sleazy way. He would smell like grease and engine dirt and Mennen Speed Stick deodorant, even though it's not available in Europe. He would run his fingers through his filthy hair, bat his sleepy (and slightly bloodshot) eyes at me and say, *"You, little lady, do something to me, and it ain't just the shoes. Come on up here and sit next to me; I'll let you drive the train."* He would never once mention the terms MILF or cougar.

I go on and on like this, eyes closed, deep in a menopausal *Thomas the Tank Engine* fantasy. Funny isn't it, how one lascivious look from a train engineer could set me off this way. I have gone from Great Aunt Edna to Sydney Leathers in a mere ten minutes. The words to "I've Been Working on the Railroad" flash through my brain. "Someone's in the kitchen with Dinah" . . . ah, a mid-September reverie. I wonder if I should wave to him when I get off the train. Or leave a trail of breadcrumbs.

Just before I get to the "Dinah won't you blow" part of the song (an ill-advised lyric if there ever was one), I open my eyes to see how close I am to home.

"Holweide. Next stop Holweide," says the computerized voice over the PA system.

"*Holweide?*" I say to no one in particular, but everyone hears my panic.

I am on the wrong goddamn train.

That goddamn dirtball Axel, or whoever the hell he is, tricked me. He did that tongue thing, I turned into a wobbly-kneed idiot, and I got on the wrong goddamn train. He probably has a scorecard on his sooty engineer's desk, where he keeps track of how many pathetic middle-aged women he can confuse. I feel like charging into his cockpit and kicking him in the caboose.

I'm fuming. While waiting for the train to reach Holweide, I have another fantasy conversation with Axel:

"What's the matter with you?" I ask. "Do you think this is funny?"

"Not my fault you fell for it," he says. "Works every time. You cougars get all steamed up and just step right into my clutches."

"I didn't step into your clutches. I stepped onto the wrong train."

"Gotta double-check the board, lady."

"I didn't double-check the board, Axel, because you were drooling at me from your cockpit window, and I was distracted. And I am not a cougar. I am a well-adjusted and happily married mother of two grown children. I don't need looks from guys like you to feel good about myself."

"Could've fooled me. And it's not a cockpit, you know."

"Whatever."

I get off the train at Holweide, humiliated, tired, and wishing I hadn't thrown away the rest of my *Brötchen*. Axel leans out the window, doing his engineer thing, and pulls away from the platform without giving me a second glance. Maybe he never even gave me a first glance. I wonder if I've imagined the entire episode. I am now sure that my face really is falling down and that these shoes are not very cute at all.

It's not like I haven't dealt with a leering man before. It's just that it hasn't happened in ages. I'm out of shape, so to speak. I used to sit at my piano and laugh at guys who acted like Axel. Buffoons! But now, a dozen years after donning my middle-age invisibility cloak and my Great Aunt Edna shield of elegance and eccentricity, I've been reduced to blushing and performing the *Brötchen* salute. And if that's not punishment enough, I'm in some God forsaken place called Holweide, with nothing to do except wait for the train in the opposite direction to get me back to where I started.

Life. One step forward, two steps back. Just once, I'd like to go sideways.

"John," I say to my husband, "I am in Holweide."

"What?" he says. "Hole what?" The phone connection is dicey.

"Holweide!"

"What are you doing there?"

"I got on the wrong train."

"How in the world did you do that?" he asks.

"Long story. I'll tell you later," though it seems pretty stupid to tell him I got on the wrong train because a hunky pervert with dirty hair and a long tongue cast his roving eye in my direction. We hang up, and I sit and wait an hour for the next train.

I decide I must be the victim of the German version of *Candid Camera*, an awful show called *Verstehen Sie Spass?*—the English translation of which is Do You Understand Fun?

The answer is no. I do not understand *Spass*, at least not the German kind. Humor in Germany is no laughing matter.

Out of boredom I fall into a Zen-like state that's one stifled yawn short of unconscious. I wish I had another *Brötchen*. Why am I always so hungry?

A man with a shaved head sits down next to me. He wears a ribbed sleeveless undershirt—we used to call them muscle shirts back in the day: now they're called wife beaters. Tattoos cover the man's burly arms. Sadly, one of his arms stops at the elbow. Little fingers stick out of the elbow joint. The little fingers are also tattooed. I try not to stare, but I'm fascinated.

He has skulls on each of the little fingers, and right above the stump is a heart with an inscription that reads "Forever Christina."

Three Christinas in one day. Really, it's almost too much.

With his other (full-length) arm, the man removes a packet of American Mac 'n' Cheese casserole mix from his jeans pocket. Grasping the packet with his teeny tiny tattooed elbow fingers, he begins to study the instructions. The package has little American flags on it and a photo of a delicious-looking bowl of macaroni and cheese on the cover. I have nothing with me to read, so I'm grateful to look over his elbow and read along with him.

This is what happens to women who end up in Holweide. It seems a fitting punishment for my gullibility.

Finally, the train arrives. I nod a silent good-bye to the muscle man (he is still memorizing the Mac 'n' Cheese packet), take the train back to the main station, and begin waiting again. Twenty minutes later, the train to my village arrives. The engineer drives right past me—no leers, no looks, and I'm glad for it. Because this is Europe, the brakes do not squeal, and the doors open efficiently. But no seats are available—the car is packed with boisterous young people returning home from the gaming trade show, an annual spectacle that features the latest ways to waste time and have fun shooting virtual bad guys. I have wasted a lot of time today myself, but I didn't have any fun, and I certainly didn't shoot anyone, although at specific points in today's voyage I might have been tempted. My feet hurt, my back aches, and I just want to sit on my living-room sofa and eat a bowl of Mac 'n' Cheese. But I don't eat cheese anymore, so it would be Mac 'n' Mac.

"Excuse me, madame," says a teenage girl in a tight black miniskirt—exactly the kind of thing I would have worn at her age. She radiates confidence and youthful energy. "Would you like to sit down?" She jumps up and fluffs her hair. "I've been sitting all day, and you look like you could use a seat." I sit back and settle in. In the course of two hours, I have traveled back and traveled forth, on the rails and in my mind. I have lost and regained three decades. I'm exhausted.

"Thank you," I say in my best Great Aunt Edna voice. "Thank you."

Twenty-Seven

Baubles, Bangles, and Queens

My daughter, Julia, and I climb the staircase to the Cologne Musical Tent, a temporary structure on the Rhine that has become a semipermanent part of the skyline.

We're headed to *Werq the World*, a live show featuring top performers from RuPaul's *Drag Race*. Julia has convinced me to buy tickets for tonight's shindig. She's thrilled, but I'm in my seventh decade of life, half of which was spent in piano bars, so this is hardly my first drag-queen rodeo.

Some of my earliest gypsy-in-my-soul performances on the professional stage—back in the late seventies—included playing the piano, singing, and dancing in an old-fashioned burlesque show that featured a couple of queens. First lesson learned: never stand next to anyone, male or female, who is blonder or thinner. Second lesson learned: always make friends with the drag queen—she'll keep you laughing, teach you how to touch up your roots, and let you cry your broken heart out on the padded shoulder of her Joan Crawford suit jacket.

In 1982 I worked as an actor on a horror film outside of Baltimore (*House on Sorority Row*). We were in production at the same time as Barry Levinson's *Diner* and John Waters' *Polyester*—a trifecta of cult films in three different genres. We visited each other's sets, and a couple of times, I had lunch with

Divine. I found myself wishing she had been cast in our "chop up the college girls" classic—she would have made a great house mother. Divine was divine.

During my years in Manhattan, while playing piano at the Grand Hyatt, I marveled at "Night of a Thousand Queens," an event that attracted hundreds of chiseled men in drop-dead gorgeous evening gowns. Upswept hair, spackled faces, butts and fake boobs cranked to stunning heights, baubles, bangles, and queens. On my break from the piano lounge, I sat in the granite lobby pit on a brown pleather sofa and gaped at the razzle-dazzle parade. In my drag-wannabe Piano Girl high heels and black tulle, gold-spangled Betsey Johnson skirt, I envied their heat-seeking confidence and queenly defiance. Like a pack of fierce, stiletto-footed wolverines, they stalked the lobby and left a trail of undulating optimism in their collective path. We didn't say "you go, girl" back then—we said, "Work your show."

Somehow, these guys had survived the eighties. Everyone I knew during that dark decade in Manhattan had lost friends to AIDS. The Hyatt horde of queens turned the lights back on, at least for a few hours. They were rage turned inside-out, dressed to the nines and ready to fight back.

So here I am tonight, three decades later, prepared for another shimmer-shine extravaganza. Julia and I have opted to wear simple black dresses with tasteful accessories. No bling for us. I learned my lesson years ago—no matter how many leopard-print accessories or junk jewelry bracelets you own, you can't upstage a queen on a mission. Her false eyelashes will always be longer, fluffier, and tinted to the perfect shade of midnight; her iridescent eyeshadow will have more glitter than yours. The drag queen colors the world with a different, more vibrant box of crayons.

The press page blurb for *Werq the World* says this: "Over-the-top production numbers that will leave fans gagging." Tonight we're scheduled to see Aquaria, Asia O'Hara, Detox, Kameron Michaels, Kim Chi, Monét X Change, Naomi Smalls, and (my favorite name) Violet Chachki. The queens, led by *Drag Race* den mother and jury member Michelle Visage, will attempt to rescue the galaxy from who knows what. The galaxy needs a lot of help these days.

As we head inside, I wonder if we're in the right place. The squeaky-faced youngsters around me look like they're headed to a church picnic or next week's performance of *Bodyguard: The Musical*. But we turn a corner, and bam! An Amazon queen—in a blonde wig and head-to-toe silver sequins—poses for photos with awestruck teenagers.

"Yep," says Julia. "This is the right place. Just wait until you see Asia O'Hara and Kim Chi."

"Kim Chi?" I repeat. "Like the Korean pickled cabbage?"

"Exactly. She is spicy."

We hand our tickets to a man in a blue coat and enter the theater. The music thumps and bumps so loudly that I can feel it jack-jack-jackhammer my heart. Is this necessary? Too much bass in the place. Scary. I put my hands over my ears.

"Mom," yells Julia. "This is way too loud for you. Wait here, and I will go to the lobby and get you earplugs."

"What?" I ask. "Did you say earplugs?" I wish I had brought my noise-canceling headphones, but then I would have looked like an oversized, menopausal toddler dragged to a rock concert by her aging hippie parents.

The German word for earplugs is *Ohrstöpsel*, right up there with *Dudelsack* (bagpipe) and *Kaiserschnitt* (C-section) on my personal list of great translations. I wonder where Julia will find *Ohrstöpsel* in the lobby, but she returns with a small sealed package.

"They're required to have them at music events. I think it's a law," she says.

The foam plugs help. Now that I'm no longer worried about drag-show-induced deafness, I'm free to look around at the other audience members. Along with the churchy looking youth groups in pressed pastel oxford-cloth shirts are stout boys with artsy tattoos and rainbow hair, bearded men wearing suit jackets and skirts (the Billy Porter influence has hit Germany), straight couples in nuances of navy, and young women (I think) with bouffant hairdos and killer waistlines.

As far as I can tell, we're the only mother-daughter team in attendance. I am easily thirty years older than everyone else around me. Once again, I have clearly entered Great Aunt Edna territory. Old Edna goes to the drag show. But it's nothing Edna hasn't seen (or heard) before—just a lot louder.

The curtain goes up. The audience gasps. The queens enter, one at a time, wearing space capes (remember the galaxy theme) that, when stripped off, reveal a rainbow of spectacular costumes. Even though I know these ensembles are the work of a crazed costume designer toting an oversized glue gun on each hip, from a distance they look couture.

The queens lip-sync, prance, look fabulous, prance some more (the show features an extraordinary amount of prancing), and are occasionally joined onstage by real dancers. Kim Chi does one number with four acrobats underneath her skirt. Aquaria, with turquoise hair, hangs upside-down from a rope. Asia—a Donna Summer clone—works hard for her money. The audience goes nuts. I spy people weeping with joy. Or maybe it's relief. These queens—silly, slutty, and over the top—give us permission to feel good about how we present ourselves to the world. Black pantsuit or lavender sequined ball gown—it's all good.

In the midst of all this fakeness, the air hangs thick with authenticity.

"See, Mom? I told you. These queens inspire tolerance."

I wonder what would have happened if I had seen this show in the seventh grade, when I was bullied by a gang of nasty girls for playing Bach on the piano and wearing the wrong outfit (plaid skirt with fabulous matching green shoes). Tonight's message might have made it easier for me to sashay away from those tyrants with my dignity intact. Instead, I got dragged down the steps by my hair and kicked in the ribs. And then I stopped wearing plaid skirts.

In the midst of all the galaxy saving, trapeze work, and satin cape waving, Michelle Visage, the only person in the theater close to my age, walks center stage, screams, "Hello, bitches," and proceeds to talk about having her breast implants removed—she had the "enhancement" in her early twenties because she felt she needed big boobs to play the Hollywood game. Years later, after dealing with serious illness that the implants caused, she had them yanked out.

"Breast in peace!" she shouts to her young audience. Michelle speaks pointedly about never allowing society to dictate the way we look. She talks about body image, eating disorders, and the difficulty of raising teenagers in a culture obsessed with standardized perfection. It's a missive we don't hear often enough, certainly not one I anticipated at a drag show.

I'm awestruck by the love in the hall. By the time the show is over, I'm transformed, not by the blow-your-balls-off bass lines, the Cher-on-steroids costumes, or the razor-sharp highlighted cheekbones—but by the subtle way the queens have taken an edgy, brash, in-your-face drag show and turned it into a gentle lesson in how we can live better, more authentic lives.

Werq your show. Save the galaxy with compassion. Love is love. Be yourself. As RuPaul would say, "Don't fuck it up."

Twenty-Eight

Playing Nice

Another Sunday. It's New Year's Day, and I'm headed to my steady gig at a fancy hotel in Cologne. Royal Afternoon Tea with solo piano music. I pull into the parking lot of the Honrath train station a few minutes before my scheduled train connection at two o'clock. I roll down my window. The day, unseasonably warm, pulses with the promise of spring, even though winter has yet to arrive. The air smells toasty—a peculiar mix of burning branches and freshly baked bread.

I close my eyes and think about the refugees who have arrived in Germany from Syria and other war-torn countries in the past month—what it must be like for them to start a new year so far from home. Frightening, exciting, frustrating. Maybe feeling safe overrides any other sensation. I've never been a refugee, but I understand what it's like to move to a foreign country. I had every possible economic advantage when I moved here, but it was still complicated, challenging, and, at times, a little scary. The language, the culture, the change. I can't imagine what our new neighbors—chased from their homes by brutality and fear—are experiencing.

From the warmth of my car, I check out the action on the platform. Look there—it's Jamaican Guy! Jamaican Guy, with waist-length dreads, stands next to the ticket machine, trying

to make sense of an über-complicated set of German instructions. Over the years I have seen Jamaican Guy several times in
Wahlscheid, the quaint village where I live. Although Wahlscheid
has become more colorful due to the recent influx of Syrian and
African refugees—it's still pretty much a *Sound of Music*-looking
community. Whenever I spot Jamaican Guy strolling through
our little town, I feel an urge to say hello. The village Rasta!
Surely, he's a musician. Or maybe not—just because a Jamaican
man has dreadlocks and looks like the coolest person this side
of Paris does *not* mean that he once played sessions with Bob
Marley. Maybe he's not even Jamaican. I scold myself for making generalizations and keep my comments to myself. Still, I
can't help imagining the strains of "Edelweiß" arranged for steel
drums and alphorn. Fusion at its finest.

As I sit here watching, an elderly woman—wearing a pink
coat and a baseball cap—hobbles over to Jamaican Guy and
begins waving a ticket at him. I sense a potential language breakdown and hop out of my car to see if I can help.

"Please," says the woman, who looks to be at least eighty. She
is spright, fidgeting, and speaks German in a booming voice, the
way people do when they want to be understood, as if shouting
might somehow make the person on the receiving end suddenly
grasp the many nuances of a foreign language. "PLEASE, DO
NOT SPEND YOUR MONEY ON A TICKET. Save your
money for food and shelter. Today is a holiday, and I am permit-
ted to take a guest with me on the train. Let me help you."

I translate this into English for Jamaican Guy, leaving out
the part about food and shelter. He looks at me, smiles, and says,
"She thinks I'm a refugee, doesn't she?"

"Uh, yes." OK, he might be a fish out of water, with limited German language skills, but he hardly looks like a refugee.
I guess in the eyes of this well-meaning woman, his dark skin
and stylishly ripped jeans mean he has just gotten off a boat and
walked halfway across Europe with his belongings in a plastic
sack. Perhaps she hasn't noticed his distressed leather man-purse,
his Nikes, or his Rimowa suitcase.

She really wants to help him.

"Well, fine with me! I can be a refugee if it makes her feel better." He turns to the woman. "Happy New Year, Madam! *Danke!*"

Madam beams, her cheeks blushing as pink as her coat. "My pleasure," she says.

I have wondered about Jamaican Guy for years. His occasional presence in my village offers a welcome distraction from a neighborhood that seems, at times, way too predictable. Now's my chance to talk to him. We introduce ourselves. His name is Andru; the German woman calls herself Frau Baumgartner. Together, we climb onto the train. Frau Baumgartner sits across the aisle from us and stares at the beautiful countryside as it sweeps past her window.

"So many shades of green," she shouts in German. "Strange for this time of year."

"Where do you live?" I ask Andru. "I've seen you in Wahlscheid and have always been curious about you. We don't have many Jamaican-looking guys in town."

"I have children in Wahlscheid—I come often to visit them. But my other homes are in Manhattan, Tokyo, and Kingston. I travel a lot for work. I'm headed back to Japan today. Every place is home for me—but no place is home, if you know what I mean."

"Yeah. I really know what you mean. So, I have to ask—are you a musician?"

"Yes," he says. "And a songwriter."

"Me, too. How's it going for you?"

Turns out my new friend Andru is a pretty big star in the reggae world after all, with several gold and platinum records to his name. And he did work with the Wailers.

"I'm sorry Frau Baumgartner thought you were a refugee," I say as he collects his belongings and prepares to get off the train—he's connecting to another train to Frankfurt International Airport.

"She's a sweet lady," he says. "It's the dark skin. Sometimes we all get lumped together. But, you know, she's playing nice. It's all good." He doesn't come right out and start singing "One

Love," but it would be a fitting musical sentiment at this particular moment.

Don't worry, be happy.

We exchange cards, he says good-bye and *danke* to Frau Baumgartner, and disembarks.

"*AUFWIEDERSEHEN!*" she yells.

I immediately pull out my phone and do a Google search. Impressive. I find a YouTube video and slide over to Frau Baumgartner's side of the aisle to show her.

"Look," I say. "The man you helped today is a big star. He is flying to Japan this afternoon." I show her a video of Andru performing in Moscow. She smiles, then her eyes widen.

"What a pity," she says, speaking at normal volume.

"What do you mean?" I ask.

"What a pity that he is now a refugee. No one is safe in this world."

I think about this for a minute. "I suppose you're right," I say. "What brings you into Cologne on New Year's Day? Are you meeting friends?"

"Oh no, dear. I am alone. But I like to get on the train and see what happens. I bring a bag lunch. I like getting out of the house and collecting adventures. Today has gotten off to a good start. A refugee who was once a star! Imagine! I hope that young man will be safe in Japan. I hope the Japanese are good to refugees."

I don't have the heart to set her straight. She has done her part, and I should do mine by not shattering her illusion. We have been an unlikely trio—a blonde American pianist, a Jamaican international reggae star, and a kindly German woman in a pink coat.

I get off the train with Frau Baumgartner, and we say cheerful good-byes. She totters into the balmy winter afternoon, an old woman with a youthful willingness to help, a need to be needed, and a day of adventure—and shifting colors—ahead of her.

Twenty-Nine

Runway
Tempest Storm, High Heels, and the Adventures of an Aging Model

*L*ike so many of life's great stories, this one starts with a pair of shoes.

Cruising around on Facebook one morning when I'm supposed to be practicing the piano, I'm distracted by a fabulous pair of pumps, way too high-heeled, and, I assume, way too expensive. Pale powder pink—austere but hopeful—the color of a newborn's cheek, with a small platform, a little bow on the vamp, thick, towering high heels, and an ankle strap. They would be perfect shoes for a dress I don't yet own. On the chance that I may be suddenly booked to play for a Parisian garden party or get an invite to summer tea in Vienna, I decide to track them down.

I see the shoes on the fan page of a store called Fusskleider, a pricey boutique located in Bergisch Gladbach, Germany, a posh neighborhood near Schlosshotel Lerbach, where I play the piano every weekend. The Bergisch Gladbach community is about twenty kilometers outside of Cologne.

I send a message to Dörthe, the store's owner and wife of a jazz pianist I know—which somehow makes us part of the same club. She tells me the price, but I remember we're paying college tuition for our son and saving for our daughter's education. These kids—Curtis is working toward a career as an AI strategy consultant, and Julia is a budding filmmaker with activist tendencies. The next ten years are going to be pricey.

Investment in pale pink platform shoes is perhaps not the wisest choice.

With a heavy heart I tell Dörthe that the shoes are out of my budget.

"Well," she asks, "want to model? I'll pay you with the shoes."

Hmmm.

I consider this with great interest.

I am no stranger to the "singing for my supper" barter arrangement. Several times I've exchanged my music or writing skills for beach vacations, wine, or spa treatments. But shoes? This sounds like a perfect deal.

Then I come to my senses.

"Are you crazy, Dörthe?" I ask. "I am fifty-five years old, not even close to a size extra-extra small. I am, in fact—god help me—a medium. I've avoided Botox, I have wrinkles and all my original parts."

"Perfect," she says. "Except for the Botox, you're like most of my customers."

"Are you sure you don't want to hire my daughter instead? She is sixteen, five foot ten, and, you know, model material."

"If I put a sixteen-year-old on the runway, my customers will not be happy. A sixteen-year-old looks good in anything. But you, now, that's another story. If they see you looking good, they'll figure there's hope for them."

Hmmmm.

I think this is a compliment, but I'm not sure; it may be an accidental insult. Just the other day someone told me I looked good in a photograph because the camera was so far away from me. Little things like this creep up in my life all the time. Little stabs disguised as compliments. I've gotten used to being over fifty and invisible—I've even grown to enjoy it—but that doesn't mean I have to wear a burlap sack and hide in the bushes, does it?

There is the issue of my titanium foot. At this time last year, I was recovering from joint replacement surgery on my right foot. I had to go up and down the stairs on my behind, and I wore a Frankenstein boot for six weeks. How can I possibly model for a store that showcases tight jeans and high-heeled shoes? Then I remember Heather McCartney and her appearance on *Dancing with the Stars*. She did turn out to be the heel in the McCartney marriage, but I figure if she can win a dancing contest with a fake leg, then I can be a runway shoe model with a fake toe.

"OK," I say, "I'll do it."

I'm skeptical about removing my invisibility cloak, but I'm not at all nervous about the show. This will not be my first catwalk, although I am several decades out of practice.

I modeled in my younger, thinner years in Pittsburgh, where I did informal modeling for Saks Fifth Avenue. I even walked in a runway show for Donna Karan when she was starting out as a designer for Anne Klein. The show was at Pittsburgh's Carnegie Hall, and the clothes were works of art. She was nice to me. I was nineteen at the time.

Then, disaster struck. The events manager at Saks discovered that I was willing to wear costumes, that I had no problem at all dressing up as Mrs. Santa Claus, Tanya Baum the Talking Tree, Cupid, or the Easter Bunny. I became the Saks "costume model," which sounded good, paid better than the standard modeling jobs, but kind of crushed my fantasies of working in high fashion. *All* the models wanted to wear Dior and YSL, but I was the only one willing to sport a cupid costume. On Valentine's Day 1977, I pranced through Saks in a red leotard and wings, shooting rubber arrows at unsuspecting customers.

The next time Ms. Karan was in town, on Easter, I had to walk the runway in a rabbit suit.

Carnegie Hall, in a rabbit suit.

Not many models can boast of such an achievement. But I was making a living, hopping and hoping that my career in fashion might help pay the bills while I worked on my acting and music skills. Occasionally the Saks fashion director would take pity on me, scoop a designer dress out of her designer trunk, and toss it at me like a designer bone. But most of the time the fine ladies of the fashion office costumed me in some type of synthetic fur with matching ears. I wanted Chanel; I got Peter Rabbit.

Eventually I moved to New York City, where I decided to stick to the piano. Manhattan had tens of thousands of aspiring models but only a handful of female pianists. Who knew? I like to tell people I quit the modeling business, but it would be more honest to say that it quit me. I escaped the world of fashion and planted my skinny behind on a piano bench, a decision I've never regretted. Now, the only time I wear a designer dress is when it's black, loose, and easy to accessorize. If you're willing to be invisible, you have a surprising assortment of choices.

With my runway gig as an elder model here in Germany, I'm making a comeback from a career I never had. I'm thirty years too late and thirty pounds too heavy. I don't know if the shoes are worth the catwalk down memory lane. But I'll be damned if I'm going to let that Heather McCartney get ahead of me.

I tell my family.

"You? On the catwalk?" my two kids say in unison, a teen-age chorus of horror and disbelief. At least they're not laughing.

"Sure!" says John, coming to my defense. "Your mom is more than a piano player. She's a good walker. Just watch her walk!"

I pull in my stomach, toss my hair, and do a couple of loops around the dining room table, simultaneously sashaying and serving scoops of lentil salad. No one seems very impressed, by either the walking or the salad.

"You know," I say to the kids, "I trained with one of the best walkers in the world: Tempest Storm."

"Here we go," says Curtis, rolling his eyes.

"Tempest Storm?" asks Julia. "What a name! Was she a model? Was she a weather girl?"

"Was she a runway trainer? Like Jorge?" asks my son, who is a big fan of Jorge Alexis Gonzalez Madrigal Varona Vila, the *Germany's Next Top Model* runway coach, a tall, skinny Cuban guy who wears towering high heels covered in sequins, speaks broken German, and shouts things such as *schtrut your schtuff Chica, Chica!* at the girls as they *schtruggle* and *schtumble* on their platform shoes. It is impossible to not like Jorge.

"Well," I say. "Tempest Storm was neither a model nor a runway coach. She was different from Jorge. She was, uh, a stripper."

A moment of awkward silence.

"A stripper? You took walking lessons from a stripper? Was she also a pole dancer, Mom? Modeling in public is weird enough, but if you say you're going to take your clothes off and pole dance, I'll have to go to school with a bag over my head."

"No, Julia, no pole dancing. I don't have the upper body strength," I reason. "Anyway, many years ago—OK, like thirty years ago—I was hired as an actress to play the part of a piano-playing stripper in an old-fashioned burlesque show. Tempest Storm was an aging but very famous real-life stripper. She was also in the show, and she gave me walking lessons."

"Like Jorge!" says Curtis. "*Chica, chica!*" He is beginning to see the light.

"A little," I say, "but Tempest had a tad more, shall we say, 'experience.'"

Tempest Storm, whose career as "The Queen of Exotic Dancers" spanned sixty years, boasted a curriculum vitae that included headliner appearances in America's best burlesque houses, along with starring roles in films such as *French Peep Show*, *Striptease Girl*, and *Buxom Beautease*. My favorite Tempest fun fact: her G-string is in a glass display case at the Burlesque Hall of Fame in Las Vegas. She might be the only woman in the world with her underwear in a museum.

I still remember Tempest standing behind me during a rehearsal at the Folly Theater in Kansas City, Missouri, her hands on my hips, whispering "toe heel, toe heel" in my ear as we coasted in sync—a tag-team stripper machine gliding like twin Dorothy Hamills across an iceless stage floor.

The follow spot threw blue light on us. Tempest was wrapped in a white satin robe with marabou trim; I was wearing rehearsal sweatpants, a Pittsburgh Pirates T-shirt, and high heels. She was fifty-three; I was twenty-three. She had a curtain of red hair trailing over her graceful shoulders, breasts that defied gravity—I could feel them poking into my back—and the sexiest walk I have ever seen. I coveted that walk.

Tempest and I slithered to stage right and slid stage left—the key, she said to me, was to create a flow to my movement, to never let the audience sense that my feet were hitting the floor. I should float above the stage, she said, my arms hovering like wings, my pelvis guiding each liquid step to a seamless soft landing on the scarred hardwood floor.

I stood backstage every night and watched her. She was the opposite of invisible. She was a star, a floating star. I practiced and practiced and never got it right.

"Don't worry, darling," she said to me when I expressed my frustration. "It's like playing the piano; you need thirty years of practice to find out if you're any good. I could teach you how to crawl, too, but that's a lot harder."

"Now's my chance," I tell the kids. "I'm going to channel Tempest Storm on the runway!"

"Forget Tempest, Mom," says Curtis. "Go with Jorge."

I show up on the day of the fashion show and relax when I see that the clothes are hip and figure friendly. Except for the jeans.

When did it happen that blue jeans, once the comfort pants of choice for leisure time and outdoor activities, became modern-day persecution devices? The jeans assigned to me feature spaghetti legs and a zipper that's about an inch high. Really.

These jeans are so low that my butt crack is showing. I look like a plumber, or an extra on the *Prison Break* set.

"I think you need a smaller size," says Steffi, the dresser for the show.

"NOOOOO!" I am scandalized. "These are, uh, perfect. I can't sit down in them, but they are perfect for, you know, walking." The jeans are paired with very high-heeled green shoes. The shoes are *fantastico*. I am also wearing a loose orange cotton cardigan. Lucky for me, it disguises the muffin top created by the "waistband" of the jeans. A festive scarf—bright orange, grassy green—ties everything together. I do so love a festive accessory.

It's almost time for the fashion show to start.

And there's news. Heidi Klum's mother is in the audience. I've played the piano a handful of times for the Klum family. I like them, mainly because they like music. But the idea of having to model in front of a supermodel's mom strikes me as bizarre. All of a sudden I feel kind of vulnerable without my piano. I feel sort of, well, visible.

I text Curtis to tell him that Heidi's mom is at the show.

"Ask her if she knows Jorge," he writes back.

The other models, Andrea and Anke, are also "real" looking models, but they're a little less real-looking than I am, mainly because they are a good fifteen years younger. Maybe that's what happens to women as we age. We become more real. The thought comforts me, even though I now feel like a human version of *The Velveteen Rabbit*.

These jeans are killing me; I'm being eviscerated by the crotch seam. Death by denim. But I am double-Spanxed and determined to stay positive.

The things a girl will do for a pair of shoes.

The store is small, the runway is more of a gangplank than an actual catwalk, but Bergisch Gladbach's most elegant ladies have shown up for a glass of champagne, a cupcake on a stick, a strawberry dipped in chocolate, and a chance to see the spring collection.

Here we go.

I fling my scarf dramatically over my shoulder—inspired by Jorge, the absolute master of scarf flinging—and plop onto the runway on my green high heels. The music blares. My titanium foot is holding up, my ankles aren't wobbling, and I've got enough oxygen to suck in the muffin top for the three minutes that I'm in the spotlight. So far, so good.

"Robin is wearing jeans by *Stretto e Stretto* of Italy," says Dörthe. "The 'boyfriend-jean look' continues this spring—loose, relaxed, and comfortable."

I'm glad they didn't give me the *tight* jeans. Good God.

Chaos reigns in the dressing room. Three models, one dresser, heaps of clothes on racks, in piles, on tables. It looks like my daughter's bedroom times three. Shoes and straw handbags sit on every surface. Steffi holds it together, but she counts on us to stay organized.

Once I peel off the jeans, I'm in heaven. Now I get to wear silky tunics with ankle boots, stretchy dresses with leather jackets, full skirts and linen tops, and . . . "the shoes."

I'm in a footwear-induced twilight coma—wondering which pair of these shoes I should select for myself when I'm finished with this gig. I could barter for the clothing, too, but the shoes are why I'm here. I'm falling in love with this little pair of perforated leather Chelsea boots. Soft as butter. I step onto the runway in a taupe silk shift with a crisp leather jacket. Gorgeous. I smooth down the dress and realize I've put it on inside-out. Not good. What to do.

"Look—it's reversible," I say. No one seems to mind, the champagne is flowing, and to tell you the truth, the dress looks pretty good no matter how you wear it.

I also have a misstep with a shoe that's not properly buckled—the powder pink pumps with the ankle strap, the very shoes that seduced me into this situation! Once I reach center stage, I realize that my foot is flopping around in the shoe. I can't walk properly so I have to slide and shuffle to make my way. It is a high-risk maneuver. Too bad I never mastered crawling with Tempest Storm. It would come in handy right about now.

Chica, chica!

We are scheduled for two shows. On the break in between, I take myself out to lunch. It's probably not very model-like to have a pig-dog lunch in the middle of a fashion show day, but I am starving. Besides, I know that I'll have to put those jeans on again in a few hours, and I'll need the energy to get them over my hips. So, I order a salad and a giant baked potato. There.

I sit in the chichi restaurant by myself, watching beautiful women out for a Saturday latte or espresso. The land of Heidi Klum has so many of them, each one thinner, taller, and more picture-book lovely than the next.

The smaller the town, the tighter the pants. The higher the heel, the younger the girl.

Not one of them can hold a candle to Tempest Storm.

They enter the restaurant and look around, waiting to be noticed. I wonder, if like me, they will need three decades to figure out that it's way more fun to be heard than it is to be seen. I doubt that Tempest, Heidi, Heather, or Jorge would agree with me, but I can't wait to get back to the piano.

I dig into my potato, take out my notebook, and start writing, grateful, once again, to be invisible.

Thirty

Pretty, Pretty
Piano Girl versus Trump

My hair is big. My dress is too tight. It's 1986. I'm sitting at a Steinway on a Saturday night in Manhattan. I'm back at Trumpet's—Donald J. Trump's quasi-namesake lounge, more or less a gift from his old man, who was actually successful at the real estate thing, in a highly disagreeable, tycoon kind of way. With the sponsorship of his evil father, the Donald had partnered with the Hyatt Corporation to build the glass-and-granite behemoth currently hovering over Grand Central Station. I can't imagine receiving a midtown Manhattan hotel as a college graduation present. I got a Peavey amp, a Shure SM57 microphone, and a gentle reminder to treat people with respect. I straighten my spine, curve my fingers, and remember that it doesn't take talent or hard work to inherit money.

I play "Misty" or "All the Things You Are" or some random Elton John song. Who's listening? No one. Tourists from one of the Dakotas sit in a dark velveteen corner sipping Diet Coke. I can hear them talking about the matinee performance of *Arsenic and Old Lace*. Tonight, they're headed to see Shirley Bassey . . . on Broadway. I play "Goldfinger," but they don't notice. I see reflector stripes on their puffy white shoes.

Two other couples, most likely Connecticut commuters conducting illicit affairs, grope at each other with the desperation of teenagers trying to cop a last feel before their parents show up. They are probably headed home to monotonous marriages, mortgages, and backyards that need mowing.

Waitresses, shiny and skinny and sporting slinky black stain-repellent costumes designed to entice titans of industry, balance glasses of over-oaked chardonnay and bowls of smoked almonds on glittering silver trays. Smoked almonds make me a little queasy these days. I must have consumed about two million of them over the past year—the starving Piano Girl's version of dinner.

I haven't eaten at all today, but I'm still worried that I look bloated. Maybe I have an almond allergy. No one has yet figured out how to incorporate stretch into velvet, and my dress, unforgiving and stiff, pulls at my waist and puckers at my hips. My bra strap threatens to slip over my shoulder.

"Don't take a break," says the food and beverage manager, a short man with gelled hair who once told the lobby jazz trio that they were not allowed to walk on any carpeted areas of the hotel. I am used to going along with his ridiculous directives, but I have been playing for an hour, and I need a potty run.

"Why? Not much happening here tonight, unless you're waiting for the live sex show that's about to start over at table thirteen. Those two need to get a room."

"Mr. Trump is coming in," says the food and beverage guy. "Stay at the piano and look pretty."

I do not blink or take offense. Look pretty. Sure. I tuck in my bra strap, fluff my hair, and play. This is the eighties, and this is what female employees do when Mr. Trump shows up. We primp and prepare and pray we pass the "pretty" test.

Mr. Trump arrives. He hovers for a minute by the bar and scopes out the room, his shifty eyes taking in all of us to make sure we are looking at him. I smile. *Yes, Mr. Trump, we notice you.* Once he sees me look at him, he ignores me. He is my employer. I need the money. I'm grateful for the job. I play the piano and play the game and play along with his need to be the most important person in the room. This is part of the gig.

It finally occurs to me that the name of the lounge—TRUMPet's—makes us seem like Donald's version of Playboy Bunnies or Penthouse Pets. Some marketing genius came up with this. Nice.

Because it's the eighties, I know a lot of guys who behave like Trump. He doesn't strike me as anything special. He doesn't really stand out at all. He's just another obnoxious rich guy, a professional progeny with a huge ego who demands that I notice him and smile.

Deep down I know two things, not just about Donald, but about many of the men I work for during the eighties: If I look good, they'll hit on me; if I look plain or chubby, flat-chested or fat-assed, they'll fire me. I grew up with feminist parents, attended a very fine women's college, studied hard, worked my tail off, can play everything from Mozart to "MacArthur Park," and I still have to put up with guys who judge me by the way I fill out my cocktail dress? I have become an expert in the art of flirty, diplomatic turndowns.

A few years later, long after I left the Hyatt (I was replaced by a piano-playing waitress who was having an affair with the general manager) and moved to another Manhattan hotel, I run into Trump again. I have just flown into Atlantic City on Trump's private helicopter with Allan, my wealthy compulsive-gambler boyfriend.

We dine in an upscale gourmet restaurant in one of the Trump casino-hotels. Allan, who has turned the peculiar shade of gray common to gamblers itching to get back to the blackjack table, seems uncomfortable when Donald comes to our table to greet us. Trump loves guys like Allan—they show up in his casino and lose more money in a night than I earn in a year.

I am twenty-three years younger than Allan. Donald looks me over and gives Allan the "thumbs-up" sign. We all laugh. It's the eighties. I play the trophy bimbo-girlfriend role with style even though I know it's not who I am. It's shameful.

"You know, Mr. Trump, I used to work for you," I say. "I played the piano at the Grand Hyatt."

"And just look at you now," he says, "Unbelievable. Really. Unbelievable. Tremendous. Wow, wow, wow." He stares me up and down, as if working for him has catapulted me into the sparkling, sleazy world of inappropriate relationships and casino fine dining. I have landed in the lopsided lap of luxury. Really. Just look at me now. Wrong, wrong. It's all just wrong. I know it, and yet here I am. It's the eighties. I eat my Caesar salad and hope I don't look fat.

Fast-forward a few decades. I recovered from the eighties by the skin of my laminated teeth. Some of my friends weren't so lucky. AIDS, eating disorders, drug addiction—for many of us, it was a decade of catastrophes, even if we were smart enough to avoid shoulder pads and Spandex. Everyone claims they had fun in the eighties, but for many of us it was a nightmare cloaked in gold spangles and hype. We dealt with a lot of unethical stuff. Sometimes we even participated.

Things are different now. We have options. We have chosen natural fibers and approved of political correctness. We have the Marriage Equality Act. We have honest conversations about body image and sexual harassment and holding men and women to the same standards. We make progress in a way that is too slow for most of us but enough to give us hope.

We are not stuck in the eighties, a decade of mean-spirited, pseudo-glam nonsense. We trashed our tight dresses and low self-esteem. Despair might have propelled us into the nineties, but we entered the new millennium with a newfound sense of cautious optimism. And we're not going back.

Pretty, pretty no more. Shout it out. Want amplification? I've got a 1980 Peavey amp and a Shure microphone you can borrow. But I suspect, eventually, the volume of our united voices will be loud enough.

Thirty-One

Hold the Zucchini

Dear Fabian and Becky,

Thank you so much for inviting us to the after-concert dinner at your apartment next Saturday. Backstage catering is the worst, and we're ever so grateful when patrons of the Piano Girl concert series take the trouble to prepare a tasty late-night meal. Steve and I are truly looking forward to your "June Moon" menu. A clever theme—you know how I adore a good clean rhyme! And it's very kind of you to ask if we have any food allergies or dietary restrictions. Not every host bothers to inquire, and, after several recent trips to the emergency room (following meals at the homes of former friends and fans), we welcome your concern. You may have heard that South-North Airlines refused to let us fly last week simply because we complained about pretzel dust in the air. The incident was humiliating for poor, asthmatic Steve, who did not for one second enjoy being hog-tied and carried off the plane by security thugs. The sound of his wheezing still haunts me. Will his trombone playing ever be the same? Doubtful.

Potato chips are fine, as are GMO-free, organic Doritos (but not the nacho ranch flavor). We'll discuss dip later.

Like most folks in our musical-culinary circle, Steve and I follow a gluten-free, peanut-free, dairy-free, half-pescatarian, low-sodium, no sugar, vegan diet—except that Steve occasionally eats onion bagels and medium-rare roast beef. I enjoy a doughnut now and then (rainbow sprinkles, please), but for the most part, I avoid all grains. As a singer of traditional Albanian music, I'm allergic to anything bland or boring, so forget about rice, unless it's the rare purple type found in the part of the Maldives that is not yet underwater. Purple rice (served on ivory china) dances off the plate when combined with root vegetables. No carrots, though—Steve hyperventilates and has "bodily fluid" issues when exposed to anything orange. Orange is the new death, at least for Steve. I've been told that he is not alone.

A word about plate design: I like my rice choreographed. No overlapping, please, and make sure the grains are all facing the same direction, west to east, if possible. Poorly arranged food can trigger rage, depression, and the gag reflex. Why take the risk?

Hold the zucchini. Or any type of squash for that matter. I'm not technically allergic to squash, but it gives me the creeps. And speaking of creepy, I can't abide dried fruit, wasabi nuts, or anything in the "pudding" category. I'm not a picky eater, but I have my limits.

Most vegans refuse to eat fish, but—outliers that we are—we'll occasionally dine on organically sourced steelhead trout, as long as it's from the greater Pittsburgh area and cooked in a wood-burning stove at precisely 483 degrees Fahrenheit. Don't try to get by with charcoal—that sneaky Sally van Sutherland from the Newport Jazz Festival served us charcoal-baked farmed trout last summer, and I ended up with spontaneous conjunctivitis, hair loss, and an infected gallbladder. All of this happened before dessert—a mousse of chestnuts and air that made Steve's head blow up to the size of a pumpkin. That was quite a night. Steve and I, side by side in a Rhode Island ambulance, clinging to life, cursing Sally van Sutherland and swearing that we would never again eat trout. Sad. Sally ruined trout for us for at least nine months. The lawsuit should bring us some comfort.

Note: Pumpkin—orange!—is also a no go.

Really, is there a person alive who can tolerate chestnuts? I think not.

Crispy duck is OK for Steve (another vegan exception). I refuse to eat the "cute animals"—duck, lamb, or rabbit. But I will gladly slurp down that yummy hoisin sauce as long as it is MSG-free. In 2013 I suffered from MSG-induced leg paralysis. The restaurant, Ho Ho Fu on the Upper East Side (now out of business), blamed my inability to stand on the two bottles of Riesling I consumed with the meal, but paid experts later testified in court that my hoisin-induced MSG levels were "off the charts."

After the concert, Steve likes to drink Diet Dr. Pepper, but I prefer Mr. Tom's Bloody Mary mix with Absolut vodka once the wine has run out.

You might be thinking we're a couple of complicated divas, but we're not! Just last week Bruce and Gladys served a divine Sunday brunch after our "Albania Meets Jazz" performance at the Newark Holiday Inn. Except for Steve's projectile vomiting (caused by a hidden piece of yam in what was supposed to be an orange-free dining experience), we very much enjoyed the selection of gluten-free, vegan delicacies alongside the roast beef, trout, and rainbow-sprinkle doughnuts on the bountiful buffet. Too bad Steve's overly enthusiastic spewing caused the other guests to flee earlier than planned—they seemed like nice people, especially the Bolivian taxidermist (we can gossip about him when I see you—tightest pants ever). Anyway, I suspect that Steve ruined Gladys's beautiful Swedish table linens, but she has only herself to blame. Everyone knows Steve suffers from yam intolerance.

Egg whites are fine, but quail eggs only.

Please, whatever you do, NO BREAD BASKET ON THE TABLE. This is very important. Steve has psychotic episodes when he senses an overabundance of carbs. A few months ago, our agent took us to dinner at Chez Norman (Michelin two stars, so they should have known better). Steve attacked the basket, dug out the inside of a baguette, and rolled the dough into tiny balls. This would not have been so bad, but he stuffed the bread balls up his nose and almost died of carb asphyxiation. I rode next to him in the ambulance. Steve sneezed (what a mess that was), we veered into an Uber car, and I dislocated my shoulder.

When you see the cast on my arm on Saturday, please don't mention the booking agent or the carb incident—Steve still feels guilty.

You're probably aware that I only have one eye—Lisalotte Lux, that anorexic oboe player from Teaneck, threw a fork at me several months ago after I complained about her pesto. I told her about my pine nut intolerance, but she said she forgot. Forgot? Those hives felt like hamsters crawling up my butt. I refused to suffer silently, so I spoke up. Lisalotte got pissed and threw the fork. End of story. End of eye. Lisalotte has a few years remaining in her jail sentence, plenty of time to reconsider her pesto recipe.

Please note: because I'm half-blind, I prefer my meal to be visually balanced. Diligence can be a matter of life or death for me, and I can't very well patrol my plate if I can't see it. Candlelight? No, thank you.

French onion dip is fine. So are grilled raspberries, truffle enchiladas, and deep-fried baby asparagus (only the white kind, not the green).

Steve will tell you he can eat pork rinds, but don't listen to him.

Looking forward to Saturday. Let me know if we can bring dessert. My shoulder is still healing, but I can manage carrying a doughnut or two.

Hugs and kisses!
Piano Girl

Thirty-Two

The Summer of Love

I perch on my padded piano bench, inhale the mingled scents of jasmine, Jo Malone, and musty French cheese. I sip a glass of Agrapart champagne, contemplate the months ahead of me, and marvel at my good fortune. The summer of 2011 offers more than the average number of castle weddings. This year we'll host a multitude of international couples—they'll tie the nuptial knot in a location that exceeds storybook expectations.

I've reached the point in my career where I'm playing for the second weddings of some of my previous clients. Creepy. But this summer—all newbies! First timers with a peeled-egg patina of loveliness, pretty children dressed for adulthood, a wash of youthful optimism in a world grown sour. I cannot think of a better way to snap out of my middle-age funk than sitting behind a grand piano and playing songs to accompany the hopefulness of young love.

I have musician friends who play for weddings in barns where guests end up naked and dancing on rooftops. I know of one wedding that featured an ensemble of a hundred elementary school flutists, standing in a field, playing "Moon River." My father once played for a Fourth of July wedding that included the reenactment of Slovenian immigrants arriving in America by boat—a group of babushka-clad women (including the bride) rowed across a swimming pool in a rubber raft to simulate their ancestors' arrival on American shores.

I do not play for these kinds of weddings. I would, but no one asks. My weddings tend to be subdued, upscale, and elegant—the kind of events where everyone eats and drinks for hours, but no one suffers from bloat. My weddings are studies in silk shantung, seed pearls, and restraint. Picture an English garden in a German castle. Roses, lavender, fifty shades of ivory. Multilingual servers in dark suits pass trays of tasty tidbits to bejeweled guests who never seem inebriated, despite bottomless glasses of pricey swill.

For most of these events I sit in the corner of a fancy hall, a hotel lobby, or a garden and play *"tinka, tinka"* for serene, occasionally joyous guests. Let the summer of international weddings begin.

Today's Turkish bride has requested John Coltrane. This is oddly hip, and it alarms me, as I am not a jazz musician. Coltrane's interpretations of standard tunes can be discordant and challenging to those who don't like jazz, but I shall play "My One and Only Love" and "Angel Eyes" and hope for the best. The bride also requested "Greensleeves." She has hired a DJ for the Turkish-music part of the program. Something for everyone—a musical potpourri.

The ceremony takes place at the Bergisch Gladbach city hall, home to one of Germany's finest Steinways. I adore this Model D—I've gotten to play it a handful of times, and it's like coasting on a cloud. The local music school uses the town hall for recitals, so they keep the piano primped and primed for action.

The crowd gathers as we wait for the downbeat. How nice to see two cultures colliding in a good way. German groom, Turkish bride. Anticipation builds. The groom's family, conservatively attired in dark suits and chalky linen dresses, hovers across the aisle from the Turkish contingent, which features older women in embroidered head scarves, younger women in jewel-toned silky dresses, and men with biceps bulging under their snug suits.

Here they come. The bride and groom march in together accompanied by a recording of a Turkish love song. The Turkish side cheers. I sit at the Steinway and wait for my cue. I love this.

I play "My One and Only Love" to polite applause, but alas, no cheering. I play "Greensleeves" about as well as I can play it. I cruise through "Over the Rainbow" and Bach's Air on a G-String. We finish with another rousing Turkish recording of celebration music. More cheering. The Turks have it going on. Weddings should definitely include more cheering.

I love the Cookbook Guys. I have played for this persnickety and wonderful group of food writers for nine years. The gentlemen always book overnight rooms at the castle, dine at the Michelin three-star restaurant, and then, after they've consumed ten courses of broiled quail's eggs and skewered truffles, come to the bar for cognac and whatever. I'm the "whatever" part. I play for them from midnight until two in the morning. Each year the event is quiet and classy and—even though it's way too late—a delight for me.

This year, when I arrive at the castle at 11:30, I'm horrified to see a conga line of wedding guests (from another party) snaking through the main hall of the castle, around the very grand piano I am scheduled to play. The bride—an American woman wearing what looks like a 1975 Bob Mackie creation, leads the line. She is skunk drunk and singing "I Will Survive" at the top of her very developed lungs. June is bustin' out all over. Chaos at the castle. Who is responsible for this madness, and why is the bride wearing beaded fringe?

What will happen when my suave Cookbook Guys catch wind of this?

The cacophony comes from the back salon, where a musician is running his keyboard through a flanger. Waa-waa-glub-glub. He cranks the wedding party into a squealing frenzy by performing to a taped medley of German carnival songs and Gloria Gaynor disco hits. Oh, my God, is that a smoke machine?

And a disco ball? The piano man is just doing his job, but because I am about to do mine, I'm tempted to cut his cables.

My Cookbook Guys, slightly snooty and the type of men who generally try to avoid the Macarena and the mass consumption of tequila shots, are currently in the gourmet restaurant, blissfully unaware of the Studio 54 misfire happening in the lobby. Like every year, they expect to stroll into the bar to listen to delicate music and sip their hundred-euro brandies.

What to do.

My colleagues are the best. I grab the banquet director by the shoulders, tell him we have a looming disaster, and persuade him to wrangle the bride and her braying group of line dancers back into the private salon. The bar manager, who quickly becomes my hero, single-handedly moves the piano (a Yamaha C5) from the lobby into the bar—a job that involves rearranging the heavy bar furniture, removing one of the French doors to the room, and taking the lid off the piano. After the big heave-ho, he replaces the lid, flicks his wrist, tosses some rose petals on the piano, and lights a dozen votive candles. The Cookbook Guys sashay into the bar, completely unaware that they were seconds away from walking onto the set of *Nightmare on Disco Street*.

I put on my calm piano-hostess face and greet my Cookbook Guys. The adrenaline has woken me, and I get through the late-night gig without my head crashing onto the keys. Periodically I look over my shoulder, through the closed glass doors, and see the bouncing bride and her cohorts cavorting through the lobby in drunken clumps. But it remains quiet in the bar—just me, a very large piano, seventy-five Salvador Dali lithographs, and twenty-two Cookbook Guys.

On his break, the musician from the wedding stops by to say hello. "Wow," he says. "It's really quiet in here. Too bad. We've got a real party going on next door."

Before I leave, I stop in the salon to say good-bye to him. Consider it a professional courtesy. He is playing "Mandy," and the bride, nearly popping out of her Cher dress, dances alone in little circles around his keyboard. She sings a different song—I don't know what it is, but it's not "Mandy." Maybe it has some of the same notes.

While saying good-bye to the musician, I accidentally step on the train to the bride's dress, causing her to stumble.

"I'm so sorry," I say.

"Ah, that's OK. I'm sick of this fucking dress anyway." She strips off the bodice. I marvel at her glittering strapless bra.

"Enough of this 'Mandy' shit," she says to the keyboard player. "Play something raunchy. You know, stripper music."

I sneak out the back door, even though the real show is just now starting.

The next weekend, I play for an exquisite Indian wedding reception. Wow! I have never seen such beautiful attire—saris in bright silks—saffron, emerald, magenta—with elaborate embroidery. Handsome Indian bodyguards loiter around the piano. They are protecting someone important. I spend much of the gig trying to guess which guest is the VIP, a fun little Piano Girl game I like to play in a crowd like this. The guards stand with their arms across their chests, without ever blinking. I love a man in uniform, even if the uniform involves a saber. I try to get them to smile, but to no avail.

I can't help but feel like I am the wrong musician for this job, but the gathered crowd seems appreciative and happy. The bride's aunt has requested "A River Flows in You." A lovely piece, but I wish I knew an Indian folk song or two. I should have invested in that "Bollywood's Greatest Hits" fake book.

As is often the case at high-society events (Indian or otherwise), a metaphysical barrier sits between the guests and me. The piano pulls focus at the center of the room, but I'm bubble girl, encased in a haze of subordination to the upscale people paying my salary for the evening. This sounds icky, but it's not—a certain emotional freedom comes with staying firmly on my side of the Steinway. Idle chitchat isn't so important; it's enough to communicate with music.

This afternoon the societal barrier is securely in place. I'm more curious than usual about this particular crowd and why they have traveled from Mumbai to my corner of Germany for a wedding reception, but it's not my place to ask questions—I'm just the piano player. Here they are, oozing elegance. Here I am, providing the requested ambient cushion of sound. And here comes the bride. Just as she arrives, a ray of sunshine pierces the cloudy day, gleams through an oversized window, and illuminates her flawless skin. Her sari sparkles. We are blinded by the light.

The Japanese bride at tonight's wedding looks like a hummingbird wrapped in meters of expensive white tulle. The German groom, normal size by German standards, seems hulk-like next to his fragile wife. We're celebrating in a baroque castle nor far from where I live. I don't like the pianos in this place. Call me a diva, but I can't stand playing a Kmart piano in a venue that charges eighteen euros for a piece of cake. Thankfully, the gracious father of the groom likes my music and has insisted on renting a good instrument for the evening.

The bride's favorite song is "Fly Me to the Moon." I play it straight, but she doesn't recognize the melody. Lost in translation, I guess. Poor thing. She has been decanted into a wedding dress with a corset so tight that it may well have cut off blood circulation to her brain.

I've never seen a fully formed adult with such tiny features—button nose, wee hands, and feet the size of my fists. Why does a woman this small need a corset? She is ethereal, translucent, Disney-like. If it weren't for her puffy gown, I could slip her into the lining of my suit jacket and take her home with me.

Pocket Bride's white dress has a mile-long train on it. Her dear mother has to tame the train every time her daughter stands. They are seated next to the piano, and one stumbling incident almost results in the three of us being smothered by Pocket Bride's dress. Death by tulle. There are worse ways to perish.

Before I know it, it's speech-making time, and if a wedding musician must know one thing, it is the importance of plotting

an advance escape route for the speech-making portion of a wedding reception. Once a speech starts, you can't sneak off the bandstand without looking arrogant, obnoxious, or downright rude. If the speech begins before you get out of Dodge, you are stuck onstage forever, forced to smile politely at endless stories about people you will never see again. Great Uncle Wolfgang's delightful reminiscences of a 1957 hiking trip to Schweinfurt might amuse members of his own family, but to you, the hired help, these charming recitations feel like verbal torment, especially if you need a potty break.

At this particular wedding I ignore my own advice. I'm trapped onstage between Pocket Bride's dress and a towering arrangement of white orchids. No escape.

Several translators have been hired for the evening. Each formal speech—and there are dozens of them—is slowly and painfully translated into Japanese. The Japanese speeches are translated to German. It's like the United Nations, except without the little earpieces and notepads. One gift exchange ceremony takes about two months. My cheeks cramp, and my face freezes in a smile position.

Pocket Bride's mother gets up, successfully navigates her way past her daughter's dress, and comes to the piano. She bows. I bow. Ah, she wants to play. She sits on the bench and plays a dirge-like piano solo that is very beautiful, very Japanese, but the most mournful piece of music ever played at a wedding. I can't leave the bandstand, so I stand to the side, nodding solemnly and pretending to understand the artistic intention of her solo. Did someone die? A grandparent? Maybe I missed something when I zoned out during the speeches.

And now, how about dessert?

I play my last notes of the evening. For the sake of Pocket Bride, for the sake of all of us, really—I hope love will find a way.

I bow twice and say thank you three times.

Doumo arigatou. Thank you. Danke.

Thirty-Three

Holding On, Letting Go

The first time I went to IKEA I was thirty-five and about ten months pregnant. I had my arm in a cast, the result of a slapstick tumble I had taken a few weeks earlier on a rain-slicked street in Astoria, Queens. I had been on my way to a piano gig at the Manhattan Grand Hyatt and was wearing a black chiffon Zsa Zsa caftan and a parka. My belly was so huge that I couldn't see my feet, let alone the slippery wooden ramp propped on the curb. Down I went. A chorus of Greek women, concerned about the baby, surrounded me and called an ambulance. One of the emergency medical technicians made a joke about needing a crane to get me onto the gurney.

The baby was fine; the arm, cracked at the elbow; the ego, deflated—due to all of the above, my piano-playing career, a very real tether to my own unreality, was going to be on hold for a few moments.

What better time for a little shopping?

"Enough of this indignity," said my Swedish-American friend Lesley as she looked at my cast. "Über-pregnant *and* maimed? This is pathetic. You are two weeks past your due date and need to have this baby *snabb!* A trip to IKEA is in order. A magical Swedish folktale claims that Swedish meatballs are known to induce labor, produce strong Viking progeny, and save the kingdom from the plunder of, you know, 'foreigners.' Swedish meatballs are mystical."

Lesley, a jazz singer who was smart, helpful, and funny in a quirky, dry, Swedish Albert Brooks kind of way, had given birth six months earlier. She was anxious for me to join the New Mother Club.

Let me say this and get it over with: I didn't like being pregnant. A tiny but ham-fisted, steel-booted trampoline artist had invaded my previously lithe body, and the ruckus in my belly drove me crazy.

My feet swelled every time I ate.

"Why bother with shoes?" said Lesley. "You could just wear the *skokartonger*."

"The *skokartonger*?"

"The shoeboxes."

Lesley tried to help me get labor started. She suggested Swedish saunas, a tiny glass of Aquavit, videotapes of Swedish erotica. Even swimming—she insisted a proper fjord was absolutely necessary, but I settled on the Holiday Inn Crowne Plaza Health Club pool. Apparently, not the same.

I was waiting in line at the liquor store—not a good look for a pregnant woman, I know, but I was buying a bottle of champagne for a friend's birthday—when my water broke. I called John and raced to the hospital, only to be told that the imagined amniotic fluid was just pee—a bladder malfunction. The doctor sent us home to wait it out.

"Ja," said Lesley, Swedishly. "The third trimester Walk of Shame. You need meatballs. In Sweden everyone knows this."

Sure, I thought. *Why not?*

"What if I go into labor in IKEA?" I asked Lesley.

"Don't worry," she said. "They have everything."

And, so, we drove to IKEA, and I ate the damn meatballs (*Köttbullar*, $3.99). At that point I would have gotten on my hands and knees and assembled a bedroom set for triplets if I thought it would speed things along.

Köttbullar aside, I loved IKEA. The musical, whimsical Scandinavian names of household articles large and small—named after towns and people—were a linguist's fantasy. To entertain myself I wandered through the store, inventing my own names for merchandise. In the children's department I spotted a plastic bib (*Sloppgard*, $1), a set of tiny wooden blocks (*KinderChöke*, $2.99), and an adorable crib that would later convert to a real bed (*Nytemäre*, $49.99).

I was so intrigued by the living-room department I forgot about my pregnancy. I shuffled my swollen feet past affordable sofas (*Näpp*, $169) and practical coffee tables (*Crapholdor*, $29.99), mentally decorating rooms I didn't own, marveling at fabric combinations, and occasionally lifting my plastered broken arm, pointing to a display, and saying things like, "Look. They even make colorful soup ladles" (*Glop*, $1.39).

Long Island mothers pushed parade-float strollers through aisles of baby items—*Bratsy, Dipewop, Spitlik*—and I wondered if I would ever have my own bundle of *glädje*, or if I was destined to forever roam the IKEA showroom floor like a pregnant zombie, staring longingly at childproof flatware (*Stabsma*, $2.99) and searching for my former self (*Svelte*, out of stock).

I bought numerous *Slopskid* towels and a *Ristsprane* bookcase for the baby's room.

When I arrived home, my patient husband wedged me into the bathtub and washed my hair, carefully avoiding the cast on my arm. He dried my back with the *Slopskid*, then, using the special IKEA Allen wrench, assembled the *Ristsprane*—the first of dozens of IKEA storage units he would build over the next few decades.

"I don't think the baby will need a bookcase, like, right away," he said. "This might be a bit optimistic."

"We can store other stuff on it. Music books, for instance," I said. "Why do they call this screwdriver thing an Allen wrench? Was it named after someone named Allen? Woody, maybe?"

"Maybe Steve?" he said as he twisted the screws into place, stopping periodically to stretch his cramped hands.

I watched him, grateful to be married to a jazz bassist willing to risk his livelihood by building a bookcase for an infant. I waddled across the room, plopped my blimpish body on the piano bench, noodled a lame one-armed melody, and sobbed.

The final throes of pregnancy test even the strongest women.

"This is God's way of making you ready for labor," said Valentina, a supposedly good friend who was at our apartment, sporting a super-slim pencil skirt and crop top, balancing a chilled martini in one perfectly manicured hand, an unlit cigarette in the other. A year ago, I had looked like her. Now I looked like four of her. I wanted to karate-chop her chiseled midsection with my cast, but I had already peed in public once this month; a second round seemed distasteful.

"I think it's God's way of making me want to shoot myself," I said. "But thanks for the support."

"You know," Valentina said, glancing with obvious disdain at my IKEA bookcase, "I *adore* IKEA. They make such cute cardboard containers for accessories (*Sluttbox*, set of three, $2.99). Maybe you could use them for baby jewelry or something."

"It's a *boy*," I said.

"It's *New Yawk*," she snapped. "Try to have an open mind."

"I feel like this will never be over," I said.

"Well, no one stays pregnant forever. At least you stopped working for now—you wouldn't want that baby born in a piano lounge."

Actually, I could think of worse places to enter the world.

It took almost thirty hours of labor, a Philippine nurse who liked to perform selections from *Madame Butterfly* under her breath, a lot of medication provided by an anesthesiologist who resembled the neighborhood crack dealer, and, when it became apparent that the baby was not anxious to vacate a perfectly comfortable piece of NYC real estate, a C-section.

After a lot of hoopla, I was allowed to hold our son. In a heartbeat I forgot the swollen feet, the broken arm, the sore back, and aching legs. I looked at him and turned into a joyful, maternal cliché.

Lesley brought me homemade soup in an IKEA container (*Likuidgladje*, $1.69) and wine in an IKEA sippy cup (*Drönk*, $1.20). And she admitted that she made up the Swedish meatball story.

"*Svensk saga*," she said. "A Swedish fairy tale. We had to do something to get you to the other side. Welcome to motherhood."

IKEA, for better or worse, has become a big part of my motherhood story, but it recently occurred to me that I've never purchased anything in an upscale "real" furniture store, nothing that hasn't required an Allen wrench. Our home is decorated with an eclectic and lovely mix of New York City dumpster-dive finds, antiques of negligible value from family and friends, gotta-leave-town-fast spit backs from American expat families, dining chairs from a castle where I used to perform, and paintings from the Washington Square Art Show. Even my grand piano, cigarette-scarred and elegant, was purchased secondhand from a jazz guy in Pittsburgh. The piano has survived numerous moves, including a six-week odyssey across the Atlantic. The ship docked in the port town of Bremen, and the piano was lovingly transported to my German home by three movers named Hans, Hans, and Franz. They wore matching blue coveralls that were too tight in the crotch, and they used a wedge of wood and an old stick to put the legs back on the piano. "Look Ma, no Hans."

But the rest of our furniture, the stuff that binds the raveled seams of our lives, comes from IKEA. The store has never disappointed me, even when I've been particularly susceptible to disappointment. If I'm having a bad day, I stroll through the IKEA showroom, fantasize about loft beds (*Krässh*, €129.99) and pick up a lawn chair (*Gartenswäag*, €19.99), a night lamp (*Elderblynd*, €24,55), or a toilet brush (*Covfefe*, €6.39).

I have an IKEA Family Card, and I always, always stop for the complimentary hot beverage (*Söpewasser*, free).

Our adult children have recently left home to start their own lives and careers. To help them with their new apartments, we have made a record number of trips to IKEA, buying mattresses (*Bäkkpadd*, €119.00), dressers (*Jammkräp*, €54.99), curtains (*Pervstopp,* €14.99), and dishes (*Ramenscoop*, set of four, €4.00). The kids each have their own starter sets of *Ristsprane* bookcases, lovingly assembled for them by their devoted father, who might as well keep an Allen wrench in his back pocket, just in case.

The original IKEA *Ristsprane* shelf—where I once stacked cloth diapers using an arm in a cast—looks forlorn. Over the decades this shelf has held Lego cabins, school reports, Donald Duck comic books, Batman action figures, Harry Potter volumes in two languages, a stuffed dog named Ruby, an autographed photo of basketball star Steve Nash, a replica of a Chinese Terracotta Warrior, handcrafted heart-shaped figurines, and books about Steve Jobs and Eleanor Roosevelt.

I think back eighteen years, to when our daughter was a toddler. While I was in a decorator stupor, distracted by an area rug in an unusual shade of taupe, she disappeared into the IKEA Marketplace. I raced around the showroom searching for her, sick with worry. After the longest ten minutes of my life, I found her in the lighting department with a lampshade on her head, singing a German song about a rabbit.

"Look, Mommy," she said, "a party hat!"

Pregnancy ends with the birth of a child. Childhood ends with the birth of an adult. Motherhood never ends, but it sure seems different these days. I miss my kids. It's a new phase for me—fraught with opportunities for redecorating, renovating, and reinventing myself. It's a little lonely, but also a little exciting. Maybe I'll head back to IKEA and buy myself a *Sluttbox*.

Thirty-Four

Remember Me

A Gentleman, a Steinway, and a Couple of Stubborn Ghosts

Manhattan, with its counterpoint of horn blasts, sirens, grumbles, whispers, and roars, performs a deafening sonata. I feel energized, defeated, inspired. I wonder how I ever lived here, or why I ever left.

To celebrate the publication of my first book, *Piano Girl*, Henry Steinway and Steinway Sales Representative Betsy Hirsch have invited me to present a solo piano concert and reading tonight in the famed Steinway Hall Rotunda. I open the heavy door of 109 West Fifty-Seventh Street and step from the bashing, flashing, pulse of the city into an embroidered oasis of tranquility. The high-domed ceiling, hand-painted by Paul Arndt in 1925, seems to scrape the sky. "*Reach high,*" it says to me. Maybe I'll touch something worth remembering.

Betsy hugs me. "Ready for tonight?" We walk down a portrait-lined corridor to a practice room so I can prepare for the main event. Irene Wlodarski, a fiery redhead who looks like she could have been a Rockette in a former life, jumps from her desk to greet me. I feel at home.

Some buildings are haunted in a good way. Steinway Hall has always been such a place—a luxurious monument to the skilled artisans and musicians who have dedicated their lives to the complex mechanics of simple beauty. It's not simple to build a piano; it's also not simple to play one.

I met Henry Steinway last month, when I was in town to tape NPR's *Piano Jazz* with jazz legend Marian McPartland. As Betsy escorted me back to Henry's office, I felt my face burn and my hands tingle, the early warning signs of impostor syndrome wrinkling my newly pressed black suit. Back in the eighties, when I was working as a cocktail pianist in Manhattan hotels, I had been too intimidated to step into Steinway Hall. It seemed like a place where "real" pianists hung out—an elite club for the chosen few, a secret den with a painted ceiling that was home to the world's best pianos and artists.

Betsy introduced me to Henry, a perfect gentleman with an affectionate handshake and a huge smile, then left us alone to chat for thirty minutes. Henry, the last member of the Steinway family to serve as the company's president, quickly put me at ease. How I loved listening to him talk about making pianos. He had always maintained a deep respect for those on both sides of the piano business—the makers of pianos and the makers of music. Artists might receive standing ovations, but Henry made sure his craftspeople heard their own share of applause.

Henry had read *Piano Girl*, so we had a long talk about the hotel music business, the tricky art of playing quality music when it seems like no one is listening, the joy of playing a great piano, even in a cocktail lounge full of chattering tourists and businesspeople. "Music is so very personal," Henry said to me. "Every skilled pianist has something unique to say—it's up to us to give them the means to say it."

We talked about craft and skill and talent. We talked about imagination and the critical role it plays in all aspects of the piano business. We talked about writing books. Henry told me he wanted me to meet his brother-in-law, the great author William Zinsser, the author of *On Writing Well* and a hero of mine, whom he would invite to my concert the following month.

Henry Steinway, William Zinsser, Marian McPartland—I felt as if a golden triumvirate of nonagenarians had been appointed to guide my career. I discovered that Steinway Hall was also entering its ninth decade. Perhaps ninety would be my new lucky number. I floated out of the hall that day after playing a dozen pianos, each one with a special historical pedigree, sensing that I had been dropped into a fantasyland of wood and wisdom, pins and hammers and perfect sound, all brought to life by an aging gentleman with an ageless vision, wearing a bow tie and holding court in a regal office that seemed more like a home than a workplace.

"Here," Betsy says, on the eve of my performance. "You can warm up here. It's Henry's special room." The piano technician tweaks a few last notes and then, after wishing me luck with my concert, leaves with Betsy. This is hardly a practice room; it's a small recital hall with a perfect Steinway B, a warmhearted piano that makes an audience listen. It's a piano with no wrong notes, a piano that takes a decent player and makes her music sing. I love it here. I love the carpets, the oil paintings, the smell of the wood, the mantle of hope that cloaks me as I sit down to practice. A buzz in the air is comforting and energizing all at once. Ghosts of concerts past? Maybe.

While warming up for the main event, I allow my mind to wander. My nerves jangle. I take some deep breaths. Decades of musicians have played in the Rotunda. Decades of edgy preperformance sweaty-hands, jelly-knees, dry-mouth tension. Decades of genuine passion, decades of accidental bravery. In an attempt to muster some courage, I try to summon the ghosts of concerts past. I tell myself the acoustic underpinnings of disappeared music—pirouetting silently down the staircase in double time—will carry me through the night. But musical ghosts don't really exist. Or if they do, the minute I sit down to play the Steinway D in the Rotunda, they'll flutter away and leave me to fend for myself. No help from the ghosts. Henry was right: music is personal—that's the glorious (and scary) thing about it.

I leave the practice room and stand on the balcony overlooking the concert space, peering down through the prisms of the enormous crystal chandelier onto the coiffed and stylish heads of the guests below. It is time. One hand firmly on the railing, I descend the long, curved staircase, greet my audience, greet the piano, and begin. I read my goofy *Piano Girl* stories about hotel piano bar shenanigans and play my sincere solo-piano compositions with titles such as "Twilight," "Peaceful Harbor," and "Mountaintop." I say what I need to say. It's hardly a perfect performance, but it's better than it should be because I'm assisted by this marvelous instrument in this magical place. I am now part of a Steinway Hall Rotunda tradition that all of us think will last forever.

Years later, when I learn that Steinway Hall has been sold, I'm overcome with sadness, a grief deepened by the recent loss of Henry. If walls could sigh, if corridors could cry, if chandeliers could sing forgotten compositions and repeat familiar refrains, what would they say to us? Move on. Music doesn't live in buildings, even the ones with fancy oil paintings and domed ceilings. Music is human. It lives in the craftspeople charged with making these pianos; it lives in the hearts and souls of the musicians who play them. I imagine the ghosts of concerts past on moving day, teary eyed and a little belligerent about leaving but eager to catch up to the parade of vehicles departing from West Fifty-Seventh Street.

And then, dancing in time to piano music only ghosts can hear, they'll follow the vans and trucks to Steinway Hall's newest home. There, a little disgruntled and perhaps missing the hand-painted ceiling, they'll do what ghosts do best—they'll take revenge by resorting to ghostlike skullduggery: they'll rattle the chandeliers, flicker lights, send a cold breeze from nowhere to freeze the trembling hands of an on-deck performer, disconnect a sustain pedal or cause a key to stick—probably a B flat—to completely screw up anyone's attempt at sounding good. Or maybe, they'll stop their yammering and haunting, and listen to the music they helped create, hoping to hear a little of themselves in someone else's playing, because even ghosts have big egos. Music past and music present—all of it very personal, some of it worth remembering.

Thirty-Five

My Celebrity Endorsements

*H*alfway through the 2018 Christmas season, while running a Google search on my name (I only do this once a month, I swear), I stumbled upon my original composition, "First Snow," included on a Spotify playlist put together by Kourtney Kardashian (or, more likely, by her "people"). For me, a sixty-two-year-old solo pianist with no people and a decidedly non-trending repertoire of soothing music, this came as a bit of a Yule-time shock. Hark! Jingle! Ho! A Kardashian Kristmas! For a moment I considered changing my name to Kobin Koldsby.

Worlds collide, thanks to the quirks of social media. Finding myself on the playlist of an Insta-princess such as Kourtney did wonders for my ego. How did this happen? I have neither the whittled waist nor the plump cheeks that Ms. Kardashian boasts. I am plenty old enough to be her mother. Her Kristmas photo featured her in an itsy bitsy teenie weenie silver leatherette bikini. My Christmas photo showed me wearing enough red velvet to cloak the wings of the Shubert Theatre. But, OK. She also featured Bing Crosby (let's call him King Krosby) on her Kristmas playlist, and he is hardly kurvy of butt or young of years. In fact, he is long past his kancellation date, which makes me a spring chicken in komparison.

Perhaps Kourtney was simply listening to the music instead of looking at the musician? Works for me. A new concept: music for listening. Our world has become so fixated on the visual that we often forget we have ears.

The Kardashian brush with fame got me thinking about the many celebrities who have tap-danced through my life. I've played the piano in a lot of upscale joints over the past forty years, many of them populated by the world's movers and shakers, has-beens, and shooting stars. Hotel musicians, you might guess, have curbside seats at the promi parade. Star spotting is a minor fringe benefit of the job, along with the free drinks and unlimited pretzel nubs. We take what we can get.

Note: celebrities come in all shapes and sizes, but most of them are thin.

Here's where I start the heavy name-dropping. Forgive me, but this is fun.

My initial brush with on-the-job fame occurred during one of my first gigs at the Pittsburgh Hyatt. Jonathan Winters (not thin) and Art Garfunkel (thin) were at the bar—an unlikely pair, but there they were. They offered me a drink. I was underage—eighteen—and requested an orange juice. Mr. Winters ignored my drink request and sauntered over to the piano carrying a large vodka with a splash of orange. He laughed when I nearly choked on it and sputtered my thanks. I played and sang "Fever" for him, a song that no self-respecting teenager should have in her repertoire.

At that same bar, I met Henry Mancini and pounded out one of his famous songs, "Charade," in 5/4. He introduced himself as Hank and was very pleasant even though I had mangled his tune. He did not buy vodka for me.

The Pittsburgh Hyatt also hosted visiting National Hockey League players in town for Pittsburgh Penguins matches. I am sure they were talented skaters, but a handful of them were also hard-drinking, loud-mouthed apes. Back in 1978, if a famous athlete Sasquatched his way to the piano, grinned at me, and said, "Hey, nice tits," I smiled nervously and thanked him, because I didn't know what else to do. These days I'd probably end up doing at least five minutes in the penalty box for cross-checking.

Back then I wore tube tops and halter tops and evening gowns with low necklines and lower backs. Fashion wise, I was sort of a Kourtney Kardashian for the seventies. When I see her posts, I recognize some of my old outfits—although I never had the guts (or the six pack) to wear a leather bikini. I wonder if Kourtney ever took piano lessons. Anyway, I was skeptical about hockey players until I moved to Manhattan and met Wayne Gretzky, who hung out at a swanky hotel where I had a regular gig. A true gentleman.

Since we're on the topic of athletes and manners, let me mention that baseball star Jerry Royce was a noble chap, and handsome. He liked my version of "So Far Away," probably because he was on the road so often. New York Yankee's manager Billy Martin was not so refined. He treated me with relative respect, but he often got into boozy fistfights at the Grand Hyatt bar, my favorite, of course, being the time he punched George Steinbrenner in the nose during the Glenn Miller/Beethoven medley. The brawl made the papers, but sadly, no one mentioned my piano accompaniment, not even the part where "In the Mood" slides headfirst into the *Moonlight Sonata*. Admittedly, it might have been a bit much for the sports pages.

When I lived in New York City, the rich and famous became recurring, familiar characters in my struggling-artist story. It's hard to live paycheck to paycheck when surrounded by pomp, privilege, and prosperity. Playing the piano in a posh Manhattan hotel constantly reminded me that even though I was the focal point of the cocktail lounge, I remained on the outside looking in, a wallflower at the celebrity ball, a little drunk on the mingled scents of arrogance and smoked almonds.

Trumpet's in the Hyatt at Grand Central—a smoke-filled lair of debauchery—provided a hideaway for prominent people who wanted to smoke cigars and avoid the paparazzi. In contrast, the Marriott Marquis at Times Square served as a playground for celebrities hoping to be seen. *Look at me, look at me, look at me now.* I met Rosemary Clooney there. She seemed grateful that I knew she was a legendary singer and not the lady from the toilet paper commercial. Oscar-winner Anthony Newley— worshipped by David Bowie and many other songwriters—was a frequent guest, generous with drinks and praise, and inspirational for a novice songwriter like me. Neil Diamond seemed a little neurotic and very concerned with his comb-over. Who could blame him? He was headed to the unveiling of the newly renovated Statue of Liberty and it was windy on the harbor, a disaster in waiting for anyone sporting a toupee or fretting about bald spots.

My all-time favorite Marriott glam guest was Tina Louise, Ginger from *Gilligan's Island*. Talk about thin. I watched a division of the New York City Fire Department—called to the hotel to investigate an alarm—drop their axes and gawk at her as she strolled through the hotel lobby. Fire? What fire? Twenty years since she got off that island and she still had it going on. I don't know what she is up to these days, but I bet she's still wearing her Ginger wig and that mink coat. That has to be a wig, right?

I played at the Marriott for seven years and had a theory that eventually everyone in the world would drift through that atrium lobby. Tumbleweed clumps of humanity—not just celebrities, but also crazy people and old boyfriends—fluffed past the Yamaha grand. I'm grateful that no one took a shot at me; I was a sitting Piano Girl duck in that vast lounge, surrounded by dying ficus trees, last-gasp celebs, the occasional dipsomaniac pornographer, and balconies that turned out to be perfect launchpads for projectile objects and a couple of suicide attempts.

Living in New York City eventually immunized me against celebrity crushes. I often spotted Christopher Reeve on Fifty-Seventh Street. Every single time I would think: *Wow, that guy looks like Superman; oh wait, he is Superman.* Any New Yorker will tell you that Robin Williams sightings were once common. I would see these guys, register their greatness, and keep moving. No eye contact, no weird vibes, just a potholed concrete playing field upon which we lightly treaded.

After moving to Europe, I spent fourteen years playing at a German castle—an exclusive hotel property that attracted a discerning clientele. Over the years, Bono, Robbie Williams, Daniel Barenboim, and heads of state from numerous first-world countries stayed with us or dined in the Michelin three-star restaurant. Lionel Richie was a frequent, cheerful guest. *Hello? Is it me you're looking for?* Evidently not.

During the World Cup championship, the entire Brazilian soccer team lived in the castle, hung out next to the piano, and applauded politely while I self-consciously plowed through my limited list of Jobim tunes. Then they lost a crucial match and went home without saying good-bye. Heidi Klum and Seal, who showed up every now and then, once stopped by the piano so Seal could sing "Greensleeves" to his daughter, the Baby Seal. He was wearing a white suit, a good wardrobe choice if you have skin the color of polished ebony. He was the most dashing, dazzling man I'd ever seen. And he could sing.

Celebrity hat trick: one night I played for Queen Silvia of Sweden, a German Olympic swimmer named Franziska van Almsick, and Nick Nolte, who entered the bar with his own pre-made cocktail in a sippy cup. He looked sinister and handsome in his black trench coat and aviator shades, and he grumbled a few words of encouragement in my direction. I was grateful for his attention because neither the queen nor the swimmer had registered my presence.

During this same period, an Omani princess was residing at the castle in a group of suites that the royal family had rented for several months. She listened to me from her private indoor balcony and sent notes and requests via her security chief. Before the princess returned to her heart-shaped palace in the middle of the desert, she gave me a chunk of gold the size of my thumb. And now she sends me a Christmas card every year. I have yet to receive a Christmas card from Mr. Nolte or any other Hollywood celebrity, but I remain optimistic.

I do not kid myself; I know, and have always known, that I'm in the service industry.

My recent foray to Buckingham Palace to play for Prince Charles is well documented, as is my NPR *All Things Considered* appearance opposite Bill Clinton, and my five-minute concert performance for Angela Merkel (she smiled at me one time and was wearing a lavender blazer). I've whipped these stories into frothy musical tales that work nicely at dinner parties when there's a conversation lull.

I still play for VIPs and pop-up legends as they traverse my musical sphere and do whatever it is that famous people do. But times have changed. The presence of a pianist in a five-star hotel lobby seems shocking these days, even to those accustomed to daily pampering. Now we're a rarity—petite, long-fingered dinosaurs gracefully fighting extinction.

But there's hope. Music may have taken a heavy hit in the live-performance category, but it's more available than ever in the streaming world. And that's how I've found myself on the playlists of lovers, dreamers, and stars. This sounds like a rejected lyric from "The Rainbow Connection." It's not.

My old friend Tobin Bell, the generous, talented star of the *Saw* psycho-drama horror film series and my former partner for the Holocaust Remembrance Day songwriting gig, often tweets about my music to his gazillion followers. As a result, I have a cult following of *Saw* fans, most of whom are under twenty-five. Having a teenage audience might not keep me young, but it's given me some street cred with my kids. Maybe I'll get a gig scoring horror films. After years of working in cocktail lounges, I'd probably be good at that.

I have a recurring nightmare that all of the B-list celebrities I've run into over the years show up at the same cocktail party. I'm playing, and there they are, clustered around the piano, sipping Aperol Spritz, and throwing obscure requests at me—Larry Hagan, David Hasselhoff, Joey Reynolds (talk-radio pioneer and author of the memoir *Let a Smile Be Your Umbrella But Don't Get a Mouthful of Rain*), Gary Player, various *Sesame Street* stars, Mr. McFeely, Buttercup Blondeau, Ron Popeil, Bruno Sammartino, Marie Osmond, Gene Simmons (without his Kiss makeup), those damn hockey players, Joe Franklin, the entire cast of a German soap opera called *Lindenstrasse*, and Lloyd Bridges. I wake up from the nightmare—before the room gets too crowded—with the "Theme from Sea Hunt" banging in my ears.

Speaking of banging, legendary piano basher and free-jazz wizard Cecil Taylor, master of chord clusters and intricate poly-rhythms, was, for about six months, a fan of mine. Musically, Cecil was my polar opposite. He used to sit by himself next to the white grand piano in the white lobby of the Omni Park Central and sip drinks, listen to me play my timid tinka, tinka arrangement of "Love Story," and say, "Yeah, baby." I asked him to sit in one time, but he demurred, claiming he'd wreck the piano, and I'd probably get fired. I got fired anyway, but it had nothing to do with Cecil.

Smokey Robinson kissed me on the cheek one time, but I was nine years old, so maybe that doesn't count.

Greg Allman hung out at my gig at the Waterbury, Con-necticut Holiday Inn. He sat next to the spinet piano, and I was tempted to run my fingers through his long, blond hair. He was that close.

Evander Holyfield, the Real Deal, was pleasant and liked piano music, possibly more than he liked Mike Tyson.

I could go on, so I will. My music is featured regularly on archconservative and conspiracy-theory superstar Glenn Beck's playlists. I can't help but wonder why a self-proclaimed "angry man"—whose latest book is called *Addicted to Rage*—would include my placid arrangement of "Feed the Birds" on his list of favorite tracks. Maybe he needs to balance all that wrath. I'm happy to help. Maybe he'll fall asleep and stop ranting.

Forget the celebs for a minute: I regularly receive mail from non-famous listeners who have used my music for childbirth, funerals, hospital stays, and weddings. A twenty-two-year-old university student reported that my music helped her get through a grueling final semester. My supersmart lawyer friend Peter has played my albums to help him stay calm and prepare for his own classical piano recitals. An elderly woman named Margie claimed my music improved her bowling scores. I just received a letter from a man who has been listening while rebuilding his life after the recent fires in California ravaged his home. These endorsements are of the highest order, and I treasure each one of them.

Then there are the deathbed testimonies.

"Exactly what track was Mr. Eggrich-Bimmelstein listening to when he passed away?" my husband once asked (with raised eyebrow). As mentioned earlier, I had told him about the death of one of my elderly fans—a ninety-six-year-old gentlemen who crossed over while listening to a specific tune of mine, on repeat for his final forty-eight hours.

See, that's the thing—when faced with an important transition in life, most of us choose to listen, not look. Mr. Eggrich-Bimmelstein wasn't staring at Instagram photos of bikini-clad sex kittens when he slipped away—he was listening to a piece of music that helped him move forward. In this case, it was one of my tunes. But it could have easily been Bach or the Beatles.

And so, we circle back to Kourtney. Her photos make me uneasy, or envious—or a little of both—but I admire her audacity, her willingness to celebrate her sexuality, the irony in her face-tuned "casual" photos, her desire to stand apart from the roaring, boring crowd. If Instagram had existed when I was her age, I might have done the same thing; I was thin enough, and I would have looked great with that Valencia filter. Instead, I played the piano—my launchpad into adult life. It helped me figure out who I wanted to be. It still does. Ms. Kardashian, using a different platform, has embarked on a similar voyage of self-discovery, one that involves hashtags and lash extensions. Good for her.

How does my low-key music fit in with Kourtney's razzle-dazzle, hip-hopping, ab-pumping, leatherette lifestyle? A desire for simplicity, perhaps? A higher bowling score? Or maybe, like the rest of us, she just needs some downtime and a way to move forward, gently. All that posing can be exhausting.

Thirty-Six

I'll Take Manhattan

My taxi from JFK into Manhattan sits in traffic outside the Queens Midtown Tunnel. Every few minutes we creep forward a few feet. A pale sky frames vibrant billboards that advertise luxury condos and cosmetic dentistry.

Concrete, steel, cranes. The only humans I see are stuffed, like me, in cars—their tiny heads bowed to check text messages. Maybe they are praying for their exodus from Queens.

I lower the window, and a warm February breeze, greasy and choked with exhaust fumes, teases me with the promise of something better on the other side of the river.

Lunch? Egg salad on an everything bagel sounds nice, but I'd settle for a knish with mustard. Yeah.

If we moved any slower, we'd be going backwards.

New York City doesn't play nice with musicians. It never has. When I moved here in 1980, at the age of twenty-one, I knew the city's reputation for crushing careers. Still, I showed up and managed to claw out a successful life for myself.

Manhattan was like a strutting, strung-out, skulking bad boy in a distressed leather jacket, and it hypnotized me. Now and then I snapped to my senses and considered leaving, but the sexy bad boy, aware of my displeasure, would toss a half-full swag bag in my direction—a piano gig in a sleazy hotel bar, an audition for a job as a piano-playing stripper, a songwriting assignment for Holocaust Memorial Day—and convince me to stay put. The stench of ambition wafted up Madison Avenue and lulled me into a state of contented numbness. I probably stayed longer than I should have.

I played the piano in hotels that offered live music as a perk for their five-star guests. Hotel musicians like me had decent health insurance, a pension plan, and enough money to cover rent, an occasional new pair of glitzy shoes, and countless diner breakfasts. Over the course of fifteen years, I may well have consumed two thousand plates of poached eggs on toast. Coffee, regular.

Those years were terrible and wonderful. And fun.

I left in 1994 at the age of thirty-seven. I flew away, victorious, to Europe with a bassist husband and toddler son. I felt strong and lucky. I had survived a minor eating disorder, a major Valium habit, way too many of those poached eggs, a borderline-dangerous serial dating habit, and aching loneliness. I had also fallen in love, polished my music skills, and learned how to say no with confidence.

Countless people—some of them beautiful, some of them crazy, criminal, or worse—had passed my piano over the course of fifteen years. I played. They listened. They ignored me. I played some more. Back then, music floated through the lobbies, restaurants, and cocktail lounges of upscale Manhattan hotels. The piano soothed, entertained, and reminded guests who were paying too much for a hotel room that a nice song can do more for the soul than a double shot of Ketel One Citron and a bowl of salty nuts.

I'm returning to the city this afternoon on the heels of a short East Coast concert tour. I won't be playing any gigs in Manhattan, but I will visit friends, infuse my drowsy spirit with the city's energy, and hear some music. Two decades after I started a calmer, more creatively productive life in a foreign country, I want to see what I left behind.

Except this tunnel is taking forever. What was that movie back in the eighties? *C.H.U.D.* Cannibalistic humanoid underground dwellers. Why do I remember such things?

At last. We come up for air, and I see this is how the bad boy gets you—he makes you drive through a stinky, gloomy tunnel thinking you're a cannibalistic humanoid underground dweller, then waves a couple of brownstones and a ginkgo tree in your face and tempts you back into his tattooed arms.

My husband, John, will arrive later this afternoon. Our good friends Norman and Ellen, the kind of hip, warmhearted, smart people you'd expect to meet in the world's most sophisticated city, will host us for the next three days. Their Fifth Avenue, window-lined apartment—with guest room, a New York rarity—has offered a welcome refuge to many of their artist friends over the years.

John shows up, as fresh as one can be after a nine-hour flight from Berlin. In the past five days he has been to Maastricht, Bielska Zadymka (Poland), Berlin, and now, Manhattan. I have been in Charleston and Pittsburgh. He wins.

We haven't seen each other for three weeks, and we have a lot to talk about. The last time we were in New York together without kids was twenty-five years ago.

We walk a couple of blocks to the Knickerbocker for dinner, a place where John used to play duo gigs with some of the greatest pianists in the world. The place is packed, but tonight there's no music. The grand piano sits in the corner covered with a gazillion mid-priced bottles of liquor. I can hardly see the top of the instrument. A baby stroller the size of a Hummer is parked where the piano bench should be.

The food is great, the wine is fine, but where's the music?

The next day we visit the new Whitney and walk the length of the High Line. We meet a street poet named Mary, who improvises a poem for me on the word of my choice. I choose "John," and she goes to town:

When he's gone,
There is no dawn,
That's the way you feel,
About your John.

I love the Thirty-Fourth Street grunge-themed Greek diner where we have lunch. It reminds me of a place on Eighth Avenue where a street person once blew his nose right into my friend's plate, then, when we recoiled in disgust, grabbed Danny's BLT and ran out the door. I'm not sure why I'm nostalgic about health department violations and street poets.

We walk and walk and walk. Later we meet Norman and Ellen for dinner at Joe Allen, where—much to Norm's delight—one can still order warm fudge cake with coffee ice cream.

Norman and Ellen head home. John and I begin our evening tour of places where we used to play. We stroll through the pedestrian park that used to be Times Square. It feels familiar but slightly off—like a cheesy waltz version of a piece meant to be played in a bashing, odd-meter time.

Where are the cars? Why does it look like Las Vegas for children?

We enter the circular band of elevators at the Marriott Marquis and run around trying to find an available lift to take us to the eighth-floor lobby. I played here for seven years, starting in the mid-eighties. Eventually Marriott management replaced me with an awful-sounding player piano and a tuxedo-clad crash-test dummy.

The dummy and the piano have vanished. I walk to the middle of the Atrium Lounge, stand right where the piano used to be, and look up. I remember the waitresses in their casino-inspired, organ-grinder's monkey costumes, the greeter who had a dwarf phobia, the breakfast buffet on top of the piano, the ladies' room attendant who sold me silk evening gowns from her "shop" in the handicapped toilet stall, the stalkers, the moguls, the hookers, the stars.

But mostly I remember music. Seven years of solo piano—that's a lot of notes. The current silence fills the lobby with despair. It seems hollow and pointless here—like a hospital cafeteria trying too hard to be cheerful.

Onward. We wait for an elevator but give up and take the stairs.

Next stop, the Algonquin, Dorothy Parker's former residence and home of the famous Round Table. The Algonquin, renowned for its literary history, also hosted New York's finest cabaret stars. I spent many serene evenings in the Oak Room, listening to John accompany Susannah McCorkle. The Oak Room was Manhattan at its best. You could order a martini, listen to some Gershwin, and slip into your most divine self.

We ask the concierge about music.

"No music," he says. "Sorry."

"No music?" John and I respond in unison, a Greek chorus of disbelief.

"Sorry."

"But this is the Algonquin," I say.

"New management," he says. "The Marriotts took over a couple of years ago. Sorry."

Those damn Marriotts. Replacing the pianist with a mannequin was bad enough, but closing the Oak Room? A scandal.

"So, the Oak Room is dark?" John asks.

"Yeah," says the concierge, who seems to be doubling as a doorman. "Sorry. Now it's a conference room. Go see for yourselves."

We peek inside and gasp. Flourescent lighting, a fake wood conference table, folding walls, a beamer. They might as well call it the Plastic Room.

"And the Round Table?" I ask. "Please tell me it's still here."

"Yeah," he says, "but they closed the library bar. Now it's in the breakfast room."

"Like Dorothy Parker ever ate breakfast," I say.

"I used to play back in the Oak Room," John says to the concierge. "With Susannah."

"God rest her soul," he says. "I loved her. That 'Waters of March' recording is still my favorite."

"I played that with her a bunch of times," John says.

A moment of silence for Susannah, for Dorothy, for the confused cabaret and literary ghosts roaming the hotel lobby. A few choice words from Jobim's "Waters of March" run through my mind. Sticks, stones, and slivers of glass. Life, knife, and the end of a run.

"Hey," says the concierge, "we still have the Algonquin cat."

"That's something," I say. "At least there's that. There's the cat." I sound like Mary the poet.

Onward.

We head to the Grand Hyatt, where John and I played for years. He worked with a jazz trio in the lobby; I played in the velvet-and-leather cave known as Trumpet's. Back then the hotel was owned by professional son and future U.S. president Donald Trump.

John and I met at this hotel. The Hyatt Corporation had a catchy slogan in the nineties. "Welcome to the Hyatt. Catch the wave." John and I caught the wave. Twenty-six years have passed. That was a big wave.

We're not expecting any music when we walk through the glass doors—we knew the Hyatt music policy had ended years ago, but if the Marriott now looked like a hospital cafeteria, this place looks like a mausoleum. This hotel was never a Mecca of good taste, but now it's sterile and a little creepy.

Where's the crystal fountain? Where are the crazy lobby people who hid behind fake ficus trees and muttered absurdities at the musicians? Where are the pornographers and dancers and brawlers and hulking security guards who occasionally belted out Frank Sinatra tunes during the trio's last set?

Gone.

It's shiny and sterile and corporate in here, a polished-stone shrine to mediocrity. We walk down the empty corridor to Trumpet's, a bar I used to poke fun at for its eighties upscale lounge-lizard vibe. Trumpet's once featured music six nights a week, five to midnight. We catered to Grand Central train people. I spent years at the Trumpet's piano, finding my musical voice and fending off guys who sent me vague musical requests along with their room numbers.

"Oh, no," I say when we reach the entrance to the former cocktail lounge. Another stupid conference room. It looks like a sheetrock shoebox. Remembering that this is where I fell in love with John, I try to conjure a little romantic nostalgia for the Hyatt—but I come up empty.

I never really liked Trumpet's, but this nondescript space is beyond depressing. Just for a second, I'd like to catch a glimpse of my former self, the younger, skinnier, goofier model, tossing bouquets of notes to a half-grateful crowd.

Onward.

Next stop: the Waldorf Astoria, home to one of the last hotel piano gigs in Manhattan. The Waldorf was recently purchased by a Chinese insurance company called Anbang and will close its doors for a three-year renovation that will turn the hotel into a condo residence for rich-and-famous globetrotters.

My pal Emilee Floor has been playing at the Waldorf for the past nine years. John and I, along with several of my good friends—my former agent Harlan Ellis, Greg Thymius, Carole and Emilio Delgado—will be there to send her off in style. A few of the Waldorf's other musicians, past and present, also show up. Daryl Sherman and Debbie Andrews, both of whom worked with me back in the eighties and early nineties, wander into the lounge, looking a little wistful. Piano girls forever, I guess. We may all be twenty years older and a few pounds heavier, but we still have closets full of evening gowns, fleeting fingers, and too many songs left to play.

Emilee plays the 1907 Cole Porter Steinway, a gorgeous, blond mahogany instrument that needs a serious, expensive overhaul. It hurts to play this piano, which some of us call the Tendonitis Steinway. The Hilton Corporation, which manages the property, likes to brag about the piano's pedigree, but they have never seen fit to invest in its restoration. It's plopped in the corner of the lounge, facing exactly the wrong direction. Emilee, a singing-playing wonder in a purple sequined cocktail dress, does her best to capture the mood of the room.

John and I listen and watch as a sloppy, irritated woman in a business suit at least a size too small staggers to the piano and begins harassing Emilee. Smiling, Emilee chats between phrases and does that thing that great hotel players know how to do. It's like watching a munitions expert disarm a bomb. The woman chills out and wobbles back to her Bacardi and Coke.

Emilee conquers the evening with her free-spirited, uplifting vocals and lissome piano arrangements. Her music paints the lounge with light, but the night hangs heavy. We have visited four hotels, three of them without music, one of them about to close its heavy brass doors.

What will happen to the Cole Porter Steinway?

I fear the Hiltons, or the Chinese Anbangs, or whoever is running the place will shove it, unceremoniously, into a storage locker meant for cans of lard and bed linens. In three years, following the hotel renovation, they'll have housekeeping dust it off. An overworked, deadline-crazed, junior interior designer with no clue about music history will say, "Oh, that's cute" and place the piano, unrestored and out of tune, in a nook of the lobby surrounded by velvet ropes. It will bear a meaningful plaque. The piano, silent and stuck without a player in a cone of corporate silence, will become a museum piece. Occasionally, an underpaid food and beverage trainee will use the closed piano as a surface to hold bottles of sparkling wine or a large vase of calla lilies.

I don't think Mr. Porter, who would have adored Emilee Floor, had this in mind when he bequeathed the piano to the hotel.

"*Get that piano in shape,*" a modern-day Porter might have trilled. "*You spent forty-thousand to reupholster those ugly-ass sofas in the ladies' lounge, the least you can do is fix the damn piano. And hire some musicians to play it. What good is a silent hotel lobby? Get the wine off the Steinway and put it on a table where it belongs. And for God's sake, lose the calla lilies. It's not a funeral.*"

Live music has always been a glossy thing. Slippery, almost. It flows into the night like a delicate river and rolls forward into an ocean of collective memory. The loss of music in Manhattan's hotels might seem inconsequential, but it's not. The retreat of song marks one more indignity in an era clouded by corporate folly, desensitization, and greed. The river is running dry.

By discontinuing their music policies, Manhattan hotels have officially insulted their guests—a subtle slap in the face of expense account clients and international tourists hoping for a little New York City enchantment.

When you take away music, you take away magic. That simple.

Enough.

Onward.

Over the next few days, we see a Broadway play, attend an Emanuel Ax rehearsal at Carnegie Hall, go to lunch with our niece, hang out with Betsy Hirsch at the new Steinway Hall, visit some Village jazz clubs. Yes, New York City remains jam-packed with fanciful things to do and see. But I've come to realize that— had I stayed here—my career as a hotel musician likely would have fizzled and died. I would have found something else to do, because that's the way it is when you live and work in New York City. You keep on keepin' on, even when you're tired and feeling like a C.H.U.D.

I love it here; I hate it here. We leave town on a Wednesday and get stuck in traffic, this time on the Manhattan side of the tunnel. It's hard enough to get into the city, but I have to fight my own demons every time I dare to leave.

This Piano Girl life of mine. Pittsburgh, New York City, Europe. My world overflows with booming bass lines, tricky harmonic structures that I'll never completely understand, effervescent melodies that fly and fall from my fingers and land nowhere. Where do all the notes go?

I look at my handsome husband and think about our adult kids back in Europe, our home, our lush careers. The piano, at times, has almost cracked me, but it continues to push me to the other side of who I'm supposed to be, offering an expectant soundtrack that accompanies every good thing I know. It's the first of March. We travel under the East River and start our long trip home.

Acknowledgments

*I*t has been a joy to share my musical stories with you. Many thanks to John Cerullo at Backbeat Books for guiding my project and to author Mike Edison for jumping onboard as my editor. Mike, you added the Edison Edge to my Piano Girl prose. I'll be forever grateful.

Hats off to the Piano Girl editorial and marketing dream team, including Barbara Claire, Carol Flannery, Jessica Kastner, Della Vache, and Joanne Foster.

I remain thankful to editor Richard Johnston, who, back in 2005, recognized the potential of my stories to throw light on the behind-the-scenes lives of working musicians. Five books later, here we are.

How about our illustrations? I adore Julia Goldsby's inspired book cover, especially because she gave me angel wings, a champagne glass, and Beyoncé thighs. And I love how the piano keys dissolve into stardust in the indigo sky.

My loving family—whose support, humor, and readiness to give me *just a few suggestions*—means everything to me. My husband, John, is more than the love of my life; he is my in-house bassist, chord doctor, the strongest guy I know, and a shining example of how to face life's challenges and keep swinging. Our kids, Curtis and Julia, have their own wonderful lives now, but they show up when we need them (with *just a few more sugges-tions*).

Many thanks to my dear friends, in particular Leslie Brockett, Robin Spielberg, Pinky Rawsthorne, Debra Todd, Margaret Melozzi, Andrea Aldrup, and my FAWCO sisters around the world.

Much love to my parents, Bob and Ann Rawsthorne, and my sister, Badass Randy—the reigning Chatham Village beauty queen (even though she cheated).

Thanks to Steinway & Sons for making incredible instruments and to Henry Steinway for inviting me—many years ago—to be part of the Steinway Artist Roster.

A shout-out to Frank Baxter and the pianoworld.com global community of piano professionals, hobby players, technicians, and fans; to Kathy Parsons at mainlypiano.com for her commitment to the art of solo piano music.

To my fellow musicians—this book is for you. Thanks for continuing to inspire me. We are a noble group, and I'm honored to be part of the club.

The final edit of *Piano Girl Playbook* was completed in April 2020, during the first stages of the pandemic lockdown. Editor Mike Edison and I, despite a potentially paralyzing sense of low-grade panic and confusion about the state of the world, managed to laugh, cry, and work our way through each of my essays. Mike encouraged me to finish strong.

My last pre-pandemic gig was March 15, 2020, at the Excelsior Hotel Ernst in Cologne, Germany, where I've been performing for the past five years. As usual, I played solo piano music for a grateful audience of guests of all ages, most of them enjoying one last outing a few hours before lockdown. We already seemed nostalgic for something we knew was slipping away—the chance to gather, listen to music, remember, forget, drift. I played original music from my *Magnolia* album along with a few standards and closed the set with Billy Joel's "And So It Goes." My guests were strangers to me, but for the three hours we spent together that afternoon, we bonded. Maybe it was even a little *magical*.

I could have played the *Titanic* theme, but I didn't.

When I covered the Steinway and left the hotel, part of me thought I was walking away from a joyful forty-five-year career in live music, one that has grounded me, given me wings, and provided a livelihood for my family. But the survivor part of me, the Pollyanna Piano Girl who has never lost faith in the ability of music to unite hearts and minds, resorted to *talking out loud* to the piano.

"Don't worry," I said, "I'll be back."

My gratitude to all of you for believing in the beauty of live music. Keep listening.

Index of Song Titles

Index of Key Terms

About the Author

Robin Meloy Goldsby is the author of *Piano Girl: A Memoir*, *Waltz of the Asparagus People*, *Rhythm*, and *Manhattan Road Trip*. She has appeared on NPR's *All Things Considered* and *Piano Jazz with Marian McPartland*. Goldsby is a Steinway Artist and cultural ambassador with artistic ties to both Europe and the United States. Robin currently performs about two hundred live piano gigs a year at Excelsior Hotel Ernst in Cologne, Germany, and tours internationally with her popular concert/reading program.

robingoldsby.com

About the Illustrator
Julia Meloy Goldsby is a freelance visual artist living in Cologne, Germany. In addition to her illustration projects, she is an award-winning documentary filmmaker.